John Carroll

Father Corson

The Old Style Canadian Itinerant

John Carroll

Father Corson
The Old Style Canadian Itinerant

ISBN/EAN: 9783337216160

Printed in Europe, USA, Canada, Australia, Japan

Cover: Foto ©Lupo / pixelio.de

More available books at **www.hansebooks.com**

Rev. J. E. Hunter.

"FATHER CORSON;"

OR,

THE OLD STYLE CANADIAN ITINERANT:

EMBRACING

THE LIFE AND GOSPEL LABOURS

OF

THE REV. ROBERT CORSON,

FIFTY-SIX YEARS A MINISTER IN CONNECTION WITH THE CENTRAL METHODISM OF UPPER CANADA.

EDITED

BY THE REV. JOHN CARROLL, D.D.,

Author of "The Stripling Preacher," "Past and Present," "Case and His Cotemporaries," "The School of the Prophets,"
&c., &c., &c.

"Not with excellency of speech or of wisdom," "but in demonstration of the Spirit and of power."—ST. PAUL.

TORONTO:
PUBLISHED BY THE REV. SAMUEL ROSE, D.D.,
AT THE METHODIST BOOK ROOM.

1879.

DEDICATION.

TO

ALL THE SURVIVORS

OF THE

EARLY CANADIAN PIONEERS,

BOTH IN CHURCH AND STATE,

AND TO THEIR DESCENDENTS,

This Book

IS RESPECTFULLY INSCRIBED

BY

THE EDITOR.

PREFATORY PLEA.

A published life of the Rev. Robert Corson has not been undertaken because he was considered a great man, in any one respect. And if he had been considered as merely an average good Methodist preacher, his biography certainly would not have been written. There are hundreds of average preachers, as good and devoted as he, whose lives it would not be worth while to publish. "Father Corson's" life is essayed because, while he preserved a spotless religious reputation for over three-score years, there was something in his spirit, manner, and doings, which caused him to be "the observed of all observers" and led to his being loved above many, which has begotten a desire to retain the genial old gentleman still, in some form, among his friends.

But the unusual structure of the book will strike the reader, and perhaps make it the occasion of confronting the EDITOR with not very approving criticism on the part of some. Some of these probable grounds of attack may be anticipated. Each of the unusual features, therefore, I shall make to stand out by itself for a moment.

First, I have made the several stages of his public life to coincide with the several epochs of Canadian Methodist history. In justification of which unusual plan I have to say: If this distribution of his life-work and progress will answer as well as any other division of his career, who has a right to object? But I have done more: I have given such incidental references to all passing occurrences in Provincial Methodism, that, while lured on by the story of a humble itinerant, "the general reader," who could not be induced to encounter an elaborate history, because something too formidable, will, unknown to himself, be getting informed on all the essential outlines of that history.

Here some one of those who always know how a thing should be done better than the person who has made it a special and delighted study, will ask: "Why connect the history of the Church with so obscure a person as Mr. Corson? It would be very well if he had been a leading influence like some of the learned doctors, but not with a humble labourer like him. Nay, his very humility, which led him to labour on in an overlooked career, was one of those very things that made his efforts as valuable to the Church as those of almost any of the doctors. Besides, it must not be forgotten that Robert Corson did take a noticeable part in the deliberations of Conference itself; and, in his own peculiar way, his course was an influential and useful one. Further, he could not help having been brought into the Church before any of the great crises in its history transpired ; and he had the rare merit of clinging to the main cause of Methodism in this Province, through weal and woe, until all the difficulties it had to confront were tided over ; such as the first Missionary aggression ; the organization of the Canada Annual Conference ; the separation from the States ; the first state of independency ; the union with the British Conference ; the disruption of the union, and the separate action of the two sections of *Wesleyanism ;* the happy reign of the restored union ; and the final work of organizing a Methodist church for the whole Dominion of Canada. And he took a profound interest in every useful movement, as it transpired, if nothing further. Why, then, may we not notice these instructive events as we drift along down the stream of this old minister's long public life ? Why ?

But some may say that I have dealt in materials below the dignity of such lofty themes. Truly, some of the incidents would have been too homely and familiar, if dignified history had been my main object. But, on the contrary, my principal design was the portrayal of an individual, and he one of the most unpretentious and pleasantly accessible of men. And, as I had to describe a bush-born preacher, destined to be a pioneer nearly all his public life, who was borne up and along in his toils and privations by the exuberance of his joyous, playful spirits, I have concluded, that a style of phraseology and illustration suited to rude scenes through which he was called to pass would be the best adapted to recall those times; and would best befit the genial, unexacting, and almost rollicking good man I was trying to present to my readers. In short, I wished to make his "old companions in distress" live their lives over again along with him; aye, and cause this generation also to live that peculiar life along with him and his compeers.

I wish to present a Robert Corson, or a "Father Corson," whom his friends, old and young, would know and recognize again. Such a one, I believed, would be welcomed back with open arms, while any other would receive the proverbial "cold shoulder." In pursuance of the above intentions, I have gone farther and used the colloquialisms and *patois* of former days; presented old-time pet names, some of them rugged enough (albeit Mrs. Robert Corson herself, from her native delicacy of taste, disallowed their use among her third generation of Corsons); described the homely scenes of the rude heroic age of Canadian history, civil and ecclesiastical, to do which I have preserved snatches of doggrel poetry, one at least smacking a little of profanity, because I thought a legitimate description required them.

I have no sympathy with those scarcely honest people who would make out all their ancestors to be of gentle blood and manners; and who think it imprudent to hint that a minister (I beg their pardon, "a clergyman"), ever did so sordid and vile a thing as to perform manual labour —those persons I mean who have so much conceit and affectation that they can never do nor say a natural or sensible thing; no, I care not for their criticisms. Of their attacks, I am prepared to say to the whole army of exquisites, "*Come one, come all*," *and as soon as you like!*

> "Believe us, noble Vere de Vere,
> From yon blue heavens above us bent,
> The grand old gardener and his wife
> Smile at the claims of long descent:
> Howe'er it be, it seems to me,
> 'Tis only noble to be good,
> Kind hearts are more than coronets,
> And simple faith than Norman blood."

And I embrace this opportunity to take *on* myself, as EDITOR, and *off* my contributors and publisher, all the odium for all things *homely, quaint, unusual* and *outre*. But if any person, in a friendly spirit, will point out anything slip-shod, or in *really* bad taste, I will promise to try and amend my ways.

Another objection may arise, namely, that I have reproduced myself, in adopting portions of my "BIOGRAPHICAL HISTORY" and sundry other works of mine, which related to Mr. Corson, in this memoir of him. My plea, if this charge should be made, is this: It has been only gathering into this what was dispersed abroad in those, with the additional merit, that I have corrected, condensed, or amplified, as it was needed.

1*

There are some sanctimonious people who will, no doubt, say my book is not *religious enough;* that is, it is not so grave and demure as it should have been made. To such and to all I solemnly declare I have sought to subserve the interests of earnest religion in all I have done, to quicken the ministry, and to promote the welfare of the Church at large.

With these explanations I commend my peculiar featured little offspring to the care and direction of THAT GOD who created, with their respective idiosyncracies, both ROBERT CORSON, the subject of the book, and

JOHN CARROLL,
The Author.

Don Mount, April 22nd, 1879.

EDITOR'S OBLIGATIONS.

For the large amount of matter furnished by the accomplished sons of the deceased, and for their suggestions and criticisms, I am under unspeakable obligations. To those who, whether requested or spontaneously, furnished contributions for this work, I wish publicly to tender my thanks. And, especially, I must not forget to acknowledge that the excellencies of the book, if it have any, both literary and mechanical, along with publisher and printers, are largely due to the REV. DR. WOOD, often before my co-labourer in similar efforts, by going over it carefully while passing through the press. Even the watchful care of the Rev. Mr. Matthewson, as the copyist of a small portion of it, has been of service to me. If there are others to whom I ought to have acknowledged obligations, my omissions must be ascribed to want of thought, and not to design. J. C.

PRELIMINARY SURVEY.

Methodism, if we have judged aright, was a revival, a renewal of true Christianity—in its doctrine of salvation by grace through faith—its self-denying sin-hating spirit, and its lovingly aggressive advance against the darkness, misery, and ignorance of a sinful world. That movement, begun in England early in the eighteenth century, had established itself, and taken form and consistence in the old American colonies, or at least, it arose coincidently with the existence and independence of the United States; and before the century was finished its heralds had crossed the waters which constitute the dividing line between the new republic and Britain's still newer colonies, north of the latitude forty-five; and great were the successes of this form of Christianity in the "two Canadas" during the first twenty years of its provincial existence.

Then, alas, came the unnatural war between the parent and the child; or the two sections of the Anglo-Saxon family, the elder with its adherents, and the newer one. Every religious interest suffered in the British colonies, especially in Canada, and those of Methodism among the rest. But after the "deadly blast" of "war" was "blown" over, the recuperative power of this vital form of Bible religion began to assort itself in renovated societies, extensive revivals, and the upraising of instruments to carry forward these Gospel conquests.

The Methodist revival may be said to have produced its own preachers. "When God gave the word" of free grace, "great was the company of them that published it." It was so in England, as exemplified in the raising up of a Maxfield, a Mitchell, a Nelson, an Oliver, a Storey, and scores of others. So also it was in America, both before and after the Revolution; God providing a Watters, a Gatch, and a Garretson, native Americans, to carry on the work, which the few British preachers could have never overtaken. These men knew the Anglo-American mind and manners, and were better adapted to be useful in the States than any laborer, however devoted, with none but old country ideas. And Canada was no exception in this respect to Methodism in all other places where it had been planted.

In the last century, Sylvanus Keeler, if no others, had gone forth into the field from the wilds of Canada; and early in this century a Bangs, a Perry, a Picket, a Prindle, and others of Canadian growth, recruited the ranks of this sacramental host. But, especially, Methodism showed its productive energy and resources during the war of 1812-15 (when many of the American preachers were withdrawn, and there were no opportunities of receiving contingents from that side of the line), in manning the walls of the Methodist Zion with good men and true, who sprang to the rescue from out the fields and workshops of Canada itself; take the cases of Reynolds, Adams, Culp, Covenhoven, Hopkins, Harmon, Swazey, and Youmans. After the war the necessity for home-bred preachers was none the less than immediately before. That strife had created a prejudice against American citizens, at least in the minds of many, and even the American church authorities saw the importance of supplying the Canada section of their work with British subjects; and the Great Head of the Church provided for this demand by raising up men whose minds were not only in harmony with the government of the country, but men also, who knew the manners and customs of the land, and were inured to the hardships of this then newly-settled country. From 1815 to the Conference of 1822 Canada had produced (not to mention any that failed early) two naturalized Americans, two Irishmen, one Englishman, and two native Canadians, eight in all, three of whom, Ferguson, Peale and Wilson, had known the hardships of military service. William Brown and John Ryerson were the native Canadians.

But at the next Conference (the one for 1823) Canada produced no less than seven laborers to cultivate her own moral wastes, all of whom were either born in Canada, or thoroughly acclimated to it, two or three of whom were able and willing to perform its roughest kind of work. The list of names was as follows:—William Ryerson, William Griffis, Joseph Castle, Jacob Poole, David Wright, Solomon Waldron and Robert Corson. The three last were specially of the character just indicated; but neither of them was so pre-eminently adapted to the hardest work in the hardest places as ROBERT CORSON, whose life and labours myself and co-biographers are now to portray and detail. Mr. Corson and several, if not all, of the other candidates had performed circuit work under a Presiding Elder, for one or more years before that Conference, but they came now *officially* to view for the first time.

Mr. Corson's life, from his birth to the Conference of 1823, from the Conference of 1823 till that of 1858, when he superannuated, and from the Conference of 1858 till 1878, when he died, will constitute the plan of this book. These general divisions each will admit of all sorts of particulars necessary to illustrate our subject, in the form of subordinate divisions.

TABLE OF CONTENTS.

I. WHAT RELATES TO ROBERT CORSON PRIOR TO 1823.

1. *Events before his Conversion:*

Paternity and birth-place—Hard work and plain fare—Virtuous youth—Homely pleasures—Mrs. Force's testimony—Causes of youthful popularity—Religious leanings.
The War and his services therein—Volunteers and serves six months—A cowardly comrade—His own brief statement—His song-singing capabilities—Snatches of patriotic songs, C. Flumerfeldt's.
Dismissed, and salt-making—His residence at the salt-works leads to his acquaintance with Emma Freeland—The emigration of her family from New Brunswick—Toilsome journey—Meets the Editor's family in Niagara—Grounds of attachment between Robert and Emma—Marriage and conversion.
Revival under Joseph Gatchell—"Bob will be a preacher"—Emma Corson's usefulness—Their religious associations and privileges while at the "Thirty"—Camp-meeting at the "Fifty"—Self-tuition.
Resume of these events by Dr. J. W. Corson—Gov. Carlton and his daughter—Antecedents of the Corsons and Freelands—The country and its settlers—The early itinerants—Corson's travels anticipated. From page 1 to 19.

1817-1822.

2. *From his Conversion until his going out on a Circuit:*

Joined M. E. Church in 1817—Warren, Byham, and Ferguson—Removed to Oxford in 1818.
Licensed to preach in 1820—Preachers on the Long-Point Circuit—Operations of exhorters and local preachers then—Local preacher two years—Jackson, Williams, I. B. Smith, Culp, and Ferguson.
Serves as a junior preacher on Westminster Circuit under P. E.—Long absences, and severe privations to Mrs. C.
Quotations from "Itinerant's Memorial"—Salary—Recommended for probation. From page 19 to 24.

II. FROM THE CONFERENCE OF 1823 TO THAT OF 1858, WHEN HE RETIRED FROM THE ACTIVE MINISTRY.

[*Distribution of this part of his life.*]

1823-24.

1. *Mr. Corson's Ministry from 1823 to the formation of the Canada Annual Conference in 1824:*

Westmoreland Conf.—Last U. S. Conf. for C. preachers—Did Corson go?—MS. Journals of old Genesee Conf.—Candidates: Griffis, Waldron, J. Poole, Castle, Wright, Wm. Ryerson, Corson.
To labor alone on the New London Circuit—What townships it comprehended—Labors—Gains. From page 24 to 27.

1824-26.

2. *Mr. Corson's Gospel Labours from 1824 to 1828*:

Hallowell Conference—Meeting at York, on the way down—Who present—Garb of some preachers—His appointment necessitates a move—Dumfries Circuit—Its character and extent—Interesting details from his own pen—Henry Chrysler's recollections—Dr. W. Corson's statements—Builds two chapels—The Ellises—Squire Kilborn's letter, describing Mr. Corson—Immersing a big Dutchman—Editor's recollections of the Yonge Street C. M. and R. C.—Increase—Full connexion and deacon's orders—His old parchment—The "Fifty Conference full of suggestions. From page 27 to 34.

1826-27.

Hiatus between *Dumfries* and *Westminster* Cts. filled with Hamilton (township) Conference particulars—Conversion of an Indian tribe or band—C. goes to Westminster—Quotations from "Itinerant's Memorial"—A bachelor colleague—Small collection—Getting a wedding suit under difficulties, and losing the bride—Ticklish baptism—Paid in lumber—Small allowances, but wins souls—Running down a squirrel. From page 35 to 41.

1827-28.

Conf. at "Springer's Meeting-house"—Anxious one—Ryan retires—Corson ordained *elder*—Goes with Griffis—Neither servile nor aspiring Quotations from "Case and Co."—Increase—Corson's private memoranda—Incident at Woodhouse church. From page 41 to 43.

3. *From the founding of the Canada Church to the Union with the British Conference.*

1828-29.

Memorable Conf. at "Switzer's Chapel," Earnestown—Last jurisdiction of an American bp.—Routine—Conf. resolves itself into an independent Church—C. acted as usual with the majority—Taken ill, and a weary ride home—Mammy Gilbert pronounces the preacher "wery sick, or else was a creat crunt"—Appointment and move to Whitby—Its extent—Includes the Scugog Indians—Union revival—Aaron Hurd—Editor and E. Evans overtake Corson—Dinner at S. Holden's—The Editor meets Mrs. Corson at the log parsonage door—Not the mother of the Gracchi, but of five sons called after as many ministers—Presque Isle C. M.—Preaching and doings there—Lorenzo Dow—Corson and Ferguson's preaching, respectively—Plenty of water without immersion—Corson's vivacity. From page 43 to 55.

1829-30.

Conf. at "Bowman's Meeting-house"—Incidents of the Conf.—Read off again for Whitby—His MS. "Sketch"—Circuit enlarged by adding part of Cobourg—Vandusen called out—Anecdotes of Van.—Meet them at Presque Isle once more—All the labourers but the editor gone. From page 55 to 58.

1830-31.

Kingston Conf.—Adjourned to Belleville—Member of General Conference—Appointed to Toronto (township) Ct.—His own account of it—Names of the four "log churches"—Increase—Salary—H. Shaler—Primitive Methodists—Preachers help to harvest J. G.'s wheat crop. From page 58 to 60.

1831-32.

York Conf.—Revival time—Continued on T. Ct.—No less than three several colleagues—McNabb, Rose, Kennedy—First marriage ceremony performed by R. C.—Names of parties and copy of certificate—The Foster Family—Recollections of Mr. and Mrs. W. Foster and other old friends—Question of height—J. W. C. *From page 60 to 65.*

1832-33.

Hallowell Conference—Initiation of first Union—Corson favourable—Yonge St. Ct. with D. Wright—Pronounces his Ct. "one of the best"—Enjoys showers of blessings—Particulars—Long and Gatchell—Names of Local Preachers—Resides at R. Hill—Neighbours. *From page 65 to 68.*

4. *Mr. Corson during the seven years of the first Union :*

Unifying Conf.—E. Ryerson—Messrs. Marsden and Stinson—Unanimous vote—Change of name—Re-appointed to Yonge Street—J. R., P. E.—Centre of discontent—Organizing of a M. E. Conf. at Cummer's chapel—The churches of that vicinity—Corson loyal, but liberal—His course with regard to office and office-bearers—A humourist philosopher. *From page 69 to 74.*

1834-35.

Newmarket Circuit—Kingston Conf. in 1834—Revs. Messrs. Alder and Grindrod—"*Inexpediency* of ordaining any more local preachers"—Mr. C. begins to take a part in Conf. deliberations—His junior colleague, T. F.—Antecedents—Use of published letters—Family residences traced, and recollection of neighbors, by Dr. W. C. Corson—Attempt to get a "local habitation"—The new farm at German Mills—Heroism of the mother—Homely pleasures of a retired family—Details of revivals and their promoters on the N. Circuit and its vicinity. *From page 75 to 82.*

1835-36.

Whitby Circuit—Hamilton Conf.—Many agitated, but Corson calm—Chronicles of the Whitby Circuit—Labours, revivals, gains, &c. *From page 82 to 84.*

1836-37.

Whitby, continued—Belleville Conf.—Loss of a standard-bearer—Loses Fawcett and obtains J. C. Will—T. F's marriage and the circumstances—Whitby suffers small part of the aggregate decrease—Rev. Dr. Cummings tells a good story of Mr. Corson's preaching at Cazenovia, N.Y.*—Information as to Dr. J. W. C's whereabouts. *From page 84 to 89.*

1837-38.

President Harvard and the Toronto Conf.—E. Ryerson's return from England—Resolutions on "Govt. Grants"—Mr. C.—A hoist back to Dumfries—Will, his colleague, dies—Speculations as to the supply—Gives up the farm—*Resume* and detail of residences, clearing up some obscurities, by Dr. J. W. C.—Prospective section—The children who accompanied the parents—Henry Chrysler's recollections—A wedding that "hangs fire"—A ceremony without a hitch from Squire Kilborn—McKenzie's Rebellion—Its effect on the position of Wesleyan Methodists in the country—President Harvard's manifesto, and what followed thereon—To be kept in till the Conference. *From page 89 to 96.*

---

* But Dr. J. W. C. thinks it applies to another man than his father.

1838-39.

Conf. in Rear St. Church, Kingston—E. Ryerson made popular by M. S. Bidwell's defence—Appointed Soy.—Discussion of the late action of the President and Editor—A sharp debate, which is ended by an explosion of laughter, produced by a singular apologetic speech for the Prest.—C. re-appointed to Dumfries—Wm. Coleman set down as col., but placed elsewhere, and Charles Gilbert called out. From page 96 to 98.

1839-40.

Fourth subdivision of the 2nd period—Anxious Conf.—*Guardian's* course displeasing—Dr. Alder sent to subjugate the Conf. but fails—C. always with the Canadians—*Long Point* Ct., now called *Simcoe*—David Hardie, col.—Mr. C.'s own notes—Correspondence commences with the Editor—This probably the true date of the Woodhouse incident—Great connex'onal increase.
From page 98 to 100.

1840-41.

5. *The seven years of the divided Wesleyan operations:*

The Conference for 1840 (in Belleville) more anxious than the last—B. Conference makes demands which were resisted, and a delegation appointed to go home—W. and E. Ryerson—Corson with the Canadian interests—Returned to Simcoe with C. G.—Col. Neal—Corson preaches his funeral sermon—British Conf. retires from the Union, and the delegates return and convoke a "Special Conference"—Whitehead Prest.—Eleven withdrew—Separation between Corson and a choice friend—Reconstructed stations of the *London Dist.* given—Simcoe takes more territory and more work—A large nett gain on the Ct.
From page 100 to 104.

1841-42.

Conf. assembled again in *Toronto*—Several notables missed—Case, E. Evans, Stinson, Richey, Lang—Whitehead replaced by W. Ryerson—Corson to *Napanee*—Gilbert Miller—The iourney down described by his son, Dr. W. C. Corson —Mrs. C. cheered by a turtle—Residences: Napanee and Newburgh—Mr. C.'s Memoranda—A sleepy congregation awakened by silence.
From page 104 to 108.

1842-43.

Conf. once more at Picton—A. Green, Prest.—C.'s Chairman drops his standard—A tentative discontinuance of the chairmen's travels through their Districts, with which change Corson always sympathized—Re-appointed to Napanee— Changes Miller for Haw—Trying year for the Corson family—Death of the saintly wife and mother—Touching account from two sources—Vandusen, the funeral, and the burial-place—The loss abridges Mr. C.'s usefulness.
From page 108 to 114.

1843-44.

Hopeful Conf.—Great increase—Sent to *Bath and Isle of Tente*—C. R. Allison— Has to come down to $100!—Injustice of the old arrangement—Case of hardship given. Pages 114 and 115.

1844-45.

First *Brockville* Conf.—The travelling of the chairmen restored—*Consoorn* Ct.—
His own account—Colleague—Salary. Page 116.

1845-46.

First *St. Catharines* Conf.—Decrease from unfortunate political writing—Lessons to be learned—Corson appointed to Sheffield—Little progress—Lively speech—Intervention of friends to get him married—Excessive labours of the preacher, but further decrease—Determination to send a Delegation to England—J. Ryerson and Green. From page 116 to 119.

1846-47.

Kingston Conf.—Stationing Com. send Mr. C. far to the West—He indignantly remonstrates—Comforts himself with a wife—Proved a good—His own account of marriage, journey, and Ct.—Dr. J. W. Corson's advice—Some account of the second Mrs. C.—Parries a question—Dr. W. Corson's account of his stepmother—Information gained by the Editor by succeeding to the London Dist.—Mr. C.'s description of his two several wives—Their privations and shifts on the *Adelaide Mission* -Rev. Thos. Williams—Amusing episode at Wallaceburg.
From page 119 to 125.

6. *From the reconstruction of the Union, in 1847, to the admission of the Lower Canada and Hudson Bay Districts into the Canada Conference, in 1854.*

1847-48.

Most relating to this year anticipated—Delegation to England successful—Union formally restored at Conf. of 1847—Mr. C. receives a British brother for colleague, and they amalgamate the two societies in the *Warwick and Adelaide Mission*—W. Ryerson their visiting Chairman. From 125 to 127.

1848-49.

Bellville Conf. and *Rev. Dr. Dixon*—*Norwich Circuit*—The travels of Chairmen terminated, and how it came about—Dr. Richey, the acting Prest., travels through the Connexion—Corson's memoranda of the year—State of the Circuit—History, character, and doings of his predecessor—How he was qualified to cope with such difficulties—Small increase. From page 127 to 133.

1849-50.

Interesting Conf. at *Hamilton*, in '49—Corson returned to *Norwich*—Editor attended his August Qr. Mg., and the observations he made on Mr. C.'s management and general success—Numerous pastoral visits—Comforts of his home—Visit to a discouraged brother—Services of the Quarterly Meeting.
From page 133 to 136.

1850-51.

Second Brockville Conf.—Dr. Baugs—Death of *Healy* and *Metcalf*—Went to his home in the West, and then further west to *Gosfield*—Its geographical position—Mr. C.'s own account—Feels the burden of local difficulties—Amusing way of referring to them. From page 136 to 139.

1851-52.

Toronto Conf. and *Crowland Circuit*—Young Irish colleague, W. C.—Under the Editor's chairmanship—How I found him—Very observant—"Bishop's Sermon." From page 138 to 140.

1852-53.

Kingston Conf.—Returns, but name different in the Minutes—Desire for change—Promise a sprightly young colleague—How I obtained one, and who it was—A long letter from that colleague, R. Clarke, full of interesting particulars relative to Mr. Corson, embracing conversation, study, visits, sermonizing, &c.—Mr. C's habits of reading to the people—A letter of the Editor's—A MS. letter of his own. From page 140 to 147.

1853-54.

Hamilton Conf.—*Cainsville* Ct.—His Chairman visits him in his new house—The letter of an observing acquaintance relative to Father Corson, as seen for several years—Rev. A. A. Smith—Things amusing. From page 148 to 153.

7. *From 1854 to his Superannuation.*

1854-55.

Belleville Conf.—Reported increase—Hudson Bay Missions and Lower C. Dist.—Editor separated from his old friend. From page 153 to 154.

1855-56.

The *London* Conf. of 1855 memorable—Four additional missionaries for Hudson Bay—Revivals through the Connexion—Editor's own station.
From page 155 to 156.

1856-57.

Brockville Conf. and Prest. Wood, J. E. Scy.—Renewed intimacy with Corson—Both delayed after the Session—Journey up together—C. spends a Sabbath at Belleville—The pioneer and pedant pitted against each other, and success of the former—*Klineburg* Ct.—C.'s notes—Letter from a local preacher—Upsetting of a table—Becomes less observant of little matters—Way of demonstrating his capability for the effective work—"*Pen-portrait,*" by Dr. *J. W. C.*—Size—Like Lyman Beecher—Writing on his knee—Leans forward—"Smiling Minister"—Face and head—Voice—Mirthfulness -Use of his comical stories—Prayer with a R. C. (*infra*)—Dress—Like Moody—English vernacular—Paternal title—Draper in the burning ship—Letter at 84—Transitions—Parallel between him and Jay. From page 156 to 170.

III. FROM MR. CORSON'S SUPERANNUATION TO HIS DEATH; OR FROM 1858 TO 1878.

Montreal Conf.—Pleaded to continue in his work—Locates in Cobourg.

CONTENTS.

1. From his settlement in Cobourg till his removal to his house in Cainsville, a period of fifteen years.

At the *Hamilton Conf.*, in 1859, asked to resume—While pleading, the Editor sketched him—The first of the *"Conference Crayons"*—Crayon first: True Briton—Antecedents—Humour—Conference speeches—Odd juxtaposition—Wishes—His summary—His keeping a "boarding-house" vindicated—His wide acquaintance and means of usefulness (*infra*)—Dr. Chalmers and "Sandy Paterson"—Becomes polished himself in his old days—Preaches much in *person* as well as by *proxy*—Rev. W. McC.'s corn story—Pleasant badinage in Markham—Visit to the Editor at Peterboro'—Cold return journey—Rev. A. Hardie, A.M., and the student boarders—Brevity of F. C.'s prayers (*infra*)—Father Corson as a teacher of Homiletics!—His readiness—Examples—A Cobourg gentleman's testimony—Letter to the Editor—Long letter in the *Guardian*—New York—Philadelphia—Planting potatoes—Newburg- Peterboro' C. M. and old friends—Prince Albert—A. Hurd—Cobourg—Cainsville—Brantford—Dundas—Harrisburg—Guelph—Yonge Street—Visit to a sick son—Home, finishing a journey of 2,000 miles—Keeps to the old method of private conveyances and by-ways—Close of his work in Cobourg. From page 170 to 196.

2. From his return to Cainsville till the death of his second wife in 1877.

A home near his son William—Ill, and treated by his son—Supplied as "The young preacher on the Circuit"—Rev. W. Willoughby's testimony—His own sketch of *fifty-seven years* Canadian Methodist History, embracing the work in all its stages, phases, and characteristics—Strength of the several Methodist bodies—Contrasts between Methodism in 1817 and 1875—Old and new-fashioned preaching and preachers—Remembrances of some particular localities—Thrilling letter from a local preacher. From page 196 to 204.

3. From the death of the second Mrs. Corson in 1877, to his own death in 1878.

Serious blow—Obituary of Amy Lockwood Corson by Rev. W. Willoughby—History, character, and happy death—Father Corson removes to his son's at Brantford, and enjoys the kind attention and companionship of Mrs William and her little ones—Peaceful death—Funeral—Tomb—End.
From page 204 to 211.

☞ There is one thing of which I should apprise the reader, in justice, both to myself and the printer, as also for the reader's own guidance :—It will be observed by those who examine the execution of the book with attention, that its analysis and the use of CAPITALS and *italics* in the Index is different from that in the body of the book. This arose from the printer not understanding my design and, therefore, undertaking to amend copy in that particular, for perhaps one-fourth of the book. The mistake was not discovered early enough to change what had been done; but after my intention was understood, copy was strictly followed. This has occasioned a discrepancy between the earlier and later pages, and somewhat marred the mechanical effect, but it has in no wise affected the sense. Let it be remembered, however, that the TABLE OF CONTENTS presents the true PLAN of the book and distribution of Mr. Corson's life.—EDITOR.

APPENDIX, page 214.
OUR MOTHER, by Dr. J. W. Corson, 214.
HARDSHIPS do. Do. 229.
The Parting Do. 229.
Dangers Do. 232.
Joys in trials Do. 235.
Prayer for Christian Union, Do. 241.

SKETCHES OF SERMONS BY R. C., 243.
 1. Divinely Commissioned and Willing Messenger, 244.
 2. Nativity of Christ, 246.
 3. Reading and Seeking out of the Book of the Law, 247.
 4. The Reward of the Righteous and Punishment of the Wicked, 248.
 5. The Foundation Stone laid in Zion, 250.
 6. The Turning Away of God's Anger, and the Results, 251.
 7. The King's Highway of Holiness, 252.
 8. God's Command to Comfort His People, 254.
 9. The Enduring Character of God's Word, 255.
 10. The Ends of the Earth to Look to God for Salvation, 256.
 11. Is the Gospel Message Believed? 258.
 12. The Blast of the Great Trumpet, 259.
 13. Importance of Seeking God While He may be Found, 260.
 14. God's Charge to Zion's Watchmen, 261.
 15. Quietness and Assurance Attendant on Righteousness, 263.
 16. Our Stay while Walking in Darkness, 264.

FATHER CORSON.

I. WHAT RELATES TO ROBERT CORSON PRIOR TO 1823.

1793—1817.

I.—EVENTS BEFORE HIS CONVERSION

IT will be seen by statements made by other members of the family ; and especially by the elaborate papers given in by our subject's gifted and scholarly son, Dr. John Wesley Corson (which I am loath to break up into fragments and distribute into the several places to which they respectively belong naturally, and therefore leave intact, to be perused continuously as they were written) that Robert Corson, son of Daniel Corson and Rebecca Lawrison, was born in the Township of Clinton, Niagara District, then almost a trackless wilderness, his birth occurring September 12th, 1793. He knew what hard work and plain fare were, from infancy to manhood. His position and circumstances, along with a naturally docile and willing temperament, combined to give his youth a virtuous direction, making him moral, industrious, temperate, and amiable. Yet let no one think that his was a gloomy life of toil: he was contented with his lot, and entered with zest into the rude and boisterous recreations, characteristic of the youth of a new country, before they become sobered and solemnized by the influence of vital religion. His day's toil, of chopping or ox-driving, was often succeeded by an exciting walk through the dark forest, illuminated by the light of the hickory bark torch,* to attend the "husking bee," or "frolic," as it was sometimes called, which usually wound up with a supper and various sorts of plays, ending, finally, with the-not-least-pleasurable part of the programme to the boys, that of seeing the girls home to their several places of abode.

But lest I should be thought to be "drawing on my imagination for facts," I copy some written statements from the lips of Mrs. Mercy Force, a surviving sister of our venerable deceased friend, taken down by Dr. Wm. C. Corson, and afterwards affirmed to me personally, during a very pleasant interview with that old lady. Dr. William's manuscript reads as follows:—

"His moral character was without reproach; and, as a boy, he was exceedingly kind and attentive to his mother. He had no small vices so prevalent at that time, such as the use of tobacco, &c. He was very lively, however—the life indeed of any company; could tell droll stories, and sing a good song, and he was very fond of wrestling, in which he excelled. The habit of industry, which was such

* They did not always enjoy the benefit of a light. I once heard the extravagant account of an overgrown, barefooted boy's experience in returning with some others, similarly situated, from a "husking," who said, that all they had to guide their way was "the fire they struck out of the stones in the road by the contact of their toe nails!"

a prominent feature in his after life, early showed itself. In fact, even as a boy, he was never idle. He was always very tender-hearted, and at the time of any revival was greatly 'stirred' (to use the words of my aunt) showing a deep concern for his soul, years before his conversion. It was his gay and lively disposition, along with song-singing and story-telling, which made him a favorite in the company (the 'Flankers,' as they were called) in which he served, and in which he volunteered before he was out of his teens, in the war of 1812-15. His leanings were always towards the Methodists. Though his mother was a stiff Church of England woman, his father, I think, was an irreligious man, but I forgot to ascertain this from my aunt." *

With regard to the war and his services therein, his surviving sister, Mrs. Force, informed me that, as soon as the news of the declaration of hostilities reached Canada, Robert being then between nineteen and twenty, and his brother Lawrence, or "Larry," as they usually called him, being eighteen, they were, of course, subject to military service; an officer of their company came one night to the door of their rural home and announced that they were to be down at the "Big Road," as the main thoroughfare from Niagara River to the head of the lake was usually called, "by eight o'clock the next morning, with three days' provisions." The boys sprang from their comfortable beds with alacrity, impelled by the love of excitement and adventure, as well as the fire of patriotism, and began to make the needed preparations. They were eager for the

* It will be seen, by information used further on, that the Corson family entertained the Methodist preachers during Robert's boyhood.—ED.

fray, and for annihilating all the invaders in a very summary manner! It was otherwise with the dear, anxious mother, with her daughters around her in tears, as well as herself, fearing that "poor Bob and Larry" might never return from the field of conflict to the cottage on the "mountain" more; still, the preparations for their outfit went on through the too swiftly passing hours of that sleepless and agitated night—a spectacle this adapted to make the angelic messengers of "peace on earth" weep with disappointment.

I am not prepared to say whether what I am about to relate occurred the next day (or whether the volunteering took place before) and this call was only consequent upon a previous enrolment; yet, before or after, all agree that the following occurred: A certain proportion of each militia company was required for active service in the field for a certain number of months. An appeal for volunteers was first made, I presume, that if that did not produce the required number, a draft was next to be resorted to. When the appeal was made for volunteers to Captain Konle's company, to which the Corson boys belonged, Robert was the first man who stepped forward out of the ranks in answer to the call, and Lawrence was the next, and they, with others volunteering, or drafted, were marched off to the frontier, where they performed military service six months before they had the gratification of returning to their forest home on the "mountain." During the time of their service, first and last, they participated in more than one battle, such as Queenston and Niagara, or as they called it, "Missauga Point." Robert's courage was not likely to be greatly inflamed by his nearest comrade, of whom Dr. William has preserved the following tradition:

"The man who marched next to father was a great coward. At a skirmish at Missauga Point, the man would look down at himself and express aloud his wonder that he *did not fall!*"

Mr. Corson's own account, in his own "Short Sketch of his Life," is as follows: "In 1812 war was declared; I volunteered with other young men to serve my king and country for six months. When our time expired we returned to our several homes. But in 1813 we were again called to take up arms in defence of our country now invaded. When we arrived at Niagara the battle was ended in favour of the Americans. However, a few shots were fired."

It is surprising how enured men may become to danger, as exemplified in the well-known thoughtlessness and gaity of soldiers during hostilities, with the exception of the few men of pious thoughtfulness, like the praying and preaching Ferguson and Harmon, who served on that same frontier during certain parts of that war, is proverbial. Robert Corson and his comrades were no exception to the general thoughtlessness referred to. He seems to have returned home at the expiration of his term of service uncontanimated by bad moral habits (he never having been known to utter a profane expression), yet he not only joined in the prevailing merriment, but was largely its promoter and leader. Dr. Wm. Corson has already given us an account of his popularity among the "Flankers" (flank companies, composed of light active men, for quick movements on the skirts of an enemy), because of his "gay and lively disposition," joined to his song-singing capabilities.

The songs which beguiled the long evenings and the weary hours of the boys in the camp would not endure very severe criticism as to their poetical and literary merits, but the lads were not very fastidious. Dr. W. Corson has preserved a single verse of a song which served to stir the patriotism of the rustic soldiery, which, perhaps, may provoke a "disdainful smile" from those who cannot endure a homely thing. But to our specimen:

> "The lion is the king of beasts,
> And still shall be the same:
> We did maintain Old England's rights,
> And drove them from the plain."

This was probably a reference to the pushing of the invading American army over the brow at Queenston Heights when Robert and his comrades "came in on the run," after a march of sixteen miles.*

But of patriotic songs, the most elevated to which the war-period gave birth, was the one composed by CORNELIUS FLUMMERFELDT, a militia-man out of Scarborough, who also, like Robert Corson, (who, I dare say, often sang the song of the other,) became a Methodist Preacher in the Canada connexion. It related to the capture of General Hull's army. Tradition said, the inspiration came upon him while standing sentinel at night; and that he inscribed "the numbers as the numbers came," with the point of his bayonet, on the sentry-box. I have tried vainly to recover the whole of the sonnet; many of the old people remember to have heard it

---

* The following snatch of another song, although it illustrates the spirit of the times, is hardly admissable into the text, and, therefore I relegate it to the margin:—

> "There is a General Hull,
> The old numskull,
> Who thought to rule this nation;
> But General Brock,
> Hit him a knock,
> And sent him to d—nation."

sung, but none can recall the words. I have myself a single snatch of it, which has lingered in my memory since I was a child of six years. To give that verse may be the means of recovering the rest, which would be of interest, because of its author and his times. He had described the alarm created by the news of General Hull's invasion, and then followed these four lines :

> " 'Twas then our brave commander,
> Sir Isaac Brock by name,
> Took shipping at Niagara,
> And unto York he came."

The mustering of the forces, the march, and the capture, followed upon that.

This young man so ready to obey the summons of his country to the field of deadly conflict, gladly returned to more peaceful avocations when his period of service was ended. He was always possessed of shrewd discernment in business matters, and was as industrious to carry out what his mind had projected, characteristics which would have made him rich, if he had not become a Methodist Preacher. The war produced "non-intercourse" between the two nations, and cut off the supply of salt from the Province, which had been mostly from Onondaga, in the State of New York. The distress was consequently very great; even the army was sometimes destitute of this very necessary condiment. I can myself remember this destitution. My father and older brothers being in the army, and the family being dependants on military rations. I recall distinctly, that while the army lay at Burlington Heights, sometimes the person who had the contract of furnishing the bread for the troops was unable to procure salt; and as bread could not be dispensed with, whatever its defects at those times.

it was baked and served out without the necessary seasoning. Fortunately, our family had usually some salt in the house, a portion of which was sprinkled on the slices of bread before eating. There was then no knowledge of the Goderich Salt Mines, but a few "salt licks" had been discovered by the deer and the cattle resorting to them in certain places in the country, and temporary salt works were set up during the war, on a very small scale. One of those old abandoned wells I afterwards saw in the old survey of Toronto Township, about two or three miles north of the present village of Sydenham. A salt spring which was utilized in this way, somewhere in the Township of Saltfleet, or Barton, was rented and worked by Robert Corson, after his return from the wars* about the time of his majority, by which he is said to have made money, till the return of peace, when the industry was no longer paying. The war price of the commodity was ten dollars a bushel.

But young Corson's residence in that part of the country, proved to be of greater advantage to him than all the profits of his business. When my own family arrived in this province from New Brunswick, in 1809, the year in which I was born, they met a family in Niagara from the same province to whom they became very much attached, by the name of Freeland. Countrymanship and amability were the grounds of this attachment. The oldest child in his family was a daughter, then fifteen years of age, called Emma, or as the New Brunswickers pronounced it "Emmer." The family came up the St. John's River from the neighbourhood of Frederickton by boats, thence up the Madawasca

* Reference from the "Sketch" shows that, having been released from following the British army to Burlington Heights, the remainder of the war was spent in manufacturing salt.

by the same means, as far as navigable; then, they had to perform a portage of *thirty-six miles* to the St. Lawrence on foot. The youngest boy was a mere baby, whom his amiable sister carried all that distance on her back, and a great mutual attachment was the result. They joined the St. Lawrence a hundred and eighteen miles below Quebec, where they met five other immigrant families, with whom they united in the purchase of a boat, which they sailed or rowed, or dragged according to circumstances, up the St. Lawrence to Kingston. There they embarked on a sailing vessel bound for Niagara, where they arrived in the autumn,* as our family had done by another route; namely,—from the Bay of Fundy to New York in a sailing packet,—to Albany in a sloop,—and from thence we rode in a lumber waggon across the whole length of the "Empire State," ferrying the Niagara River from Lewiston into the dominion of King George. Some of the very earliest things I remember were the encomiums passed by our family on "Emmer Freeland"—her dignity of character, her amiability, and her beauty. My oldest brothers were particularly eloquent on the last theme, they very emphatically pronouncing "Emmer Freeland a nice pretty gal." This family had settled in Binbrooke, not far from the Salt Springs, and young Corson made their acquaintance. Emma was one year younger than Robert, but taller proportionately than he, and she always preserved the bearing of a senior. It is said opposites have affinity for each other; the vivacity of Robert Corson seemed to find its compliment in the quietness and dignity of Emma Freeland; and Emma's gravity found its specific in

* I owe the information given in the text to the venerable Daniel Freeman, surviving brother of Mrs. Robert Corson, the next in seniority to herself.—ED.

Robert's exuberant spirits. Certain it is, they mutually loved, and they married—married early, to be a reciprocal blessing to each other for many long years: Robert was twenty-two years of age, and Emma twenty-one. The necessity for my dwelling on the excellencies of this lady and the benefits she conferred on her husband and family are superseded by the portraiture of her by her son, Dr. John Wesley Corson, a lady of whom the Rev. Dr. Rose says, "It would be impossible to say too much." There can be no doubt but Mr. Corson owed his usefulness largely to his wife.

This marriage took place in 1815, and their first residence was at the "Thirty," near, or at, the original home of the Corsons. Though both of them were virtuous and amiable, neither of them were converted at the time of their marriage, or for some little time after. Mrs. Corson was the first to give her heart to God; she began to seek His face about three months before her husband, and found peace to her soul at a Quarterly Meeting held at the "Fifty-mile Creek," a spot where, in days of yore, scores of precious souls were born into the kingdom. Robert soon followed his wife into the fold of Jesus.

A very considerable revival coincided with their conversion in that locality. Indeed Mrs. Force said the work spread into all the townships around. The Rev. Joseph Gatchel, then in a "located" relation, resided on a farm at the "Thirty," and his zeal and uncommon powers of exhortation, along with those of his wife, (a sister of the Rev. Nathan Bangs, afterwards D.D., who was quite equal to her husband, of whom a brother, who had heard her, said that her exhortations were "a stream of red-hot lightening,") was the instrument. Prayer-meetings were extemporized in private houses around the country. At one of these, held in Robert Corson's own house, he, while engaged in earnest prayer, found deliverance. Upon receiving which blessing, he sprung upon the bench against which he had been kneeling, and began to exhort with life and energy. The unconverted lads about the door, much impressed by the occurrence, with a prescience which proved prophetic, exclaimed to each other "Bob will be a preacher!" That was the way, in fact, in which preachers were made in the days of which I write. I should not forget to say that Emma Corson was not less instrumental than Robert in promoting the conversion of souls at that time, especially among her own sex. Mrs. Force narrates that it was not uncommon to see half-a-dozen young girls, who had been more or less impressed, or benefited by her means, at the close of a meeting, clustered around her, and clinging to her for her prayers, advice, and blessing, while all the parties were in tears, and her own "face was as that of an angel."

While Robert Corson and his wife were yet at the "Thirty," not long before they removed to Oxford, they were privileged to attend one of the old-fashioned, powerful camp-meetings which characterized that day, held under the superintendence of that commanding boernergis, the Rev. Henry Ryan, then Presiding Elder on the "Upper District," mayhap, assisted by his bachelor *confrere* from the "Lower" one, Elder Case, a son of consolation. This meeting was held at the "Fifty," picturesquely situated on the "mountain" side, about half way between base and summit. Its site may yet be seen from a meandering road winding through the groves of chestnut, butternut, and hickory trees, which, happily, still adorn the steep declivity along there, and comes out near the "Fifty Church." The last, if not the only time, I drove along down that precipitous roadway, the site was pointed out to me by my obliging driver, and some of the logs, if my imagination did not do more for me than my eyes, were still remaining. I could hope that the suggestion to me of John Macdonald, Esq., should be acted on, and this old landmark, along with many others besides, be photographed for the delection of this and future generations.

But to return, an incident occurred at that meeting, which impressed the susceptible heart, and lodged in the retentive memory of Robert Corson. A local preacher, from the American side of the Niagara River, by the name of Marr, came to this meeting, and related the account of his conversion, which was rather a remarkable one. He had been born and brought up in New Jersey, but after he was somewhat advanced towards manhood, he took offence at his father for entertaining the Methodist preachers, and left home and went to his uncle's, who lived a hundred miles away. But when he arrived there he found that his uncle also had received the ubiquitous Methodist preachers, and that a young companion of his youth, Daniel Freeman, was the preacher on the circuit. A certain ball was to have taken place among the young people, and Marr was pledged to attend it. Just before it came off he went to hear his old friend Freeman, and was somewhat impressed. After the sermon the young preacher conversed with him about his soul's interests, and extorted a promise from him to go with Mr. F. to his next appointment, in another neighbourhood, and on the night of the assembly too. He called upon the "managers" to excuse himself, and to say that he was going away to a religious meeting. They, very unexpectedly to him, desired him to call on the musician on the road to say that his services would not be required, as they had agreed to give up the projected folly. They, as well as he, had been impressed with the force of divine truth. Religious meetings took the place of dancing and hilarity, and a large ingathering of souls was the result. The relation of these events at the "Fifty" camp-meeting, made a very deep impression on the people assembled, who had up to that point seemed inattentive. One good lays the foundation for another.

This is, perhaps, the place to say that schools were scarce, and poor at that; the result of which was, that Robert Corson had enjoyed only a few months' tuition, put it all together. But he had learned, at least, to read, and was always fond of a book, and eagerly perused all that fell in his way, or that he could procure. His own account of the matter is, "The country was new, and schools were few and far between; yet, we improved our time, as we had a great desire to get knowledge." Thus, deficient as some might suppose him to have been, he was in advance of many around him; and he was destined to pursue this course of self-tuition as long as he lived.

This will be, perhaps, the best place to introduce the first paper of Dr. J. W. Corson, albeit, it anticipates a few things which belong to later stages of his father's life.

"*Origin,—Sir Guy Carleton—His Daughter—Canada between the Lakes—Rich Soil and Dense Forests—People—Hardships—Methodism, its Frontier Religion.*

"Lord Clive was once a clerk; Washington grew up a land surveyor; John Bunyan was a 'tinker.' On behalf of his loving sons, we may use the plural and say that our father began life as a farmer. And it will be soon be seen how admirably his previous hardy vocation fitted him for his wonderful labours as a frontier missionary. He was honoured of God in being useful. What Felix Neff was to the scattered and benighted peasants of the higher Alps, the deceased was to multitudes of the early settlers in the little log cabins often separated for miles, amid the dense forests of what was then known as 'Upper Canada.'

"Sailors and soldiers are rarely mean. As if further to strengthen him for his work, and give a spice of chivalry to his character, he was slightly military in his early tastes. He came up in a company of volunteers all breathless on the run in the double quick march, of the reserves, in aid of the British forces at the battle of Queenston. And in that war of 1812 he served for months with the militia that bravely defended the frontier.

"We mention these historical incidents with sincere love for the two great-nations of Anglo Saxon race. Each has its necessary and independent mission in the civilization of the world. And there is ample room for both. The faith that the departed so earnestly preached, assures us that we were ransomed by the death of a divine Redeemer. And we may reverently borrow an illustration from his fervent theology, by saying that even earthly freedom is commonly bought with blood. It has been so from the days of Marathon and Sempact down to Bunker Hill and Trafalgar. Cavour began the emancipation of Italy by a Sardinian victory in the Crimea. Gettysburg and Inkerman helped to free millions. It is consoling to feel that these struggles of our ancestors were overruled by a gracious Providence, to aid in the spread of that universal liberty, which has blessed every island and continent, where either of the two flags waves. And the ties of religion and commerce have so linked us together that we can afford to look even at the conflicts of the American Revolution, and those which succeeded it as calmly as we do at the story of the wars of the roses in England.

"Daniel Corson was born in Sussex County, New Jersey, some twelve years before the commencement of the war of the Revolution.

"A few years after the conclusion of the peace, our paternal grandfather, whose name we have given, attracted by liberal grants of land, came to a beautiful farm on the Canadian side of the Niagara river. He came at about the same time with the Howells of the 'Jersey settlement,' the Aikmans, the Colemans, the Lawrasons, the Hamills, and many other names, since distinguished in the history of Canada. The Ryersons, as U. E. Loyalists, removed at an earlier day. Here the subject of this memoir, Robert Corson, was born.

"The father and mother of John Wesley differed in politics. Possibly these 'crossings' have helped to improve the race. Any divergence in our family mainly benefitted a previous generation. Our mother was the daughter of a subordinate officer on the British side in the American Revolution, named Freeland. At the close of the war which severed the colonies from the Mother country, he, with many other U. E. Loyalists, sought refuge in New Brunswick. He lived near Fredericton, about a mile from the country-seat of that famous defender of Quebec, Sir Guy Carleton. This brave officer was long remembered by the early settlers as one of the ablest and best Governors of Canada. The Emma Freeland, so dear to us, was named in honour of a favourite daughter of the good Governor. We may mention it as one of the 'Mother's Tales' of our own infancy, that when the child grew older, her fond protector used to press back her curls and caress her tenderly. This warm interest continued for years. When at last the Governor sailed for England, her faithful friends, with rare generosity, offered to adopt her and educate her liberally, as a member of the family. Our mother used, with evident emotion, to describe the struggle which it cost in her own home to decline this tempting offer.

"We record this early attachment as an incident which sheds a light on the future of this narrative. It seems a lesson to every despairing teacher in a Sabbath-school. The sower may cross the ocean; the seed may be buried for long years; and yet at the last it may yield a precious harvest. From the fruit of her teaching we have always fancied that this refined 'English Lady' was also a devout Christian. If we are not mistaken, she was unconsciously developing a noble womanly character in the confiding child, who was in the future to wield a like influence, as a faithful pastor's wife in the distant wilds of Canada.

"The Freelands at last became restless. They listened to the usual rose-coloured stories told to intending emigrants. Away in Upper Canada the soil was rich and black. Wheat waved luxuriantly in golden harvests; and on the warm shores of Lake Erie there grew even grapes and peaches. Sunsets were glorious. The stars shone out of a clear blue sky like that of Italy. Compared to New Brunswick, too, the climate was delightfully mild. They decided to remove to what in the Eastern Provinces was then known as the Western Country.

"Except John Wesley and Francis Asbury, few ministers ever travelled so many thousands of miles, or were so long 'effective' in the pulpit, as he who, in his declining years, became familiarly known as 'Father Corson.' His endurance was amazing. Including some years of preliminary labour as a local, or lay preacher; a regular pastoral service of nearly forty years; the primitive week-day appointments; and the abundant extra efforts long after his retirement—reaching in actual work to the advanced age of eighty-five—he probably averaged a sermon weekly for full sixty years.

"His itinerant parish was enormous. If the reader, not familiar with that country, will glance at a map of North America, he will notice a large triangular peninsula in the present Province of Ontario, laying just east of the State of Michigan, and like the latter, made fertile in summer and mild in winter by those inland seas, the surrounding great lakes.

"This fruitful promontory between the lakes was formerly known as the Garden of Canada. It was his field of labour. With only a few exceptions, he ranged over and over again, from Napanee, east of the Bay of Quinte, and opposite tho lower end of Lake Ontario, westward to the river St. Clair. He helped to carry the gospel to a territory nearly four hundred miles long, and averaging a little less than one hundred miles in width. Accidental causes had here attracted a comparatively choice population. Ancient Lower Canada to the east of this was almost entirely French and Catholic.

"But the region in question, or Upper Canada, was, in its earliest settlement, more purely English-speaking and Protestant than any part of the American Continent, except New England, the two Eastern Provinces, and Virginia. It was inhabited by people well versed in the Scriptures, and qualified to tax severely the resources of their first missionaries. Emigrants from England, the United States, Protestants from the North of Ireland, with Loyalists from the Eastern Provinces, and a sprinkling of retired officers from the army and navy, were blended with the descendants of those Covenanters from Scotland, who had once fought for their faith with muskets in their hands and bibles in their heads. It was no easy task to feed this motley crowd of hungry Christians.

"Then the hardships of finding them out were fearful. The country was thickly wooded. Upon a rich black mould, almost everywhere grew tall, luxuriant groves of maple, elm, and beech, with occasional clumps of hemlock, giants of oak, and frequent ridges of lofty white pines. Rivers and creeks were abundant. Deer roamed on the shores of lonely lakes. The wolf and the bear were started from their retreats by wild Indians hunting for their prey.

"As we get nearer to our Heavenly Rest we come to feel more and more that we cannot love the Saviour without loving all His children. We fully embrace the noble sentiment uttered by Dean Stanley, that each branch of the Church of Christ has some special mission. What the Baptists did for Rhode Island, the Congregationlists for the rest of New England, the Presbyterians for New Jersey, and the Episcopalians for Virginia, the hardy Methodists did for Upper Canada. They were the first messengers of the Master. Many of their preacher's were gifted with a certain rough eloquence which made them the Whitfield's of the backwoods. They forded the streams, waded the swamps, and often, by the guidance of blazed trees, they penetrated the dense wilderness to the little smoky clearings and the log-cabins, to cry, 'Behold the Lamb.'

"Into these toils the deceased entered with his whole

soul. He incessantly studied and preached. In imitation of the habits of Wesley and Clarke, he rose at four o'clock in the morning for the most of his active lifetime. Frequently he journeyed many miles before breakfast. "For the first thirty years he travelled extensively on horseback among the frontier settlements in reality as a Home Missionary. And his labours were naturally increased by the customary change from Circuit to Circuit every two years. We have known him occasionally to preach as many as four times on a single Sabbath. During this early period, either to Whites or Indians, he probably averaged nearly a sermon for every day in the year."—J. W. C.

1817-1822.

II.—FROM HIS CONVERSION UNTIL HIS GOING OUT ON A CIRCUIT.

All that we have to illustrate this period of his life are a few brief sentences from his own pen, with a very few side-lights from other sources. Mr. Corson's "Sketch" has the following: " Early in the year 1817 we both joined the Methodist Church." By which he means the "Methodist Episcopal Church," whose authorities were in the United States. Soon after Mr. and Mrs. Corson became Methodists the Wesleyan Missionaries from England, after occupying some places further east, took up ground in the Niagara country, but the Corsons seem either to have known nothing of them, or to have had their sympathies entirely engrossed by the form of Methodism first introduced into the country. The preachers labouring on the Niagara Circuit during the period now under consideration were, for 1816-17, Elijah Warren, a polished speaker, and a supply; and those for

1817-18 were John Wesley Byham and the devoted George Ferguson, between whom and Corson a mutual attachment was formed, which continued uninterrupted until the former

"Took his last triumphant flight,
From Calvary to Zion's height."

The fragmentary "Sketch" continues: "In 1818 we removed to Oxford." This removal was in consequence of his preferring a larger wild lot in the bush, to a smaller, more cultivated one at the front. It was the gift of his father. His new residence, I believe, fell within the bounds of the Long Point Circuit.

His memoranda continues, "In 1820 I received license as a local preacher." The excellent William Case was the Presiding Elder on the District for that and the three following Conference years, by whom Mr. Corson's license must have been signed. The preachers appointed for the Long Point Circuit for that year were James Jackson and William Henry Williams; but Mr. Williams, I think, was removed by the Presiding Elder to meet some connexional emergency, and the—afterwards—noticeable John Ryerson was called out, from within the bounds of the Circuit itself, to supply for the balance of the year, who was destined to be the life-long co-adjutor of Corson, and to pass away to his rest about the same time, after their several toils of fifty-eight years.

As the exhorter's office in those days always preceded that of the local preacher, nearly the whole of the time from Mr. Corson's removal from the Niagara Circuit to the Long Point, or to Oxford, our subject must have been engaged in a public capacity, at least on the Lord's Day. These Circuit officials were not then, as since and now, assigned work on a published "plan," but left to obey the calls of the people and the Circuit preachers, and the impulses of their own hearts and minds, in entering such open doors as presented themselves around them, both near and far. In that voluntary and extemporized way, much useful labour was performed in that day by the exhorters and local preachers of each Circuit, who were at once the pioneers and co-adjutors of the travelling preachers. And there can be no doubt but that important service was rendered by this zealous man of God in the newly-inhabited region around him. In the same township, but farther back in the woods, another young married man, younger by five years than Corson, began to preach as a local preacher, with uncommon pathos and eloquence, who was destined to enter the ministry at the same time as his neighbour Corson, and to occupy a wide and conspicuous sphere in provincial Methodism, co-eval with the periods of Mr. Corson's labours. This was no other than the remarkable William Ryerson, who requires very little further observation here—save it bo to say, that some obscure and unlikely places have produced some of our most conspicuous ministers—either for usefulness, like Corson, or talent, like William Ryerson. He went on a Circuit a few months before Corson was called to go.

In the capacity of local preacher Mr. Corson remained two years; that is to say, from 1820 to 1822. During that period the preachers for the Long Point Circuit were —for 1820-21, James Jackson and Wm. H. Williams; and for 1821-22, I. B. Smith, an able preacher, from whom the locals may have taken valuable lessons, and Wm. H. Williams, once more. David Gulp and George Ferguson, a fine example of zeal and diligence, were the preachers for the Circuit the year that Mr. Corson was sent by the Presiding Elder on to the adjacent Westminster Circuit himself.

His own account of his labours as a "hired local preacher," (a phrase, by the way, which did not come into use in *Canadian* Methodism till many years after), or Presiding Elder's supply, is as follows: "In 1822, I left my little family, or wife and three little boys, and commenced my journey to find my first Circuit. It was large—no chapels —and bad roads; but a warm hearted and intelligent people. I was three weeks and two days" (that is every round) "from my family. I had to ride some twenty miles in the night to get home." Observe, his family was still upon his homestead in the township of Oxford, while he was working a Circuit, which included the township of Westminster, after which it was called, London, Dorchester, Oxford, Norwich, Blenheim, and Burford.*

These long absences must have been a severe bereavement to his little ones, and a great trial to his affectionate wife; but now commenced with her that course of self-denial and staunch loyalty to her husband's vocation and duty referred to by the writer of her obituary notice, expressed in the following words: "During a period of upwards of twenty years, in which she endured with her companion the trials and privations peculiar to the Methodist Itinerancy, she exhibited, in an eminent degree, many of the virtues which go to form an exalted character as the wife of a Christian minister. She possessed the true missionary spirit. With her it was a conscientious resolution never to be instru-

---

* The reader will be interested by a most touching account of Mr. C.'s first going away from his family, several pages farther on, from the pen of Dr. John W. Corson.

mental, in the least degree, in preventing him, at any sacrifice, from fully discharging his arduous duties."

I find, by reference to my "Canadian Itinerant's Memorial," some entries relative to these, Mr. Corson's first itinerant labours, which I feel inclined to reproduce in this place, although they may involve some repetitions; yet, as those statements embrace some things relative to an earlier period of his life, which I did not recover in time to incorporate them with the earlier sections of this book, I may be pardoned for transferring a couple of paragraphs from my wider work to this more restricted one.

In the place referred to, while speaking of the Rev. James Jackson, whose name was the only one which stood in the list of stations anent the Westminster Circuit which required two preachers for the year 1822-23, I was led to say, "The Presiding Elder, Mr. Case, had furnished him" (Jackson) "with a fervent, whole-souled, and untiring colleague, in the person of a Canadian, born in 1793, in whose father's house Whitehead, Ryan, and Homes, had been entertained, when he was a little boy, and who had been early impressed under the preaching of Ca..o. He says of himself, "I first saw Elder Case at a camp-meeting in 1807. He was young, and had a pleasing address; and under his exhortation, for the first time, my hard heart was softened." I heard him again from the words, "Why will ye die?" "In 1822," (the year of which we are writing) "he was my Presiding Elder, and James Jackson was my superintendent. Mr. Case was popular, and made friends wherever he laboured. He would frequently weep over his congregations, especially at the close of his discourses."

"We are quoting from simple, honest, genial Robert Corson, who was the man sent to Jackson's aid on the

Westminster Circuit. He had a good home, and he had made the Circuit preachers welcome to that home. His gifts, graces, and zeal, as a local preacher, pointed him out to the discerning eye of Case as a suitable person to supply the vacancy, and to follow up the openings on the Westminster Circuit. True, he was married, but, for this year, his family remained at their home; and such a wife as his was likely to render far more help than hindrance to a gospel minister—prepossessing, pious, gifted, and courageous to a degree."

A further item from his "Sketch" shows that he did not greatly supplement the revenues from his farm by his ministerial allowances, but he was consoled by the salvation of souls. His words are, "My salary was small, only one hundred and twenty dollars; but we had a net increase of fifty members." Such were the circumstances and results of his first year's Circuit labours. By the Quarterly Conference of the Circuit he had served, having met their approval, he was recommended to the Annual Conference to be received on trial, which event brings me to the next division of this book, namely, to portray his life.

III. FROM THE CONFERENCE OF 1823 TO THAT OF 1858, WHEN HE RETIRED FROM THE ACTIVE MINISTRY.

The only distribution this part of his life will admit of, will be one to coincide with the history of the church of which he was a most loyal minister, namely, 1. From 1823 to the formation of the Canada Annual Conference, 1824; 2. From the formation of the Canada Annual Conference to the organization of the Methodist Episcopal Church in Canada in 1858; 3. From the founding of the

Canadian Church to its union with the British Wesleyan Conference in England in 1833 ; 4. The seven years of the first union ; 5. The seven years of divided Wesleyan operations ; 6. From the reconstruction of the union in 1847, to the admission of the Lower Canada and Hudson Bay Districts into the Canada Conference; and 7th, from the last mentioned event to Mr. Corson's retirement from the effective ranks, a period of four years.

1823, 1824.

I. MR. CORSON'S PUBLIC MINISTRY, FROM 1823 TO THE FORMATION OF THE CANADA ANNUAL CONFERENCE, IN 1824.

The session of the Genesee Annual Conference, at which Mr. Corson was received on trial, commenced its sittings at Westmoreland, Oneida County, N. Y., July 15th, 1823, the pious and pathetic Bishop George, presiding. It proved to be the last time that Canadian preachers went out of their own country to attend an Annual Conference. It was usual for the candidates to present themselves in person before the Conference to be examined by the presiding Bishop, but I have no evidence for saying that our subject was there. I suspect that he did not perform the inconvenient journey. He would have to look after his harvest for the last time ; and the Discipline provided for the examination of a candidate away from the Conference by his Presiding Elder, who, in that case, was to report to the Conference. It is very probable that several, if not all, of the Canadian candidates went to the Conference. The record in the MS. Journals of the Old Genesee Conference, relative to the Canadian candidates, transcribed by my own hand, several years ago, are very curious and interesting. Here they are:

1st. "*Wm. Griffis*, twenty-three years old, clear of debt: admitted."

2nd. "*Solomon Waldron*, aged twenty-six, unembarrassed, single: admitted."

3rd. "*Jacob Poole*, aged twenty-five, unembarrassed: admitted."

4th. "*Joseph Castle*, single, twenty-two, clear of debt: admitted."

5th. "*David Wright*, aged thirty, wife and three children: admitted."

6th. "*William Ryerson*, aged twenty-five, wife and two children, clear of debt: admitted."

7th. "ROBERT CORSON, aged thirty, wife and four children, clear of debt: admitted."

Corson was appointed to labour alone, on the newly organized London Circuit, which township had been in his last year's Circuit, and in which, if I have been rightly informed, he was the first who ever preached a gospel sermon, but previously to this. His family still resided near their farm, but they left their nice framed house for a small log one.

Here is my account of the Circuit and this year's labour, as the result of correspondence with its incumbent, then yet living. "The new organization was the London Circuit, which was placed in the hands of the laborious Robert Corson, whose acquaintance with the ground the preceding year peculiarly qualified him for this pioneering enterprise. He soon made his field of labour to include Oxford, Zorra, Nissouri, London and Lobo, with an appointment in Westminster, carrying comfort to such families as the Websters,

Warners, Willises, and others, and returned in one year 255 members."

His labours must have embraced almost continual riding, preaching, class-meetings, and visiting from house to house; yet he seems to have regarded this Circuit as an improvement on the one of the preceding year. He says, "I had a good year. I was only two weeks" (that is, at one time) "from my family. My salary was $160. Our increase of members, *one hundred and sixty.*"

1824–1826.

II. MR. CORSON'S GOSPEL LABOURS, FROM 1824 TO 1828.

There is every reason to believe that he attended the Session of Conference which took place in the village of Hallowell, during the month of August, 1824, commencing its Sessions on the 25th of that month, when the Canada Annual Conference commenced its existence, Bishops George and Hedding presiding. I am morally certain I saw Mr. Corson on the way to that Conference at a meeting held by Bishop Hedding in the town of York, although I did not then know how to distinguish him from the others. I can remember that there were several rather undersized preachers, (dwarfed all the more by contrast with such almost gigantic persons as Elijah Hedding, Nathan Bangs, William Slater, William Ryerson, not to mention David Calp and John Ryerson, who were sizable men,) file into a back seat at the left hand of the pulpit, taking no part in the discussions about the projected separation from the States, which took place after our service. George Ferguson, William Griffis, and Robert Corson were among those of the lower stature; and several of the brethren of all sizes, from the west, that night were clad in homespun, of whom, I have little doubt, from evidence I have adduced hereafter, Corson was one, thanks to his wife's industry and his own humility. The colour of these garments was mostly of a dingy quaker drab, produced by a dye made of the bark of the butternut tree. It was by men often clad in habiliments like these that the work of early Canadian Evangelization was carried on.

The reading off the Stations at the close of the Hallowell Conference was a thrilling time, and Mr. Corson received an appointment which entailed the necessity of the first move upon him and his much loved family. Alas, they were to turn their backs on their cherished home, with its pleasant orchard, to return to it only once more and that for a very short interval.

His appointment was to the DUMFRIES CIRCUIT, where he was destined to remain two years, if that could be called remaining, where he was forced to move several times to secure a shelter. This Circuit was a new creation, or as he himself termed it, "one year old." It consisted of settlements beyond the pale of previous Circuits, an organization which had been made up by the devoted Edmund Stoney, as his first year's attempt in the itinerancy, (under the superintendency of the venerable Thomas Whitehead, the place of whose superannuated retirement was adjacent to its southern border,) the year before. Mr. Corson says, it included parts of Flamboro' West and Ancaster, Dumfries, from which it was named, Waterloo, Sheffield, and one appointment among the Indians six miles above Brantford.

He said in a letter to me concerning this charge, "I was pleased with my appointment, although my Circuit was only one year old. The members were poor but pious. There were about eighteen appointments, which I attended once in two weeks,"—that is, nine appointments a week, one for each day and two over. "One of these was among the Indians, on the Grand River, though I received nothing from the Missionary Fund."

"The first year, I received, in all, $120; the next year, $160. Only a part of this was money. We had four children. We were sometimes troubled to get a house, and lived in four different ones while we were on the Circuits. The last house we lived in was pretty good, but the other three were log-houses, consisting of one room.

"Brantford was then embraced in that Circuit. It was a small village at that time. We had a class of eight members, and preached in a small, private house. The man who owned it was a good-natured Quaker; his wife was a great Methodist in sentiment. They made an arrangement that he was to take care of her preachers' horses; and she was to take good care of his Quaker preachers, and give them their dinner. He intimated to me, that his wife suspected him of giving his preachers' horses better pasture than hers. However, we soon removed into a new school-house. There were two chapels built during the two years I laboured on the Circuit. There were four exhorters; and we succeeded in getting one into the itinerant work. I allude to the late Matthew Whiting, who proved a blessing to the Church."

So much from Mr. Corson's account of himself during the two years from 1824 to 1826. Fortunately, I have other sources of information concerning that period. The venerable Henry Chrysler, now of Brantford, remembers Mr. Corson's first appearance on the Circuit, "preaching in a dark, gray, home-spun coat. His text was, Jeremiah viii.,

22, 'Is there no balm in Gilead; is there no physician there? Why then is not the health of the daughter of my people recovered?' He was very happy. After crying for joy a few times, the invitation was given, and some professing christians of the congregation came forward, and a wonderful revival took place, many accepting Christ as their Saviour. He was loved and esteemed by all. He resided in William Waugh's old homestead." Dr. J. W. Corson will give the particulars of the residences hereafter.

Dr. William Corson says of this field of labour, "No churches were built as yet, and school-houses and barns were utilized instead. The barn of Father Ellis, a man of great intelligence from the Green Isle, a local preacher, and father of several young men, is remembered as the scene of quarterly meetings of great interest and power."

But Father Corson tells us that the destitution of chapels was partly removed by the erection of two while he was on the Circuit. On this subject I find that volume III. page 15 of my "Biographical History" holds the following language: "One of the 'two chapels' referred to, and the first erected in this part of the country, was Cornell's Chapel, in Waterloo, about a mile and a-half north-west of where Preston now flourishes. It is still standing, though now unused; and the adjoining graveyard contains, 'in many a mouldering heap' the remains of some of the first members. Their names and ages may yet be decyphered on the old decaying headboards. The author spent an impressive hour one early morning in that dew-clad, lonely spot, tracing out all he could learn of their history. Several miles from there lived two brothers of the name of Ellis, William and David, natives of Ireland, who were earnest promoters of the erection of their chapel." [Years afterwards, they, their children, and neighbours erected a more elegant and substantial place of worship in their own immediate neighbourhood, now known as Zion Church.] " William was a magistrate, and David afterwards was a local preacher, and, we opine, one of Mr. Corson's four exhorters. Mrs. William Ellis was converted under Ousley in Ireland; her husband, who fired the first shot in the war of 1812, was not converted till some years afterwards. His was a most extraordinary conversion, alone on the road one dark night, on his return home from Hamilton. His wife was a person of eminent piety, and lived to the advanced age of 96, dying so lately as 1864. In an early day she used to walk six miles to meeting, carrying her child in her arms. The two Ellis' entertained all the early itinerants who came into their part of the country; and their descendants remember the tales of the horrid roads by which the messengers of the Gospel of peace reached their dwellings."

I have received a letter from an estimable magistrate and local preacher in our church, JARED KILBORN, ESQ., now residing at Plattsville, which relates to the period of which I am writing, and serves to illustrate the character of Mr. Corson and the times then passing over him :—

"DEAR DR. CARROLL,—Having noticed in the *Guardian* your request to forward to you any remembrances of the late venerable Father Corson, I send the following:—I first saw and heard Mr. Corson in the Township of Waterloo, about a mile and a half above Preston; the 'preaching place' was at a primitive log-house, the residence of the late Samuel Cornell, to which place my parents used to repair weekly for preaching and class-meeting, taking me with them—this was about the year 1824 or 1825. Memory now paints Mr. Corson as a light, nimble, tough little man, of about 125 or 130 lbs. avordupoise, with light hair and sharp, sparkling eyes. His manner of preaching was quick, bordering on the abrupt; his subjects were generally solemn; his appeals sharp; his applications appropriate; and his proofs always cogent and logical; and, I ought to add, his method generally orderly and systematic. About the time I speak of, I witnessed what, to my young mind, appeared to be a hard test of his muscular ability. At the preaching, a tall, muscular, large-boned Dutchman, lately converted, applied for baptism by immersion at the hands of our little hero. A procession was formed, headed by our preacher, arm in arm with the neophyte, followed by a singing band of brothers and sisters, who sang with power and pathos the old expressive stanza,

> 'Then let our songs abound,
> And every tear be dry,
> We're marching through Emmanuel's ground,
> To fairer worlds on high, &c.'

distance about half a mile. Arrived at the Grand River, the usual preparations were made, and a strong handkerchief was tied around the waist of the subject, which greatly assisted the officiating clergyman in restoring the disciple to air and an erect attitude. My young heart palpitated with fear for the fate of the Dutchman, but all came of well, and now both preacher and disciple are in glory."

I reserve the rest of Mr. Kilborn's letter to illustrate a further stage of Mr. Corson's history.

In the summer of 1825 I attended a camp-meeting for the first time. It was held on the land of a Mr. Cummer, about nine miles north from the town of York, and about two miles east of Yonge Street. It was a season of great power—about 140 souls were converted to God. There I heard several of our Canadian Methodist preachers whom I had not heard before, and among the rest Robert Corson. I cannot improve upon my account of my impressions of him contained in my history of "Case and his Cotemporaries." It is as follows: "His raw appearance at first damped all expectation, but he had no sooner come forward to the front of the stand, at the close of a sermon by another, to deliver an exhortation, than all began to feel the infection of his loving, ardent spirit; his word was the means of scattering a holy flame in the congregation. The same effect followed the preaching of a sermon at a later stage of the meeting. No better backwoods' preacher could be possibly conceived of than was that simple-looking, tawny man, whose hair, in neglected masses, covered his forehead. He literally carried the unsophisticated people by storm. Uncouth, you might have called him; but he was shrewd, and knew the power of religion, and taught it with power, for all that." I may now add to this paragraph, that those who knew him only late in life, could have no conception how the most moving words literally tumbled out of the man as it were to the right and left.

The net increase for the two years this warm-hearted evangelist served the Dumfries Circuit was *one hundred and two* precious souls. I now pass to another Circuit.

I should have perhaps said that Mr. Corson was received into full connexion and received deacon's orders at the close of his first year on the Dumfries Circuit, at the Conference which sat at the "Fifty Mile Creek;" the orders were conferred by the imposition of Bishop Hedding's hands. I should like to have a fac-simile impression of the little parchment certificate of ordination, so very diminutive and unpretentious compared with similar documents in this day.

In default of a lithograph, I may be pardoned for giving a copy of the wording, which I herewith produce:—

"𝕶𝖓𝖔𝖜 𝖆𝖑𝖑 𝕸𝖊𝖓 𝖇𝖞 𝖙𝖍𝖊𝖘𝖊 𝕻𝖗𝖊𝖘𝖊𝖓𝖙𝖘, That I, ELIJAH HEDDING, one of the Bishops of the Methodist Episcopal Church in America, under the protection of ALMIGHTY GOD, and with a single eye to His glory, by the imposition of my hands and prayer, have this day set apart ROBERT CORSON for the office of a DEACON in the said Methodist Episcopal Church; a man whom I judge to be well qualified for that work; and I do hereby recommend him to all whom it may concern, as a proper person to administer the ordinances of Baptism, Marriage, and the Burial of the Dead, in the absence of an Elder; and to feed the flock of Christ, so long as his spirit and practice are such as become the Gospel.

"IN TESTIMONY WHEREOF, I have hereunto set my hand and seal, this Eighteenth day of September, one thousand eight hundred and twenty-five.

"ELIJAH HEDDING."

There were some things melancholy and admonitory at that Conference, and some things very encouraging, both of which, in their several ways, I have no doubt, had a salutary influence on the susceptible and improving heart of Robert Corson.

The remaining three years of this stage of our Church's history in Canada, with which I am making the divisions of my book coincide, were spent by Mr. Corson on three several Circuits, namely: the *Westminster*, the *Long-Point*, and the *Whitby*, on which last he also spent the first year of the period next ensuing.

1826, 27.

The hiatus between the *Dumfries* and the *Westminster* Circuits was filled by the Conference of 1826, which commenced its sittings, August 31st, in the township of Hamilton, Newcastle District. The place of assembling was in what was called, after the Cobourg church was built, for distinction sake, the "Back Chapel." It was a desirable seat for a Conference session, being in the midst of a very large membership, yet undivided, including the numerous societies in the neighbourhood, and the classes at Amherst and Cobourg, by whom the *forty* preachers of the Province, less or more, could be comfortably entertained.

These annual assemblies were seasons of respite and recreation to the daily toiling itinerants, who got no seaside vacations in those days; and they were opportunities of learning those things, which those otherwise unprivileged students most needed and desired to know: business, discipline, administration, theology, and how to make and deliver sermons. But our Brother Corson and his coadjutors must have found this one particularly so. This will appear from a couple of paragraphs from my "Biographical History," which I may be pardoned for reproducing:—

"It was a memorable Conference, closing a year of great numerical increase. The writer was then a member of the Church, of two years' standing, and he calls to mind the ardour which each fresh arrival of the fervent-minded preachers from the west, on their way to the place of this annual assembly, imparted to our religious services in York. The Conference was presided over by the heavenly-minded and eloquent Bishop George. The not less exemplary Case acted as secretary. Ezra Healy's diary says, 'it was a profitable Conference,' and because it was peaceful it was short. As evidence of this, I find from the same record that Healy and his friend Metcalf were conveyed away from the place by the obliging John Black, so early as the 4th of September; so that it had lasted only about five days, including Sunday. But that was a glorious Sabbath. Bishop George and Dr. Bangs preached. A message had been sent to the pagan Indians to the north of Rice Lake, who obeyed the summons,—men, women, and children travelling all night, as one of them informed me, to be there. It is to be regretted that there is a hiatus in the published journal of the Rev Peter Jones just here, commencing at the 26th of August and extending over all the rest of the civil year. It is true his manuscript refers to the published account of the wonders of that day, to be found in the *American Methodist Magazine* for 1826, page 434; but that copy of the magazine is not attainable by the writer. Yet much of the proceedings of that memorable day are stereotyped in his mind from the narration of a friend, a few days after, who chanced to be present. The converted Indians from Belleville, who had been at the Cramahe camp-meeting, which preceded the Conference, were present by invitation, and aided in this work. The Chief, Potash, and nearly all the Rice Lake band were converted. He exclaimed in his broken English, when he had obtained the peace of God, 'O ho! me never think meeting feel so good.'

"The following description of a scene at Conference, from the pen of Mr. Torry, which his book erroneously ascribes to the Conference of 1824, in Hallowell, when there was not an Indian convert in the region of the Bay of Quinté, can apply only to this Conference scene: 'At this Conference, about seventy of our Chippewas were there by invitation, who came and pitched their tents within a short distance of the place where the Conference held its sessions. During the time they were there news came to them that there was a band of Chippewas far back in the wilderness. Two or three of our chiefs immediately started out to hunt them up and invite them in. They arrived on Sabbath morning, during the hours of preaching. A meeting had been appointed in the grove, near the encampment of the Indians, and Bishop George and Dr. Bangs preached to the assembled multitudes. At the close of the preaching it was given out that after an hour's intermission there would be a general prayer-meeting at the altar. The strangers were placed in a half circle, the Christian Indians near them, while in the front were a large number of ministers. After singing, one of the Indians led in prayer, accompanied in an undertone by all the rest. In a few moments tears began to run down the cheeks of the old chief. His prayer was going up to Heaven, 'Oh, Great Spirit, have mercy on poor me! Oh, Son of the Great Spirit, have mercy on me! Jesus, come and cast the bad spirit out of my heart, and make poor Indian glad and happy.' All the Indians were so engaged that they were praying with a loud voice. Soon all the pagans were weeping and crying aloud, ' Oh, Jesus, save; Oh, I shall go to the bad place, come and save me!' The chief was still crying to God, but in less than ten minutes after tears began to fall, he began to tremble like an aspen leaf in the wind, in a moment more he fell to the ground like a corpse. One after another of these pagans fell to the ground. But the Lord passed over them and breathed upon them; they sprang to their feet giving praises to God. When the chief arose, with a heavenly smile on his countenance, he clapped his hand to his breast, saying, 'Oh, happy here! Oh, blessed Jesus, how I love thee! Oh, glory, glory!' One after another arose, until twenty of the thirty were praising God."

But then the long distance of this Conference east, combined with a long move, gave Mr. Corson a large amount of travel in the heat of summer. *He was appointed to the Westminster Circuit.* Where he located his family, at this writing, I cannot say.* In those days, as there were few or no parsonages, and the Circuit stewards never thought of providing a house, any available habitation, in almost any part of the Circuit, was usually accepted with readiness. However, both his MS. and his direct account addressed to myself, and incorporated with my history, show that he thought lightly of all his hardships.

The "Memorial" runs as follows:—"Robert Corson was Whiting's nearest neighbour, being in charge of the Westminster Circuit. His colleague's name (John Huston) does not appear in the Minutes, as he was still kept under the Presiding Elder. Mr. Corson has furnished me with a few notes of the year, in which his constitutional humour crops out a little. 'In 1826, John Huston travelled with me on the Westminster. We had a small amount of trouble on the Circuit; but on the whole, the year was a good one. Our first Quarterly Meeting was held at Westminster, in our new unfinished chapel. A good congregation—Madden our Presiding Elder. The collections on Saturday and Sunday amounted to three York shillings. Our expenses for the wine were three and sixpence, York. Another trouble; my colleague was a bachelor, and wanted a wife: a young lady agreed to marry him. He applied to me for

---

* Where he resided, will appear from statements to be made hereafter by Dr. J. W. Corson.

a wedding suit. We got some thirty bushels of wheat subscribed in one neighbourhood to make up our salaries. I had to get a team and draw the wheat to market. Obtained 50 cents per bushel, and purchased Bro. H. a wedding suit; but another trouble, the lady changed her mind, and married another man. I was requested to baptize four persons by immersion: three were so large that I could not get them out of the water, but they helped themselves. We had an increase of 70 members; and I received $170 in all. This was the highest amount I had ever received. We obtained a part of our salaries in boards, and the friends shipped them to the States, and the next year we got the money.'"

Mr. Corson's MS. "Sketch" is very cheerful. He says, "We went on our way rejoicing, trusting in the Lord, praying, preaching, and visiting from house to house; and we had a good year. Increase of members, 82." This is twelve more than the number first given to me—the second statement, probably, being the best considered.

Robert Corson was cheerful even to playfulness; and his sprightly sallies often took place in juxtaposition with solemnities of a very opposite character. These apparent contrarieties have been frankly noticed in the very appreciative sketch of him by his eldest son. The following incident was an example of the kind referred to. It was imparted to me by letter from the late Rev. Alexander Campbell, soon after my first sketch of Mr. Corson in the newspaper, afterwards published in "Past and Present," appeared. It was related to Mr. Campbell by one of the parties to the scene, many years after the occurrence. It took place not far from the shores of Lake Erie, and probably belongs to the period of which I am writing.

I have no doubt of its authenticity; for, after relating it to one of our Ministers, he told me a person gave him a similar story. Mr. Corson had attended a Camp-meeting and laboured with his usual assiduity. Several young men were at the meeting, from his own Circuit, for whose spiritual welfare he had exerted himself with great earnestness; and he had the exquisite satisfaction of seeing them happily converted to God. They all returned from the meeting in company with each other, in a very joyful and devout state of mind. Religious conversation and hymns of praise beguiled the otherwise weary distances. All at once they espied a squirrel on the fence. Every person who has lived in the country knows how exciting is the chase of one of these sprightly animals—backwards and forwards till captured. All Robert Corson's constitutional vivacity seemed to come into play at the sight of the nimble little creature. He instantly dismounted and tied his horse, calling out the while, "Come, boys, let's have some fun!" Instantly they followed suit, and with clubs and sticks pursued the animal, witnessing his leaps, and doublings, and dodges, till at length, overmatched by superior numbers, he fell a prey to their activity and perseverance. How the blood tingled through their veins and the sweat oozed from their pores, while the shouts of laughter broke forth, every one who ever engaged in the sport must know very well. The deed accomplished, with a chuckle they remounted their horses and resumed their journey, with their religious equanimity apparently none disturbed. Some might regard the affair as incongruous, or even shocking; but our rustic evangelist seemed not to perceive anything to be out of character in the escapade. He would probably think, "Squirrels are the pest of the farmer's crops; it is a beneficial work to destroy them; and if in doing it one can have a little healthful excitement all the better." Some would say, "This might have been suppressed by the editor;" but if it were, we should have one incident the less for the understanding and illustrating the character of our "Pioneer Preacher."

1827, 1828.

Mr. Corson remained but one year at *Westminster*, and at the anxious and important Conference held in the rising village of Hamilton, or otherwise at "Springer's Meeting-house," which commenced on the 30th of August, 1827, the judicious Bishop Hedding presiding, he was appointed to a new charge. This Conference was *anxious*, because of the withdrawal of one of Canada's earliest and most efficient pioneer preachers, the Rev. Henry Ryan; and *important*, because of the decision to ask the American General Conference for a peaceable discharge from its jurisdiction; and because of the appointment of Delegates to that body, charged to seek the accomplishment of that object.

At this Conference Mr. Corson received *elders*, or full ministerial orders, and was appointed to LONG-POINT as the colleague of the *Rev. Wm. Griffis*, who being a man of more education than Mr. Corson, was invested with the charge. They were of the same ministerial standing; but I never knew our subject to clamour for one moment for prestige, or priority. He was willing to work in a superior, or subordinate position. He was as free from ambition as he was from servility: he was neither proud nor mean. For this year he moved back once more to his farm.

My previously published account of that Circuit and its

ministers for that year was as follows: "Griffis and Corson were brought together from the east and the west, and met on the *Long-Point Circuit.* We have no particulars. They must have laboured hard and met with great success, for they reported nearly *one hundred* increase." ["Case and his Cotemporaries."]

Mr. Corson's private memorandum has this: "In 1827 I was appointed to Long-Point. We had plenty of good revivals; but our salaries were small, only $150"—*a-piece*, I would hope, else it were desperate—; "and we both had families. But our increase was good, as high as *ninety-four*." In view of the rich country and large number of members, 342, one can hardly restrain his indignation that all these demonstrations and professions could lead to their doing no more for their faithful ministers! But I am compelled to say it was rather characteristic of old-style Canadian Methodists, especially in rural places. Yes, sing, and shout, and pray, and "get happy;" and understand "quarterage" to mean—*a quarter dollar! O tempora, O mores!*

An incident is recorded of Mr. Corson, illustrative of his doings, but whether it occurred at this time, or whether it belonged to his second appointment to that part of the country, I cannot say; but as I have put myself in a little bit of a passion at some people's littleness, I will tell it now: it may put us in a good humour. I have it on the authority of an intelligent local preacher, long resident in that part of the country, and well posted in its tales and traditions. Thus the story runs: Every one who knows anything of "Father Corson," knows that he was punctual to the minute, but very short in his services. The latter was necessary, as he often preached four times a day. He had an appointment at Woodhouse chapel at a particular hour: he was on time, and began at the moment, and conducted a service for the few that were there—sung, prayed, preached, sung, prayed, and pronounced the benediction; and then mounted his horse and turned his head towards his next appointment. But in going out on the road, he found a much larger congregation coming than the one he had addressed. He pitied them—turned back—tied his horse once more—entered the pulpit, and went over the same routine, with a new subject: preached, prayed, and blessed,—and then, with increased alacrity, whipped up his charger for the next battle. Such a minister ought to have been *paid*, at least.

1828, 1829.

III.—FROM THE FOUNDING OF THE CANADA CHURCH TILL ITS UNION WITH THE BRITISH CONFERENCE.

The Conference which commenced this ecclesiastical year was a most memorable one. It was appointed to commence its sessions, October the 2nd, 1828, at the well-known "Switzer chapel," Earnestown, a place famous for the antiquity and strength of its Methodism. This was the last Conference at which an American Bishop presided, who, for this time, was the Reverend Elijah Hedding, afterwards D.D.; for as soon as the routine business was gone through, the Conference resolved itself into a state of independency of the Parent Connexion in the States, and proceeded to organize a Methodist Episcopal Church for Canada. I need not here go into the grounds and details of that measure, having given the law and the particulars of the case in other publications, especially in my "MEMORIAL" and my "NEEDED EXPOSITION."

Corson was there, and acted, as he generally did, with the majority. This will be a fitting place to inform the reader that, contrary to what might have been expected from his plain, humble ways, he was in nowise suspicious or obstructive; for he was not only not narrow-minded, but of enlarged and really progressive views: he gave his influence in all the great movements for extension, union, and every popularizing and liberal measure. He was far-seeing,— could read the signs of the times, and always favoured measures of preparation for each rising emergency.

His journey to and from this Conference was long and painful. His MS. says, "I was sick during the Conference." This I happened to know before reading it from under his hand. The Earnestown Conference sent me to Belleville Circuit, which included the townships of Tyandenaga, Thurlow, and Sidney, and all the accessible settlements north of that frontier, as far back as Madoc and Marmora. There was no fixed home for the junior preacher, and I was fain to spend the most of my time among the farmers in the country. One of the oldest and best stopping-places was the house of "Father and Mother Gilbert," Dutch Canadians (at least the old lady was such), the father and mother-in-law of the Rev. John Reynolds, afterwards Bishop of the re-constructed M. E. Church of Canada. They lived on the main road between Belleville and the Trent, about three miles west of the former place. They were rich, and their house very commodious; consequently, the preachers going to and from Conference, year by year, naturally turned up the lane to this comfortable hostlery. Years before, a young preacher riding up that lane, for the first time, saw a young damsel in neat, but simple attire, and therefore beautiful, standing in the doorway, and said to himself, "There is my future wife!" And so it turned out to be. As I have said, this was Mr. Reynolds.

The staple of conversation in that household was religion and Methodism, and the manners and ways of the preachers —from "Sammy Coate" and "Elder Sawyer" down to the last itinerant that had called on his way back from the latest Conference. The old lady, who wanted no waiting on herself, and had no fancy for the exacting, was quite inclined to criticise a strange preacher, who had called for a night in company with, or rather in charge of, the strong, kind-hearted Matthew Whiting, which sick preacher Brother Whiting helped off his horse and into bed, waited on him while there, and aided him in remounting his horse in the morning. Mammy Gilbert rather disliked the invalid for his helplessness. When I learned that his name was *Corson*, I stood up in his defence, saying that he was a plain, humble, whole-souled man, who would have given no trouble if he had not been ill; and succeeded in mollifying the old lady's asperity, who dismissed the case by saying, "Vell, he must have pin very sick, or else he was a creat crunt." Poor itinerants, they often received but little sympathy! Why, to ride from Long-Point to Earnestown on horseback, was enough to make a well man sick of itself; and then, to perform such a journey covered with pain and fever, and scarcely able to sit his horse, was indeed a painful ordeal. Happily the dear preachers had brotherly sympathy for each other. Had Corson been the means of bringing Whiting out of the obscurity of the "Grand River Swamp," and of introducing him into the ministry? He is now receiving the first instalment of his reward. Go your ways, ye wanderers, to your several fields of labour! Both of you are destined to be more than usually laborious, and more than usually successful in winning souls—to leave an untarnished reputation—to die in the faith—and to meet—

> "Where all the hip's company meet,
> Who sailed with their Saviour beneath,
> Where with joy each other they greet,
> And triumph o'er sorrow and death."

Mr. Corson's MS. says, "In 1828 I was appointed to WHITBY. We made some arrangements. We had five sons. My wife was a pious, talented woman, and secured friends on the several Circuits where we laboured." [Yes "WE" truly; for not only did *he* labour, but *she* also.] "But our journey of 150 miles, with bad roads, a new Circuit, no chapels, nor parsonage house" [was a little hard to bear]; "but we trusted in the Lord, and it was done according to our faith. We soon found friends that we could trust. A log parsonage was built, and my eldest son got a good place to work and learn a trade." Look at that! He who is not above the labours of a "trade" may end with a *learned profession*, and even excel in that. This was the first instance of self-reliance and self-help by a lad who graduated in medicine with honour, went to Europe and walked the hospitals of London and Paris, became an author, displayed more than usual skill in his profession, and is now aiding me in preparing these memorials of his honoured father. I made the acquaintance of the modest, god-fearing boy one year later, as a cloth-dresser's apprentice, in the village of Port Hope; but our next rencounter was in York where I found him as a student of the famous Dr. Rolph, but that was not the end of our pleasant intercourse. Precious are the memories of those days!

Mr. Corson resumes of Whitby, "I was alone—had some twenty appointments—a large Indian congregation, consisting of 200, that were members of the Church. We had plenty of work, and a blessed revival; so that our increase was *one hundred* the first year."*

It will still further serve to illustrate his character and doings, at that date, if I transfer from my " Biographical History " the account of the *Whitby Circuit* for that year :—

"The Scugog Lake Indians were placed in charge of the Whitby preacher; and the laborious Robert Corson was brought down from Long-Point to supply it. It was a heavy field of labour when he began, but he made it vastly more so before the year was ended. We remember hearing at the time, and we passed twice through his Circuit during the year, that he preached from one to four times every day; and that there were not less than forty different places where he preached. Pickering, Whitby, Darlington, Clarke, Brock, Reach, and other townships were included in his Circuit. The Scugog Lake Mission was in a very interesting and prosperous state about this time. In the early part of the year a devoted young woman, by the name of Frink, whose labours ought not to be forgotten, taught the school. At the end of her term an overgrown son of a neighbouring farmer, not more than fifteen years of age, undertook the school. He was moral, amiable, and very much interested in the Indians, but yet unconverted. Still, Mr. Case's discerning eye thought Aaron Hurd might

---

* Mr. Corson's son, John Wesley, reminds me, that his father, with his usual catholicity, co-operated in revival work with the Baptists, and reaped advantage, while he also benefited them.

be trusted, and he was employed. In the solitude of his wild Indian home, he was led to seek and find the God of his pious father. Thus was an impulse given to a mind of great natural strength, which henceforth developed fast; and had not our hopes been blasted by his early death, there was every reason to expect great results from the labours of the 'Wesleyan Student,' whose short life has been so touchingly portrayed by Rev. Dr. Holdich. Mr. Corson built a log parsonage while on this Circuit, in which his pious and strong-minded wife carried on the training of her boys in those principles which afterwards raised them all to respectability and usefulness. We cannot tell the numerical progress of the year,* the Whitby returns having been included in the Yonge Street Circuit at the preceding Conference, but Mr. Corson made the goodly return at the end of this year of 205 whites and 75 Indians, of whom there was no return the year before under this name."

It was while on this Circuit, in the summer of 1829, before the Conference of that year, that I first saw Mrs. Corson. "The Rev. Ephraim Evans and myself had ridden on horseback from our respective Circuits (he from Percy in the Cobourg Circuit, and myself from Belleville), since the previous Sunday night, meeting on the Danford Road, in the township of Hamilton. Stopping Monday night at William Fitz Moore's, we pushed on, by new zig-zag roads, to shorten the distance, aiming for the Yonge Street camp-meeting, near Cummer's Mill-Pond. About ten o'clock on Tuesday we espied before us a light waggon containing a lady, ascending a hill, and a gentleman walking, to relieve his horse. When we overtook them the gentleman proved to be the Rev. Robert Corson; and Miss Frink, the

* One hundred in MS.

missionary school teacher at the Scugog Lake, was the lady. We had their pleasant company at Mr. Sinclair Holden's, at what is now called Markham village, for dinner; and we met again before the sun went down, within the "tented grove." This was the first time I had ever been in Brother Corson's company, and then first heard some of his vivacious stories. In that day the stories mostly related to battle done with Arians and Immersionists, both of whom were obtrusive of their opinions. In his then Circuit, at a country appointment, on his road to the township of Brock, he baptized a baby; a Baptist brother present expressed his surprise and disgust that any thing so useless and absurd should be done. Let younger men, in this day, think what they please of the plain men of olden times, Corson knew our doctrines well, and the proofs and arguments by which they were supported. He was always good-natured, and could command his temper; in a very kind way he gave the Baptist brother the reasons for Methodist belief and practice on that subject. The challenger listened with candour and surprise, exclaiming, "Why, I did not know so much could be said in favour of the practice: I should like to have you come home with me to dinner." Mr. Corson accepted the invitation, as he could easily make his way among all sorts of people; and this was the beginning of very pleasant intercourse between these two Christian men of different names. I do not know that this friend gave up his Baptist views, but he learned that there was something very cogent to be said on the other side of the question.

But I am wandering from my purpose to speak of Mrs. Corson. We left her husband to make his way slowly home, as his intervening appointments permitted; and, after a Sabbath spent in York, and fulfilling an appointment made for Bro. Evans in a school-house near where Oshawa now flourishes, we pushed on eastward, and called at the door of the new log-parsonage, somewhere in the front of Darlington, I think. The preacher had not yet returned, or was gone again, if he had; but Mrs. Corson came to the door, and we had a few minutes conversation. Our interview was long enough to impress me with her fine stature and figure—her fair and florid complexion—and the saintliness of her looks, spirit, and words. We whipped up our horses, and, I am not sure that I ever saw her again. I am glad I had that one interview—not with the mother of the Gracchi, but—with the mother of the Corson boys, *John Wesley, Henry Ryan, William Case, Alvin Torry,* and *Adam Clarke.*

Dr. William Corson has furnished several interesting particulars relating to this period of the family's history, only one of which I give here. He says, "I was born in a log-house, on the *Darlington,* or "Whitby Circuit," as it is called in the Minutes. "Of course I have no recollection of our stay at that place, but I have since learned that the family passed through greater privations on that Circuit than at any other period of their history." The father, however, makes no mention of their straits.

I should perhaps say, before I dismiss this year, that Brother Evans, myself, and Brother Corson were destined to meet once more before the summer was out, indeed, not many weeks after the Yonge-street Camp-meeting: this was at the Presqu' Isle Camp-meeting, on the Cobourg Circuit, to which Brother Corson was invited by Brother Evans in the journey already described. From the time of James Richardson's adhesion to Methodism in 1818,

Presqu' Isle had been a stronghold of the denomination; and although the cause was a little enfeebled just then, it was still, because of the friends in the vicinity, its central position, and its direct communication by sailing packet with Rochester, N. Y., made it an eligible place for a Camp-meeting. There were several Methodists from the States, and among the rest, the presence of the world-renowned eccentric *Lorenzo Dow*, gave a somewhat peculiar character to the meeting. A large contingent of brethren from Prince Edward County contributed to give life and importance to the meeting, with their vehement senior preacher, the fiery little George Ferguson, at their head. Corson and he were old acquaintances, and it was a very affectionate meeting between them. Corson preached on the Prodigal Son, what I thought a moving, excellent sermon; but he seems not to have been up to Brother Ferguson's expectations. Listening eagerly behind his friend while the sermon was being delivered, he said to those around him, when the discourse was well on, " Bobby is not himself to-day, or he would have had a shout before this time."

Those old demonstrative preachers usually thought there was nothing achieved unless the congregation was put in a state of commotion. I thought Brother Corson was quite demonstrative enough. In those early days, after the example of the prophet Ezekiel, he often emphasized the strong points of his sermons by "smiting with the hand," the battlement before him, and "stamping with the foot" the floor of the stand.

But if the sermon was not sensational enough, the then invariable exhortation, which came after, made up for it. It was delivered by " Crazy Dow," as he used to be called.

It was his first address after arriving, consequently, when he arose and brought his hands beckoningly together, the people came running from all parts of the ground, and crowded from the backward seats to the front of the stand in a huddled mass around the rostrum. His discourse was a running comment on different parts of the parable on which we had been addressed. Some things that he said were most solemn and impressive, and some were irresistibly ludicrous. He said the "citizen" of the "far country," whose "swine" the prodigal was "sent" to "feed," was "the Devil." "The Devil," said he "has a great many swine-feeders now-a-days. There is one character in particular who may be denominated the Devil's swine-feeder: he frequents balls, and routs, and assemblies, and screeks on an insignificant piece of wood called a fiddle, while the people jump up and down, and turn their backs and faces, and cut up their didos." When he got as far as the "elder brother," who "was angry and would not go in," Dow exclaimed, "Oh," said he, "I guess he must have been a Close Communion Baptist!"

Speaking of exciting the congregation, Ferguson, when he came to preach on Sunday, was enabled to exemplify his own principles. Getting in what he called "one of his gales," he tore his neckerchief from his perspiring person, and flinging it back among the preachers, he walked the stand, and poured the stirring truths of the Bible upon his auditors in a way that was very moving.

The meeting wound up well with the accustomed register of converts' names, love-feast, Lord's Supper, and baptisms. But two scrupulous people, a husband and wife, very large in person, wished to be immersed, and remained behind after the meeting had broken up, to be baptized in the Bay.

The Presiding Elder, the Rev. Wm. Ryerson, had a great respect for Corson, and he detained him to assist in the preliminary service. By the way, I may as well here say, that Ryerson once declared to me, that "Robert Corson, was as good a theologian as J. R.," a man then much looked up to, "and that it was only his rustic ways that prevented his being as much esteemed." The baptism was distinguished by an incident which shows how much some people's fancies (not to say whims) have to do with their preferences for modes and forms. The husband, a heavy man, was immersed first; but the administrator was large and strong, and he could handle a subject easily, however ponderous. They walked well out into the rippling waters of the Bay, when the administrator, asking him his name, thrust the body of "John Sprung," with a noticable souse, beneath the waves. Mrs. S., though heavier than her husband, had not his strength of nerves, and when she witnessed the ordeal through which her better half had passed, felt her convictions of the indispensable necessity of plunging begin to experience considerable modification: she knew she would go down easily enough, but she was not sure she would come up so readily. She, therefore, thought it might be as truly valid if she went into the water and kneeled down, and was then aspersed with the element. Methodism is wisely accommodating in a matter of such secondary importance as the mere mode of baptism; the good Elder therefore assented to the proposition. They walked out hand in hand to the depth of about two or three feet of water, he carrying in his hand a six quart tin kettle, which, after the usual formulary was pronounced, he filled three several times, and poured it as often on her head, and "she came up out of the water" as thoroughly drenched as if she had been the subject of a trine immersion. I knew her well in after years, and respected her Christian character highly; but I never learned that she had any misgivings about her baptism, *on the score of the deficiency of water.*

Corson was full of exuberant spirits,—the very quintessence of good nature, characterized by the broadest humour. His humour was often evinced by ironical praises of himself, for his superior wisdom and ability. It was not so much what he said, as the way in which he said it, which provoked the merriment of his friends. As my object is to make our genial friend live his days over again among us, I will tell a little incident which amused us all that afternoon, after the baptism referred to, and wonderfully tickled even the dignified Elder. A group of us travelling preachers were gathered at the front of the house of James Lyons, Esq., M.P.P., then a distinguished Methodist, which fronted on the pebbly beach of the Bay. We were preparing to disperse to our several fields of labour. William Smith and myself were soon to mount our horses for the Carrying-place, where we expected to hear Lorenzo once more, *en route*, Smith for Hallowell, and myself for Belleville. Corson was soon to turn his head once more westward for the Whitby Circuit, and was desirous of company. "Why," said young Hamilton Biggar, who was then putting in the first year of his itinerancy on the Cavan Circuit, "I go your way." "I am glad of it," said Corson, "for I like to have some one along that doesn't know quite as much I do!" This sally produced an agreeable titillation all around. I would choose in those days no more agreeable travelling companion, than to ride, "cheek by jowl," alongside of "Bobby Corson." A delectable time I have no doubt they had, till the "*Guide Board*" pointed them in different directions. I have only to hope that the paths which Biggar and I have been severally pursuing, till now we are "old and grey-headed," may open out on the "heavenly plains," where we shall overtake our "glorified friend," "incapable of woe."

1829, 1830

The Conference which wound up the ecclesiastical year 1828-29, sat in the summer of the last of these two years, that is to say, commencing August 26th, 1829, at "Bowman's Meeting-house," in the township of Ancaster. Case was elected President, *pro-tempore*, and Richardson, Secretary. Several were stricken from the roll of the Conference: James Jackson, "expelled;" Isaac Baker Smith, "withdrawn;" George Farr and George Sovreign, "located;" and two brethren "left without stations for a year;" and, William Slater, gone to his last, long rest, "died." But still, with the accession of a few good men and true, one of whom was the late Thomas Bevitt, the walls were manned again with "soldiers of Christ" who did not desert their posts, one conspicuous specimen of this embattled host being Robert Corson. This Conference decided on inaugurating two measures which, despite what many might have thought of his antecedents and character, had Mr. Corson's life-long sympathy and support: these were a seminary of learning and a religious newspaper.

His name was set down once more, and read off for the WHITBY CIRCUIT. Let us see what our subject says of this year himself in his MS. "sketch:" "The second year I had a colleague; a man with a family was sent to help me. Two appointments were added from the Cobourg Circuit. My salary for the two years was $400." No wonder that a family of seven persons living on $200 a year, were sometimes "in straits."

I happened to know something of the circumstances and doings of the year myself, having begun the year on the Cobourg, which, after the first Quarterly Meeting, gave off to the Whitby Circuit not only the "two" principal "appointments" to which Brother Corson no doubt made reference, namely, Port Hope and Hope township, but two inconsiderable week-day appointments besides, known as "Dean's" and the "Danford Road." I embodied the changes and circumstances referred to in my "Biographical History," which I venture to reproduce :—

"*Whitby* began the year with its last year's minister; but from the augmentation of its boundaries, another was required, and Mr. Conrad Vandusen, a native of the Bay of Quinté, of Scotch-Dutch extraction, a man of great physical vigour, of some education, and great present zeal, being a new convert, was called out to assist Mr. Corson. He underwent herculean labours that year: the Circuit was large and his family resided in Sophiasburgh. Fortunately his ample resources enabled him to keep a good horse under him. They had lively times in the Circuit during that year. Some characteristic incidents might be told, but we pass them over."

The necessity of economising space and of preserving something like the dignity of history in the larger work, do not prohibit the use of lighter materials in the biography of a single person, which is expressly intended to be of a homely and familiar character. The two colleagues in this Circuit were far from being unsuited to each other, if they were not, indeed, very much alike. They were both thorough Canadians, both strong, active, enterprising, and enduring men. They were both possessed of exuberant spirits, and a large store of humour; both had an eye for the laughable side of the many and varied incidents constantly coming under their notice; and both loved a good story, and knew how to tell one interestingly. Several were told by Vandusen, especially. When he went for the first time to one of the most out-of-the-way places in the township of Reach, where the people, especially the young ones, were nothing remarkable for cultivation, he seemed eager and restless before the service, but, when once engaged therein, he gave them an arousing sermon, delivered with great liberty and volubility, which the rustics thought a wonderful performance. Speaking of the orator of the night, afterwards, said a great, awkward young man, "I know'd Vandusen was a good preacher, for I seed he couldn't stand still." He often said very queer things, which seemed to escape before he thought; they were the relics of his old harum-scarum way of talking, that characterized him before his conversion. Meeting the class, according to the invariable custom, one Sunday after sermon, in what was known as the "Baptist Meeting-house" in the township of Whitby, he came to a young lady, whom he accosted in the usual manner, "Well, sister, how is it with your soul?" Resenting the imputation of Church membership, she testily answered, "I'm not a sister!" "What are you then?" said Van, "a *brother?*" He had scarcely uttered the question, till he saw that would not do, and he tried, vainly, to modify and mend it; but she in the mean time showed more and more signs of annoyance, till at length she arose and went out. The preacher felt badly, and it was a source of self upbraiding whenever he thought of it during the next circuit round of four weeks; but one of the first things Bro. Moore, the leader, said to him upon his arrival the next time, was, "Brother Vandusen, that 'brother' of yours has become a *sister ;* the circumstance wrought on her mind until she has become converted to God." If I remember correctly she joined the class, and became a worthy member. I will not pretend to account for the manner in which such an odd incident was adapted to do good.

Both these brethren came a second time to a Camp-meeting at Presqu' Isle, that is during the summer of 1830, the Rev. David Wright and myself being then the preachers on the Cobourg Circuit. These and other brethren present were very efficient, and the meeting, if any difference, was better than the year before, and a revival in various parts of the country was the result. We missed Ephraim Evans of the previous year, but we had in his stead, his brother James, from the Rice Lake Indian Mission, then very much alive to God. Also, Mr. Corson brought with him his neophite, young Aaron Hurd, already mentioned, from Scugog, to whom he was greatly attached, who was on his way to the Mohawk Mission in Tiandenaga. How solemnizing to the survivors to think that every one of those faithful labourers, both old and young, has gone to his account—Wright, Corson, Vandusen, Evans, and Hurd.

1830, 1831.

The Conference of 1830 began its sessions in the old town of *Kingston*, August 17th, but it adjourned from there on the 24th to Belleville where the General Conference was appointed to sit, in order to finish up its business. Corson was at both the sessions of the Annual Conference and of the General Conference also, of which latter he was a member, by being one of "the travelling Elders, who had travelled the four years last past." The aspects of the Connexion were very encouraging at that time, and the labourers went to their several Circuits full of ardour and hope; but none of them more so than Robert Corson. He was appointed to the TORONTO CIRCUIT, including the township of that name, Trafalgar, Chinguacousy, Esquesing, Erin, Caledon, and Gore of Toronto.

His own account of the Circuit and his circumstances and successes is as follows: "In 1830, I was appointed to the Toronto Circuit. We had three log-churches" (those were 'Lindsay's Meeting-house,' the 'Four Corners' Meeting-house,' and 'Harrison's Chapel'), "I had a colleague. We found fine Societies, consisting of English, Irish, and Canadians." This was before any rivalry or division had taken place, and things were very different from the variegated Methodism of the present. He resumes, "We had some trials on this Circuit: my wife's health failed. But we had good revivals. I stopped two years" (the longest period then allowed), "and the increase during the two years was *two hundred and four*. My salary during that time was *four hundred dollars*," i.e., $200 for each year.

My gleanings relative to the first of these two years, namely, 1830-31, as set down in my "Memorial," may come in here, as illustrative of my subject. I was led to say, "The old Toronto Circuit has a new preacher in charge, in the person of the laborious Corson. Rev. Henry Shaler. after an absence of only one year, is back there again as second preacher. About this time, Primitive Methodist ministers from England began to bid for the patronage of those of Methodist proclivities in that Circuit. Some who had belonged to them in the old country returned to their first love, and some that were never before connected with that body joined them. Yet Corson and Shaler had a net gain " (the first year) " of *sixty*."

Since the above was written some items of information have reached me from various sources. Mr. Shaler, as well as himself, was married and had a small family to support; and as neither of them received more than *two hundred dollars* for the year, any means for earning an honest penny, which did not interfere with their work, was not to be rejected. In those days harvest time was a very busy season, there being then no "mowers" or "reapers" to facilitate the business. Mr. Joseph Gardiner, of the Centre Road, Toronto, had a very heavy crop, and Messrs. Corson and Shaler were skilful, active husbandmen; a friend of mine, who resided in the neigbourhood at the time, told me that the two Circuit preachers took their sickles, or cradles, and went among Mr. Gardiner's harvesters, and earned their dollar a day while the season lasted. It was a pity they were necessitated to do it; but seeing they were, it was no more to their disgrace than tentmaking was to St. Paul. One of these toiling men is still alive, but a letter, requesting information about that year, has failed to draw him out: I suspect his infirmities are too great to admit of his writing. The Master graciously help " my old companion in distress" down the declivity of life into the valley of the Jordan; and may the companion of " Father Honest " of Pilgrim's Progress, "one Good Conscience," " whom he had spoken to in his life-time," accompany him through its cold waters up on the " banks of eternal deliverance " among the "shining ones!" Amen.

1831, 1832.

Mr. Corson and his colleague had no long journey to reach the seat of Conference at the beginning of this year, for it sat for the first time, after the existence of a chapel and a Methodist society eleven years, in the good town of York. A happy Conference session it was, and crowned with a glorious revival which brought some of the most influential people of the town into the Church. Unlike Corson, I had ridden on horseback more than *two hundred miles* to be present at that Convocation, and to be received into full connexion. Where are my fellow candidates ? Two have gone to their reward in heaven ; one, highly respected, to a highly important judicial office ; only Shaler besides myself—and he, " in age and feebleness extreme"— remains with his name on the ministerial roll.

The reader is prepared to learn that Mr. Corson's name was continued in connexion with TORONTO CIRCUIT for another year. No other name than his own appears for the Circuit for that year. "Another to be employed," indicated that the Presiding Elder and the Stationing Committee had another in view. The supply was a young man of good family, good school education, and newly from Cazenovia Academy in the State of New York, a native of the town of Belleville, *Alexander McNabb* by name was he. But he was of too slight a constitution, and had been too tenderly brought up, being "the only son of his mother, and she was a widow," to stand the wear and tear of so large and rough a Circuit as Toronto, especially as planned and worked by the pushing Corson. The young man had to leave, and a place was made for him in the old Hallowell Circuit, where he found a good home at Squire

Dougal's, and a wife before the year was out. Next, a young man of very different physical stamina and proportions, brother *Samuel Rose*, was brought away from an Indian mission and placed on the Circuit. Corson, after hearing him, said, "You'll do." He was very well received and helped on with the work, while he remained; but wishing to have the benefits of an advanced school before his name was brought before the Conference for reception on trial, even he also retired from the Circuit. The balance of the year a young man from the Twenty Mile Creek, then recently the scene of a great revival, *Jacob Kennedy* by name, who though he declined entering the full ministry, at the end of the year, has proved himself, "until this day," a steadfast member of central Methodism, and an able and willing local preacher, residing still in the place of his original home. I should have been glad to hear his testimony to his former colleague, between whom and himself friendship was never interrupted. Mr. Corson's second colleague on that Circuit, now Rev. Dr. Rose, bears the highest testimony to the devotedness and diligence of his colleague of that day, showing that he preached one-fourth oftener than he expected his colleague to preach; and pronounces his wife a woman of great heavenly mindedness and sanctity of spirit and manners, of whom he says, "It is impossible to say too much."

This last year of the undisturbed independency from foreign jurisdiction and interference may be said to be the grand climacteric year of the Upper Canada Methodist Church's success. The stimulus given to every sort of useful activity was wonderful—Sunday-schools, education, and temperance. But the crowning glory was its revivals, which issued in an accession of no less than 3,714 members to the Church. Of these Mr. Corson and his Circuit furnished a generous proportion.

Some lighter matters belonging to our subject and his Circuit during this year, may now be mentioned. After twenty-five years battling for their rights, it was made legal for the ministers of the Methodist Church to celebrate the rite of matrimony, and the act went first into force during the second year of Mr. Corson's second year's sojourn in this Circuit. The first couple Mr. Corson married, I am informed by Rev. Dr. Rose, to use the celebrant's expressive imagery, he "yoked them up wrong," that is, through nervousness and want of practice, he placed the bride on the right hand instead of the groom ; this, however, is no more than I did myself with the first couple I married, from similar causes, about two years later. Through the polite intervention of the Rev. John Hunt I am able to lay before the reader and the friends and admirers of the late " Father Corson " generally, a copy of the veritable certificate given to the couple then and thus married. It is interesting and important for several reasons. I will first give the certificate, which will speak for itself, and then furnish an observation or two thereon made by Mr. Hunt.

"COPY.

" I do hereby certify that on the 28th day of December, in the year of our Lord *one thousand eight hundred and thirty-one*, George Cheaney, of the township of Toronto, in the Home District, and Abigail Walker, spinster, of the township of Chingacousy, in the same District, were married by me, ROBERT CORSON, a minister of the Methodist Epi. copal Church in Canada, in the presence of Andrew Neelands and John Rutledge, which said marriage was celebrated by publication of banns. Dated this 28th day of December, A.D. 1831.

"(Signed),   ROBERT CORSON.

"Witnesses : } John Rutledge, Andrew Neelands."

Of the parties here mentioned, my reverend informant says, "The bride is dead. Father Cheaney is living in Orangeville, married a second time, enjoying a happy old age. John Rutledge, one of the witnesses, I remember often seeing at my Father's in Toronto township. The other, Andrew Neelands, I believe is still living, near Brampton." I knew three out of the four principal parties in this business, and it effects me exceedingly to have them brought before my mind once more. May God bless the living ones ! And may they and myself be so unspeakably happy as to overtake " the friends fondly cherished, who have passed on before," including our precious friend, Corson, in that bright and blissful world, where friends in Christ shall meet to part no more ! And may the study of this life contribute to that end. I shall have at least one more curious marriage scene to describe farther on.

A little item of interest relating to the Toronto Circuit had almost escaped me. While I was labouring on the Toronto Circuit, in the summer of 1828, a highly respectable local preacher, arrived in the settlements from England, by the name of Foster. He purchased a farm, a very few miles west of his friend, Mr. Gardiner's, and identified himself heartily with the interests of the Circuit, to which his labours were of great service ; and, being favourable to liberal opinions, he clung closely to the Canadian Conference and its fortunes through all the mutations of colonial Methodism. He had several fine boys, some of whom became local preachers, and all of them decided and helpful members of the Church. One of these, now residing at Brampton, William Foster, Esq., had the "Pen Portrait" of Mr. Corson, by his son John Wesley, submitted to him, which drew forth the following letter, which further illustrates several particulars already touched upon, or yet to be mentioned. It is given below, accompanied by a note, both of which will speak for themselves :—

"Brampton, Jan. 27th, 1879.

" DEAR DR. CORSON,—I have examined very carefully the proof-sheet you sent me of your father's life, and think it very good. I have marked what I think can be improved. I fancy there is one mistake ; that is, I think, Father Corson was over medium height. His ministerial labours cannot be over-rated. Mrs. Foster remembers him very well, and can tell many hardships he had to encounter in travelling through the wilderness, carrying his saddle bags on his shoulder. The roads were nearly impassible ; he could not at all times ride on horseback. This was cheerfully done" (his trudging on foot). "Not a murmur escaped his lips. Mrs. F. remembers your dear, now sainted mother, how self-sacrificing she was. Often left alone with her little family for weeks together, yet she was never heard to say that it was hard. She bore it like a good Christian soldier, for she really was one.

"Mr. Neelands requested me to say that the proof-sheet is good, and he cannot say too much of your now sainted father. He knew him perfectly well, and often had piloted him to some of his appointments in the night by torch light.

"Mrs. Lowes also remembers him very well, for he used to preach in Father Wilkinson's house. He was a welcome messenger I assure you. Mrs. Foster and Mrs. Lowes think that the proof-sheet scarcely does him justice, as it would be impossible for pen and ink to do so; for my own part I cannot say too much in any respect of him. I wish there were more like him, as his honourable conduct was as a beacon light to all around him."

NOTE.—Father seemed taller in middle life, than as he stooped more and more in old age. J. W. C.

1832, 1833.

I am entering with my subject on the last year of a very important stage of the Church's history, and also in Mr. Corson's own ministerial life. He, and I, and my readers are now fain to take our journey to the never-to-be-forgotten Hallowell Conference, which commenced August 8th, 1832. Because of previous notification in the *Guardian*, that overtures for a union with the British Conference would probably be considered, there was a full attendance of ministers and a vast confluence of members of the church, both official and private.

I need not detain the general reader with the preliminaries, proceedings, and results of that memorable Conference, farther than to say, that it issued in the proposal of Preliminary Articles of Union with the Parent Body, which were substantially accepted by the British Conference, and ratified, in 1833, by the Canada Conference, in the presence of the British Representative. The minute particulars, with the vouchers and authorities for the whole proceedings, are given in my "Biographical History of Methodism in Canada." My present business is with Mr. Corson's relation to the measure, who was generally a middle man, independent, but peace-loving and peace-promoting. But, as far as I can remember, he was in favour of this measure from the first. And while the famous COMMITTEE OF TEN were deliberating, a caucus was held with a view of preparing the lesser and younger men for the measure, and I confess that it weighed considerably with me, that such men as Healy, Ferguson, Griffis, and Corson among the most matured of the second class of preachers, were in favour of the measure.

At this Conference, ROBERT CORSON was read off for the YONGE STREET CIRCUIT. Two more vivacious, lively, lovable men than he and his colleague, were never appointed at once to the same Circuit. His superintendent, or "the preacher in charge," as he was then termed, was the Rev. *David Wright.* Mr. Corson's temporal circumstances were to be somewhat improved for a time. He says of this appointment : " In 1832, I was appointed to Yonge Street, one of the best Circuits in our Conference. We had plenty of work, and a large number of warm-hearted friends. A gracious revival of religion took place, resulting in a net increase for the two years of *three hundred.* My salary during the two years was $560"—that is, at the rate of $280 a year, a sum which would be far from earning the meed of being "one of the best Circuits in the Conference," at the present time. How the times have changed!

My history furnishes the following particulars relative to the Yonge Street Circuit for this year, 1832-33 :—" *Yonge Street* enjoyed 'showers of blessings' this year, 1832-33. Under date of December 6th, 1832, Mr. Wright reports :— ' We have received since Conference 150 probationers, besides several by letter.' 'Our Quarterly Meeting, November 10th and 11th, was attended with the presence of the Captain of our salvation. Some found peace, others were quickened, and seven or eight joined society. Bros. Long and Gatchel's visit was attended with much good.' Later in the year, September 13th, 1833, the evangelist, Long, writes concerning this Circuit : he speaks of revival meetings held in 'Tyler's meeting-house,' 'Petch's Barn, Whitchurch,' 'Mr. Obadiah R's Barn, Gwilliambury,' 'Tecumseh,' 'Newmarket,' and 'Holland River.' Some of these meetings continued 'twenty-two days,' and 'rising of 122 joined Society' in one place. Mr. Long's sphere of labour, however, embraced part of the Albion Circuit and Yonge Street. At the close of the year, Messrs. Wright and Corson report the Yonge Street Circuit fifty miles long, and twenty-five broad. It embraced York township, Vaughan, Markham, King, part of Scarboro', East, West, and North Gwilliambury, and thirty-two regular appointments. Four local preachers, whose names we will hand down,—Holden, Watson, Moore, and Appleford,—aided them in their work. They had three Missionary Societies, nine or ten Temperance Societies, and a number of Sunday-schools. Two parsonages were erected. The net increase in numbers was 376, making a membership of 951. No wonder they exclaimed, 'Glory be God.'"

Manuscript memoranda furnished by Dr. William Case Corson, give inside views of the family and its fortunes, which, otherwise, we should not have. They seem to have resided at *Richmond Hill*. Dr. William says, "Although I was but two or three years of age, I have a distinct remembrance of one or two occurrences, such as the burial of an Indian chief with Indian rites, the long procession in single file passing our door. Amos Wright, who years afterward became member of Parliament, was our near neighbour, and his wife was converted under father's ministry; and I remember the terrible struggle she passed through before deliverance from the bondage of sin came to her. Robert Campbell, a local preacher of great acceptability, also lived near us. I had the pleasure of meeting this good brother only a few years ago at his son's, who married a cousin of mine."

1833, 1834.
IV. MR. CORSON DURING THE SEVEN YEARS OF THE FIRST UNION.

October 2, 1833, arrived. The Rev. Egerton Ryerson had returned from England with the ratified ARTICLES OF UNION, accompanied by the *Rev. George Marsden*, prospective President of the Conference, and the Rev. Joseph Stinson, the intended Superintendent of Missions; and the Conference was called to order on the above mentioned day, in Newgate Street (now Adelaide Street) Methodist Church. The Rev. Wm. Case was appointed to the chair, *pro tempore;* the report of the Delegate to England was made; the Articles, as slightly modified (all in favour of the Canadian brethren) by the British Conference, were considered, one by one, each passing by a very large majority; and then, the whole were submitted together. One minister, the Rev. James Richardson, who had been opposed to some of the details, urged "a unanimous rising vote," which was given; at least so it was pronounced at the time by the chair. The only exceptions to this were (1) a little feint by the Rev. Thomas Whitehead, which was considered as a joke (for he gave in his adhesion heartily to the measure, when carried); and (2) the voluntary absence of the Rev. Joseph Gatchell. He and the loyal, law-abiding Corson chanced to occupy the same billet during the Conference, and, as old friends, had much conversation about the proceedings. Gatchell assured his friend that though he did not like the Union, he had no intention of making dissension. This statement Mr. Corson afterwards put in writing. The chair of the Conference was delivered by Mr. Case to Mr. Marsden, and the usual business transacted under his Presidency. These proceedings changed the name of the Church from Methodist Episcopal to Wesleyan Methodist.

The YONGE STREET CIRCUIT, to which Mr. Corson was re-appointed for the ensuing year, 1833-34, was destined to be somewhat agitated by the Union measure before the year was out, and still more when it was past. The Rev. Edmund Stoney took the place of Mr. Wright, in charge of the Circuit, the "Superintendent" (for such the brother "in charge" began now to be called, in the discipline and otherwise) of the preceding having been promoted to the Chairmanship of the London District. I might say, in passing, of this latter term, "Chairman," which was used interchangeably with Presiding Elder, that during the last quarter of the year of which I am writing, it was dropped, or substituted by "Chairman" in the published list of the Rev. James Richardson, who was the P. E. of the York District, which, of course, included the Yonge Street Circuit, of which Messrs. Stoney and Corson were the incumbents, and then the example was followed by the other incumbents of the office.

I have intimated that there were persons in the Yonge Street Circuit, during this Mr. Corson's last year, dissatisfied with the Union, in sufficient numbers to make one locality in that field of labour a rallying point for the dissentients throughout the Connexion, who sought to organize and claim the title and property of the late Methodist Episcopal Church of Canada. This movement, however, did not come to a head till early in the opening part of the next Conference year. The account given of that convocation is as follows:—

"Five days after the Wesleyan Conference at Kingston

arose,—that is to say, on the 25th of June, 1834,—certain brethren, dissatisfied with the proceedings of Conference in the matter of the Union, or some of its details, met at Cummer's Meeting-house, nine miles north of Toronto, who afterwards claimed to be the legal Conference of the Methodist Episcopal Church in Canada, from which they charged the whole Canada Conference as having seceded. These men, according to the Rev. T. Webster, their historian, were the following regularly ordained elders: Joseph Gatchell, David Culp, Daniel Pickett, and J. W. Byam, deacon. There were also a number of local preachers in attendance. — We will both agree to set aside 'local preachers' as not of the legal Conference; let us, therefore, examine the claims of the rest. Mr. Byam had never been a member of an Annual Conference. He had been a probationer for membership, but was discontinued at the end of two years. He had not travelled during the past sixteen years. If he obtained orders afterwards as a local deacon, it would not have given him any legislative right or legal value. Mr. Corson says the Conference of 1825 elected him to deacon's orders. Mr. Pickett's was scarcely a better case; he had travelled nine years at the beginning of the century; had located, and had subsequently got out of the church—our information said he was expelled—and, as we have seen, preached on his own responsibility for many years, and endeavoured to raise a Society of his own called 'Provincial Methodists,' and only returned about three years before the Union, and took rank as a local preacher. His orders it may be, were tacitly recognized, but he had not been a member of any Annual Conference in full twenty-five years. Mr. Culp was more recently of the Conference, but he had located eight years before the Union.

Mr. Gatchell was the only one who could by possibility give validity to that Conference—if a Conference, which is a noun of multitude, could consist of one man. We have seen that though disapproving of the Union, he entered no protest, nor even voted against it, but withdrew from the house when the final vote was taken. His name continued in the Minutes of the Conference, and stood there at the very moment he was co-operating in the present business, and he had received the same allowance from Conference funds, for the past year, as any other superannuated preacher on the list. But Mr Gatchell even did not preside at this Conference, but Mr. John Bailey. These persons had a natural right to new-create a 'Methodist Episcopal Church in Canada,' if they preferred such an organization, but they had no legal grounds for claiming that they were the Church which bore that name before the Union."*

I have to say, in justification of introducing the above painful remembrance here, that Cummer's Meeting-house was a central spot in the Yonge Street Circuit, and had rejoiced in a very strong Society. The Cummers, who gave name to it, were a very respectable and influential family. They were the original owners of the land upon which the church stood, which, I think, had never been properly settled to the Connexion, which settlement was refused after the Union. Both parties continued to use the building for some years, when the Wesleyans drew off and opened a smaller building, which they adjusted to church purposes, and was long known as the "Parsonage Chapel." This, in its turn, has given place, for some time, to the substantial and elegant edifice at Newtonbrook. A Mr. Turner, a very

* Case and Cotemporaries.

capable local preacher, from the States, who resided on Yonge Street, bringing his American ideas with him, was one of the most active and influential in opposing the carrying out of the Union measures in that Circuit. I think George Turner became a Presiding Elder in the new organization.

This will be one of the best opportunities for saying, what I ought to mention, in justice to the memory of Corson, that although unswervingly loyal to the measures of the main central body, he was by no means bitter towards the off-shoots, but cultivated considerable intimacy with them, as he did in fact with all Protestant communities; and if, at any time, a person wished to know the condition and prospects of any of the minor Methodist bodies, he need only inquire of Robert Corson, who would usually be found posted in the facts and figures. He constantly yearned in heart towards those who had "gone out from us;" and always heartily seconded any measures, which promised feasibility, for restoring the unity of provincial Methodism. I might also say, in this connection, that he was not only thoroughly posted in the past, but the current history, or state, of Methodism, especially that of our own branch of it, in this and the neighbouring Provinces. He was very anxious to know, each succeeding year, what our increase or decrease was; and he usually learned the figures by correspondence with the several districts, or what the returns would be, before they were officially announced.

He never presumed to think he was fit for any office beyond that of a rural Circuit preacher; but he took an interest in preferring the best among his brethren to connexional appointments. His choice was usually wise, and never based on party predilections, or the offspring of party strifes. In my humble opinion Mr. Corson was a truly enlightened man, and usually in advance of current connexional opinion. Some men's reputation for wisdom is acquired by their habitual condemnation of what happens never to have been tried. Corson was not one of those: he was not scared by the prejudiced cry of "novelty," or "heresy," but was willing to view a subject on all sides, whether it were new or old. He did not get the name of a wise man by pulling a long face, looking, and talking mysteriously, shaking his head, and uttering hints and inuendoes; but if he had opinions, and he was usually made up on all subjects, he uttered them without hesitancy. He was not imprudent, but straightforward, in his utterances; and by his free and friendly discussions with the people, he did more than almost any other man to quiet those painful agitations which were born of authoritative suppression and secrecy more than of any thing else. There is nothing like the safety-valve of free ventilation, and Corson knew this secret. Our subject would have been considered wiser and weightier, by many, if he had been less jovial; and just there was their mistake. Some of the wisest things have been said in epigram, or as *bon mots*. Go to *Punch* and *Grip* if you want undiluted wisdom. Corson might have been called *the humoristic philosopher*. Before I have done with him, I hope to give some of his "lucky hits."

1834, 1835.
NEWMARKET CIRCUIT.

The Conference of 1834 sat in the town of *Kingston*, and so early as the 11th of June, in which month it was to have its sittings for the long space of forty years. This was to accommodate it to its new relation to the British Conference, which sat a month or so later in the summer, and to which it had always to report. It chanced that no less than two eminent officials from the British Conference, besides Mr. Stinson, were there. The *Rev. Robert Alder*, one of the Missionary Secretaries, who chanced to be there first, took the chair of the Conference, *ex-officio*, till the arrival of the appointed President of the Canada Conference, the *Rev. Edmund Grindrod*.

At this Conference, in consequence of the representations of Mr. Grindrod, who said the ordination of local preachers in Upper Canada was likely to produce dissatisfaction among that class of officials in other parts of their extended work, it was decided by "Resolution" of Conference, "That it was *inexpedient* to ordain any more local preachers,"—a measure which brought on a crisis, which otherwise might have been staved off, for a time at least, and greatly increased the agitation which had commenced, and which our subject and the other preachers had to meet, and which caused them much solicitude and suffering for five or six years, if not more.

In several respects the deliberations of this Conference, in which Mr. Corson now gradually began to take a part, were rather anxious, if not sometimes acrimonious. As far as our subject did take a part, from this time forward, his interpositions were always useful. He was never otherwise than fair and moderate, often talking as much on one side as on the other—giving first the "rights" and then the "lefts" a hit. But it was always done so good-naturedly as not to offend either, while his ebullitions of broad humour often "brought down the house," and broke up many a lowering cloud, by putting the angry disputants once more in good humour. Indeed, it was usually enough to see him rise, make his very peculiar bow, and utter, to secure attention, "Mr. President," and awake smiling expectation. It would often make his friends laugh, simply to look at him.

Mr. Corson was appointed to the *Newmarket Circuit* with *Thomas Fawcett* for his junior colleague, who proved himself a "true yoke-fellow." Indeed, he was a brother peculiarly adapted to co-operate with Corson; for, like himself, Fawcett was lively, loving, demonstrative, and unsparing of his pains, if labour was painful to him at all, who seemed to sport with fatigue. He was a native of Yorkshire, where he was converted and became a local preacher. He arrived in Canada timely enough in the summer of 1832, to be sent with John S. Atwood to the Dumfries Circuit. The next year, 1833-34, he was appointed to the Toronto Circuit, under the superintendency of the cultivated Zenas Adams. In both of the Circuits he must have heard much favourable to Robert Corson, becoming thereby acquainted with him by report, with whom he is now appointed to travel. Mr. Corson's manuscript account of this year is very short. "In 1834, I was appointed to Newmarket. I had a young man for my colleague, who was made a blessing to the Circuit. We had some good revivals. Our increase for one year, *fifty*. My salary for the one year, $260." Mr. Corson told the

Rev. Michael Fawcett that his brother Thomas was the only colleague he ever had who was willing to preach as often and make as many visits as he did himself.

I shall be able to give some further details, farther on, of their affairs, religiously considered, from Mr. Corson's published letters. In the meantime, we must pause and contemplate the state of his family, as drawn from the recollections of one of their number, Dr. William Corson. It seems that the family actually left Richmond Hill for the Newmarket Circuit, where, however, if I have read my materials aright, they remained for only a part of the year.

Dr. William Corson says, "From Richmond Hill we removed to Mitchel's Corners, (now named Aurora.) Here we were surrounded by those good people, the Society of Friends. Here the Hartman family lived, the father having left the Quakers to join our Church. The son Joseph rose to be a conspicuous Member of Parliament; while the daughter, Nancy, had the honour to become the wife of one of our ministers (Rev. T. Cosford). It was at Hartman's school-house that I first attended school, and Moulton was our teacher. Mr. Moulton's daughter became the wife of our distinguished Missionary to Japan, the Rev. G. M. Meacham, who also was my most intimate friend and class-mate at Victoria College, and with whom I corresponded for years, so curious are the connecting links of our history in this life. My brother John was teaching in a school-house in an opposite direction, and Moulton and he would meet at our house for a sing; and I remember to have first heard them give Pope's Dying Christian, 'Vital spark of heavenly flame.' While living there, father met that severe accident by the running away of his horse, by which one ear was so completely torn from his head as to hang by a mere shred of skin. The ear was sewed on so skilfully by the surgeon, that not even a scar remained to show the nature of the injury. This was the only time in my life that I ever saw father confined to his bed. His general health was so good that he never even complained of headache!"

In the early history of American Methodism, the allowances being so small, and no furniture awaiting their arrival on their Circuits, it became very common for a minister. when his family grew to such proportions that it was as serious a matter to move them, as it was to feed them : it was common, I say, to obviate both of these difficulties and furnish employment for the growing up boys, aye, and girls too, to select a piece of land, larger or smaller, according to circumstances and means, to constitute a homestead, where the family could be left to earn their living, while the preacher used his influence with the Presiding Elder and Bishop, or Stationing Committee, as the case might be, to station him on Circuits not too far from that sacred spot. The same sometimes took place in Canada : Ryan, Whithead, Culp, Wm. Brown, and Ezra Healy, were all examples of this arrangement, after a time.

Something of this kind was now contemplated by Mr. and Mrs. Corson while they were on the Yonge Street Circuit. Many preachers found it so hard to "make the two ends meet," that the little property they had accumulated before entering the ministry was often dissipated in supplementing the scantiness of Circuit appropriations. The late never-to-be-forgotten Henry Wilkinson informed me that the property his superior industry and business skill had acquired, while in secular life, was all consumed in the itinerancy. Fortunately, although Mr. Corson's allowances were exceptionally small, his own and wife's economy was such as to enable them to preserve the little property they had in Oxford intact. This they now sold and invested it in a purchase in a more central place, the location of which will transpire in the reminiscenses of Dr. William about to be given.

Here is the Doctor's account of the arrangement:—
"From the Yonge Street Circuit the family was transferred to a farm at the German Mills, two and a half miles east of Thornhill, while father continued the regular work of the ministry on the Newmarket and Whitby Circuits, respectively. A mother, with six boys (no girls in the family), the oldest of which only had come to manhood, settling down on a heavily timbered farm, of which only a few acres had been cleared, was an undertaking of no common magnitude. But the mother was firm, resolute, and inspiring, and she always controlled her children absolutely, though without severity. Under the leadership of the oldest son, the trees were felled and burned in log heaps; a good frame house was built, the lime having been burned and the timber sawn by what seemed superhuman exertions. A young orchard was planted, the mother holding the trees while the sons filled in and packed the earth about the roots. In the midst of this struggle the mother was calm but earnest, being the high-priest of the family, and leading the family devotions in that exalted strain of eloquence, and in cadences which can never fade from the memory 'while life and being last.' Thomas Fawcett, of precious memory, was father's colleague at this time, and here he would come to stay with us once a month or so; his visits being regarded by mother and the boys as little less than angelic. He was very pious; but he had such exuberance of spirits and such a

fund of humour, that we could only cry when the time came for him to go. Fawcett rode a beautiful cream-coloured horse, and it was his delight to place one of the boys on this spirited animal's back for a race to the watering. Here our friend first met the lovely and excellent young lady, Margaret Shaw, who was to become his wife. Before leaving the Circuit they were quietly married; and my mother related to our delectation how at the ceremony, when father put the usual question, 'Wilt thou have this woman, &c.?' that Fawcett answered in stentorian tones, 'I WILL,' thereby expressing his ardent affection for her who was to become his wife. Some of the events of the Rebellion, which took place at this time, while my brother John was absent in Toronto, will be detailed by him from information I have furnished him. One circumstance, which just now recurs to me, was, that during the highest pitch of excitement, one night the whole sky became covered by a most brilliant scarlet colour, which, being reflected back to the snow-covered earth, gave a very startling appearance to this sublunary sphere. While the children beheld this phenomenon in terrified affright, the mother, taking advantage of the occurrence, calmly pointed them, as they stood in a circle around her, to 'the Lamb of God, that taketh away the sins of the world.'"

My contributor in the above has anticipated the flight of time by two or three years, but he has written so enchantingly that I had no heart to arrest the flow of his language; besides, the unity of his subject required that it should not be broken into fragments. What a picture it presents of maternal influence on the one hand, and of filial devotion of boys to a mother on the other!

I turn now to produce some news from the Newmarket

Circuit during the ecclesiastical year 1834-35, from the *Guardian* for the spring of 1835, from among the "LETTERS TO THE EDITOR," I extract the following :—

"NEWMARKET CIRCUIT.—MR. EDITOR,—Since the commencement of our labours this Conference year, we have had some serious difficulties to encounter. Efforts have been made to create divisions; and I am sorry to say that they have been successful in two or three cases. However, in the midst of our trials the Lord hath helped us. We had some refreshing seasons in the neighbourhood where my family resides. The societies are united—they prefer union to division. In different parts of the Circuit we have been blest with an outpouring of the Holy Spirit, and a number have been brought from darkness into light, and from the power of Satan to God. We have been recently favoured with a visit from our worthy President, who attended a Missionary Meeting at Newmarket. It was considered the most interesting meeting of the kind ever held in these parts. A number of members of our society and others residing in the neighbourhood of Newmarket are much waked up to the interests of the Missionary cause.

"In conclusion I would say, that we have received upwards of a *hundred* into society since the last Conference. A few who had left us have returned. Our net increase during the year is between *sixty* and *seventy*, and we are expecting better times.

"I remain, yours, &c.,

"ROBERT CORSON."

"Whitchurch, 17th March, 1835."

It is hard to say who are the most to be commended in this virtuous and mutually attached household, the parents or the children. About the time they were first on Yonge Street, the father informed me that his son, then a mere growing boy, earned the money to purchase the grammars and lexicons necessary to begin a classical course, by "chopping a fallow" in the "heat of summer." After such herculean efforts and grand results, there is no excuse for ignorance and inferiority in this land of distinguished
5*

privileges. I hope the perusal of this Life may have a stimulating effect on many parents and children.

1835, 1836.

WHITBY CIRCUIT, (*the second time.*) The transition between Mr. Corson's year on the Newmarket and his transfer to Whitby, was occupied by a session of the Canada Conference, which sat in the town of *Hamilton*, which began June 10th, 1835, with the Rev. William Lord as President, and Rev. Egerton Ryerson as Secretary. Although that was the only Conference at which I was not present, from 1830 to 1874, I have elsewhere given a particular account of its somewhat unpleasant proceedings, drawn from authentic sources. Although many of the members of Conference were very much agitated about that time, Mr. Corson was calm, and in a state of mind to go resolutely on with his work.

He speaks of the year in his brief chronicle as follows: "In 1835 I was appointed, the second time, to Whitby, with the colleague that I had at Newmarket. We had a blessed revival. I stopped two years. Salary for two years, $520," (that is, $260 for each several year,) "Increase for the two years, *one hundred and eighty-seven !* "

The reader will still understand that he still has the genial Thomas Fawcett for his colleague; and that when he would visit his family, he must needs ride all the way to within two miles and a half of Thornhill. The eastern extremity of his own Circuit must have extended to what we now know as Newcastle, if not beyond.

The particulars of his successes from time to time reported in the *Guardian*, served to somewhat enhearten the connex-

ion at a time when prevailing depression made it cordially
appreciated. It is your laborious, soul-saving ministers after
all, who are the mainstays of the Church. Splendour of
talent may be, no doubt, put to a very good use, but *work*
and *endurance* are indispensable. The following extracts of
three letters, from that Circuit, published in the *Guardian*,
at different times through the year, I make room for, because
they exhibit the men and their work, and also refer to a
number of their old friends :—

Extracts of a letter from Rev. T. FAWCETT, *dated Markham, Nov.*
2nd, 1835.

"It will not be uninteresting to you or your readers to hear of the
prosperity of the work of God on the Whitby Circuit. We have
had an increase of about *fifty* members since the last Conference.
Many precious souls have been converted, and there appears to be
a general desire for, and pressing after, entire sanctification; and
blessed be God, some have obtained the blessing. We commenced
a meeting in Markham on the 22nd ult., which continued 12 days,
during which time many sinners were brought from darkness to
light, and 28 persons united in our Society. The services were commenced on Thursday by brother Holden, a respectable and useful
local preacher. The Rev. James Wilson arrived on Friday, and
remained with us five days. He preached with his accustomed
plainness and fervour, and his labours were rendered a blessing to
the people. Towards the close of the meeting, our much esteemed
chairman, the Rev. J. Richardson, came up to the help of the Lord
against the mighty, and concluded the meeting on the 2nd inst.

"This was the most interesting protracted meeting I ever attended. The house was crowded at almost every service, and it was
evident that a more commodious place of worship was needed. A
subscription was therefore opened, and upwards of £200 have been
subscribed for the purpose of erecting a Wesleyan Methodist Chapel.
Some of our friends have done themselves credit by the liberality
which they have manifested in this matter. To God be all the
glory!"

Extract of a letter from the Revs. R. CORSON *and* T. FAWCETT, *dated Darlington, December 13th,* 1835.

" We are glad to inform you that we have a gracious revival of religion on Whitby Circuit. We commenced a protracted meeting in Darlington, on the 28th November, which has continued every evening for sixteen days, and has been a refreshing season from the presence of the Lord. Many precious souls have professed to experience pardoning mercy, and are now walking in the light of the Lord. Between seventy and eighty have united in our Society; and our old brethren are much revived, and are anxious to have the meetings continued longer. Our Local Preachers are quite alive, and their labours have been attended with much good during the meeting. On the whole we are much encouraged, and are expecting better times. We have received upwards of 120 into Society since Conference."

Extracts of a letter from the Rev. T. FAWCETT, *dated Whitby, January 12th,* 1836.

"The cause of God is prospering on this Circuit. At the protracted meeting held in Darlington, a notice of which appeared in the *Guardian* during its progress, about 100 souls were hopefully converted, and about 120 joined Society; some of whom have since found peace through believing.

"We commenced a protracted meeting in this town on the 2nd instant, which has not yet closed. An interest has been excited which surpasses the expectations of our brethren, and several persons have sought the Lord and found favour in his sight. Last night between 20 and 30 presented themselves as subjects for prayer. Some have been brought to God in other places on the Circuit, and indeed religion appears to be reviving in the societies under our care. We are praying that the Lord will cause the work to spread till all shall know Him."

1836, 1837.

WHITBY CIRCUIT, *continued.* The Conference for 1836, sat in *Belleville,* from the 8th to the 13th of June. It was still a sifting time with the Church and its ministry. Among other things that were trying, a distinguished "standard-bearer," if he did not "faint," became weary of turmoil, and retired from the Conference, with a view to connecting himself with the Methodist Episcopal Church in the United States, which he did for one year. This was the Rev. James Richardson, for the last three years Mr. Corson's own Presiding Elder, or Chairman. Still, our subject himself did not waver in his attachment to the main central body.

He returns to *Whitby*, but he has lost him who had been his co-labourer for the last two years, with whom he never had but one "little spat," as he called it, which was soon over, and they afterwards loved each other better than ever; but he gets in his place, *John C. Will*, a young man of education and refinement, who was, nevertheless, much devoted to God, and successful in his work; a work he was destined soon to finish, and to get speedily home to "the rest which remains for the people of God."

His friend, Thomas Fawcett, was appointed as junior preacher to the Yonge Street Circuit, within the bounds of which the Corson family resided, whom he will, no doubt, often visit for spiritual conversation with the saintly wife and mother, and for an innocent romp with the boys; once in a while, a tender interview with his Dulcinea; and, at still longer intervals, a renewal of intercourse with his old favourite "Super," Mr. Corson himself. For Mr. Fawcett could not have been married to Miss Shaw till about the time of the next Conference, in 1837, when he was admitted into full connexion and ordained; albeit, his brother Michael showed me a little cottage, not very far from the German Mills, where Thomas first took his bride after their union, which would seem to imply that he must have received permission to marry a little in advance of the disciplinary time.* But to return to Mr. Corson:—

There was a large aggregate connexional decrease reported at the close of this year, but small part of it was due to any delinquency, or failure on the part of our faithful evangelist. It was quite marvellous, that in the midst of "troublous times," with an inexperienced, undemonstrative young man for a colleague, and with the "sifting" which might have been expected after the accession of the *two hundred members*, brought in by the revival of the previous year, they had so small a decrease as *twenty-three*. But favourable changes were in store for him and the connexion.

When I had got thus far on with Mr. Corson's memorial, a letter reached me from an unexpected source. The events it records must have transpired somewhere between 1835 and the date to which I have come down. It presents Mr. Corson as seen by strangers; and it furnishes some facts relative to one very dear to him, which are of great interest, and which would have been overlooked but for this letter. The letter is from one who was at that time a student from Canada in the place indicated, and has been since the President of several learned institutions. Its matter and signature will speak for themselves:

"In the early years of the renowned Cazenovia Seminary, before the existence of the 'Upper Canada Academy,' many Canadian Methodist youths repaired to Cazenovia to secure academic advantages in a *Methodist* school.

"It was quite common for the father of the student to

---

* Since writing the above, a conversation with the Rev. M. Fawcett confirms my surmises, and clears up all: by permission of his Chairman, the Rev. John Ryerson, T. Fawcett married Miss Shaw in the *April* before his ordination in *June*.

attend his son or daughter upon their long journey, to be made by stage, or stage and canal. Ministers, local and itinerant, from Canada were not unfrequently met with at Cazenovia. I remember among these the venerable John Bailey, who came to place his noble son, William F——, under the care of the Faculty. Also the Rev. James, afterwards Bishop Richardson, who left in the seminary Mary and Martha, his beautiful daughters, one of whom, in after years, became the wife of one of our Professors, the now distinguished W. H. Allen, LL.D., President of Gerard College. In 1835 a large number of Canadian students were at the Seminary. Among those I remember well were *Aaron H. Hurd, James Braden, D. C. Van Norman, JesseHurlbert, William Kingston, Wm. F. Bailey, W. H. Martin,* and many more. The pastor of the M. E. Church, then of Cazenovia, was the renowned Rev. Joseph Castle, now Dr. Castle, of Philadelphia, himself a Canadian.

"Late one Saturday afternoon Mr. Castle was seen in company with a stranger, whose appearance was so different from the average American citizen, that he attracted attention. He was in full Methodist itinerant costume. Some one of the Canadian youth recognized him as the *Rev. Robert Corson.* The Methodist Canadian boys were soon convened in Council. The conclusion had been readily reached that Mr. Corson would occupy the Methodist pulpit the next morning, and Canadian ministerial reputation was thereby to suffer greatly. The stranger had no reputation for scholarship, eloquence, or anything else, save zeal, and a good measure of success as a plain Methodist preacher. The Canadian students were very proud of the reputation of many of the Methodist ministers of Canada. They seldom, if ever, met or heard the equals of 'the Ryersons, Metcalf, Green, Ephraim Evans, and, among the juniors, of William Patrick and Lewis Warner;' and they often placed them in favourable contrast with the most gifted of the New York clergy. The more ardent and ultra urged that a committee should wait upon Mr. Castle and remonstrate against the exposure of the Canadian Methodist ministry to loss of prestige by the appearance of Mr. Corson in the Cazenovia pulpit, which always commanded the very best talent of the Conference. Some of the more thoughtful suggested that, possibly, Mr. Castle might be as suitable a guardian of Canadian Methodist honour as themselves, and that at least he should be allowed to attend to his own business.

"The conclave disbanded. Not able to bear the humiliation that Mr. Corson's certain failure must occasion, some of the Canadians remained in their rooms, but most were at the church. As was anticipated, Mr. Corson was in the pulpit, and conducted the service. His personal appearance, reading, and prayer did not relieve the Canadian students of their burden of anxiety. At the opening of the sermon he appeared embarrassed and stumbling. This, however, soon disappeared: he presently had perfect mastery of himself and over his hearers. A tide of emotion came over him, and swept over his audience. They were carried away by his vehement, burning zeal, and real eloquence. The sermon was a success. The Canadian boys received the congratulations of their New York companions, and with great pride responded: 'Why, Mr. Corson is *only one of our very ordinary preachers*—never appears on great occasions. Oh, if you could only hear one of our *really great men!*'

"The unpretentious preacher made a most favourable

impression. He left his son, John Wesley, in the institution. Like his father, he soon exhibited abilities far above what first appearances justified. That son, after completing his academic course, studied medicine; then went abroad; wrote 'LOITERINGS IN EUROPE,' a most readable book, and he is to-day among the most successful and learned of the medical faculty." [Extract of a letter from Rev. A. M. Cummings, D.D., Principal of River Side Seminary, Wellsville, N. Y.]

I have great pleasure in informing Dr. Cummings and those friends of Dr. J. W. Corson, who might be interested to know, that the doctor did "return" from Cazenovia to Canada, as he studied medicine under Dr. Rolph, in York (now Toronto); that he did practice several years in his native province, later in life; and that his residence at the present is, not "New York City," but Orange, New Jersey. All his encomiums, however, are more than warranted.

1837, 1838.

The Conference was nigh at hand to our subject this year; it sat in *Toronto*. It opened under the presidency of the urbane and pious William Martin Harvard. Several things had been done, were doing, or about to be done, to allay agitation in the Connexion, and to popularize the Conference with the country. Egerton Ryerson, who had been in England for some months, returned for the opening of the assembly, and was appointed Secretary. He brought in a series of "Resolutions" on "GOVERNMENT GRANTS AND THE CLERGY RESERVES," which, though they proved distasteful to the controlling Conference in England, gave the Canada Connexion, in the mean time, something like its old prestige before the country. Also, to give the *Guardian*, whose politics latterly had not been much admired, a sort of impersonal character, the editor's name was left off the heading of the paper. But any person who wishes to know the *animus* and details of that Conference, and their influence on our history in the then near future, must peruse my fuller account in the "Biographical History," or read the pages of the "Life and Times of Dr. Green."

This Conference gave Mr. Corson a 'hoist,' and set him down among his old friends in one of his first Circuits, THE DUMFRIES. The following are the words in which Mr. Corson himself describes the transition: "In 1837 I was appointed to the Dumfries Circuit, after being absent twelve years. My colleague died, but we had another young man sent to us." The young man first appointed was his colleague of the preceding year on the Whitby Circuit, John C. Will. Good Robert Corson's juniors often coveted to be with him still. WILL was fond of his old "Super," and desired to accompany him, but, as John Wesley rhymed of Joshua Keighly, he "found that death had swifer wings than love." Who the young man was who supplied Mr. Will's place during the balance of the year, after his being laid aside, I do not positively know, but surmise from circumstances it must have been either Mr. Byers or Mr. Newbury.

A removal so far from his homestead necessarily required the giving up of his farm, and the transfer of his family to his new Circuit, which it was impracticable for him to try to do justice to, if he gave his family any attention, while they remained at the German Mills. Indeed, his way of getting on for the last three years must have given him and his family very little of each other's society. It was to be somewhat better now. No wonder, therefore, that his son,

Dr. Wm. Corson, calls it a *re-union*. His words are, "From the farm, the father and family were re-united in the Dumfries Circuit."

Just at this point I have opportunely received from Dr. John Wesley a letter in answer to some inquiries I made of him as to the particular localities in which the family resided while on the *London* and *Long-Point* Circuits, which, if I had received before, I might have differently presented some things which have been already given. As it is, however, I decide to give the principal part of the letter now. It will serve as a *résumé* of what I have gone over, interesting to Mr. Corson's friends, illucidative to the reader, and adapted to present the too-much over-looked or forgotten hardships under which the travelling preachers and their families prosecuted their work half a century ago. Dr. Corson says :—

"I was five years of age when father left his home on the farm in Oxford, about two and a half miles from where Ingersoll now flourishes, in 1822, on the Westminster Circuit, for the first time. Mother and he both wept bitterly at the farm gate as he went away. Then mother came back, and beckoning to me to kneel by her side, prayed, with many tears, perhaps for a whole hour. That farm-house continued headquarters for almost five years, with some exceptions. Once he moved about half a mile away to a log house, near Daniel Harris's house, close to the Harris Creek, a small branch of the Thames. Our own house was a frame. We had a beautiful orchard. Then father went to the Dumfries Circuit, we resided part of the time in Jersey Settlement, close to the Church, near Daniel Howel's, in an old school-house. Then we moved to the Waughs' neighbourhood, about three miles from Ancaster. Next, we went back to the Oxford farm house." (That must have been while he laboured on the *Long-Point* Circuit.) "In the fall of 1828, the sad news suddenly came, that we must remove 150 miles, through deep mud, to Whitby Circuit."

This will suffice to clear up what was obscure in my former details. From these statements we learn that Mr. Corson occupied either his own, or a neighbouring house, while he travelled the *Westminster, London* and *Long-Point* Circuits, upon each of which he laboured a year, embracing the *first two* and the *fifth* year of his itinerancy. I defer the rest of the Doctor's letter, to form part of a section on the "Hardship of the Itinerancy."

I now turn to see what lights I can get to illustrate their circumstances during this their second sojourn in the Dumfries Circuit. Three children, I incidentally learn, accompanied their parents to that new-old field of labour, namely, Henry Ryan, William Case, and Robert, who afterwards died at Newburg; John Wesley was mostly from home pursuing his preparatory or professional studies. None of my correspondents inform me where, within the vast boundaries of his extensive Circuit, the family was located; but I surmise, from the frequent mention of "Father Ellis" and his "barn," it must have been in the township of Waterloo.

Mr. Corson's ardent friend, Mr. Henry Chrysler, says of him, "After an absence of some years, he returned. He was frequently at our house, where he was always welcome. He was excellent company." "Here, too, 'Father Long,' the Blind Preacher, with his wife, came to assist in several protracted services, which were held with great success." This retired officer of the British army, who had lost his sight in the English Expedition to Egypt, under Sir Ralph Abercrombie, and who afterwards had his eyes opened, *religiously*, and became one of the most pathetic and persuasive of preachers, did incalculable good in going from Circuit to Circuit, about this time and for years after, promoting revivals, in which his excellent lady was no mean helper. Having no children it was little matter where they were.

But our friends met with some things odd and comical as well as those that were religiously impressive. Dr. William resumes: "A curious wedding scene took place while on this Circuit, at which father was officiating. When he came to ask the usual question of the bride, 'Wilt thou have this man to be thy wedded husband?' She plainly replied 'I will not,' and immediately burst into tears. Father said, under these circumstances he could not proceed with the ceremony; and then the weeping became general. The reason given by the bride for such unusual conduct was, *that she feared she did not love her intended husband as she ought.* While the company was all confusion, a good sister made the sensible suggestion that they should, at least, partake of the wedding dinner then in waiting; and while this part of the ceremony was taking place, the bride concluded that she did love the man of her choice enough to marry him. And after dinner the marriage ceremony was completed; and a very happy wedded life theirs proved to be. A son of this couple (Clement) is now a minister in the M. E. Church of Canada."

A ceremony which went off without a hitch is recorded of the same Circuit during this period of Mr. Corson's sojourn, by the facile pen of Squire Kilborn: "When Mr. Corson was stationed in the Dumfries Circuit, about 1837 or 1838, the writer's father's house in Wilmot was a preaching-place. Word was left at the house by a bachelor to have the preacher call down on the morning after preaching, a distance of some three miles, to solemnize the marriage rite between him and his *Cinderella*. Accordingly, the horse and saddle-bags were got ready; after due inquiry as to the course the cow-path which led to the place pursued, our functionary sets out, and, in proper time, finds the 'clearing,' and our bachelor and affianced in the 'job' logging. When addressed and called to order by Mr. Corson, they dropped their handspikes, chaining the oxen to a stump, brushed off the incumbent dust and ashes, stepped into the skeleton of a log-house, literally without chinking, plaster, or chimney, and, led by our divine, mutually pledged lifelong fidelity. And all this without change of raiment, or a wedding cake. On Mr. Corson's return, my mother asked him how he had succeeded : 'I,' said Father Corson, 'I buckled them together, prayed for them, and left them in their glory.'"

There was a net gain of *twenty* on the Circuit the first year, to be followed by a larger one the following year.

During the Conference year 1837-38, the so-called Canadian Rebellion took place, although we cannot ascertain that it agitated the Dumfries country. The general facts, however, may be adverted to; for upon some proceedings growing out of the disturbances of this time, "hangs a tale" touching his simplicity and one of his lucky hits; but considerable preliminary matter must come first.

On the 4th of December, 1837, Mr. William Lyon McKenzie marshalled his insurgent forces at Montgomery's tavern, on Yonge Street, which, by the 7th of the same month, were dispersed by the few soldiers left in the Province and the loyal militia. Their leader and some of his adherents fled to the United States and soon established themselves with their American sympathizers on Navy Island, opposite Chippewa, and created a diversion sufficient to keep the country in a turmoil several months, which was of a character to interrupt all useful measures for the material and moral welfare of the Province. The way in which the Canada Connexion was affected by it is, perhaps, as well set forth in my " Biographical History " as by any new collocation of words I could otherwise employ. Here is the quotation :—

" Perhaps this disturbance rather raised the Wesleyan Conference and its adherents in public esteem than otherwise. For several years they had been charged with defection from the ranks of the party claiming to be for reform and progress in the Province. The minister who had been their leader in all public questions, the Rev. Egerton Ryerson, had predicted, when he began to falter in adherence to the extreme reformers, that their course of action would lead to rebellion. The events of this year confirmed his prophecy, and created a reaction among the truly loyal, which, now the rebellion was crushed, all were anxious to demonstrate themselves as being. This all the Wesleyans, unless a very few scattered exceptions, truly were. Therefore, when the very excellent President issued, towards the close of this Conference year, an injudiciously-published letter addressed to all the Superintendents of Circuits, requiring them to institute an inquiry in all their Societies for any who had compromised their character for loyalty during the late events, it was justly resented by the membership with indignation, and produced considerable agitation; and would have been the cause of more serious loss had not the Rev. Egerton Ryerson stepped forward with another letter, neutralizing in some measure the effects of Mr. Harvard's, and preventing its being acted upon by more than one Superintendent, who was the Rev. John C. Davidson. I regard this as the point at which the antagonism began between the leading Canadian members of Conference and the authorities representing British Methodism in the Province, which increased, by one means and another, till it issued in the breaking up of the Union. The state of alarm and excitement into which the country was thrown by the rebellion, and the militia-duty which many had to perform and the camp-life they had to lead, was woefully demoralizing and adverse to pure religion. It was well no greater loss than that of 125 members was sustained by the Wesleyan Church."

Let the reader keep the facts of the President's published letter in mind, until I furnish an account of the ensuing Conference, in which Robert Corson appeared in a somewhat serio-comic scene.

1838, 1839.

The Conference assembled in old Rear Street Chapel in the town of *Kingston*, June 13th, 1838, the Rev. Wm. M. Harvard in the Presidential chair. Egerton Ryerson, now fully restored to popular favour, by his late heroic defence of Marshall S. Bidwell, Esq., who had been illegally expatriated, was re-elected Secretary. The usual routine business was gone through with, none of which had any very significant relevancy to the subject of my memoir, till the debate which preceded the election of the editor of the *Guardian* came on. The Rev. Ephraim Evans, who had been the editor the three preceding years, had exposed himself to the criticism of some, because of two things : first, his severe expressions of disapproval uttered against the American government because of its permission of tho practical sympathy which many of the citizens of the Republic showed towards the mis-called Canadian "patriots;" and secondly, and especially, because he had not only published, but defended the President's manifesto. Thus, incidentally, the President's own official conduct, in that particular, came under consideration. Much was said on both sides ; and some of tho deliverances in opposition to the two officials were very severe. Several brethren showed that the official circular had produced a most disturbing effect on tho societies in their several Circuits.

Among the rest, Brother Corson arose and told of tho trouble it gave in his own Circuit. "Some of the class-leaders had given up their class-books," and he had experienced hard work to quiet the people. Continuing to speak he said, " I considered it very unwise and wrong to institute such a proceeding. I didn't blame Father Harvard so much in the matter as I did Brother Evans : I thought *Ephraim might have known better !* But I encouraged the people as well as I could ; and I told them *I thought we would have a new Editor.*" While the doubtful sort of plea was being put in for "Father Harvard," on the score of ignorance, the good President's smiling face was mantled with blushes ; but when Corson ended with the hit about "a new editor," the "house" was effectually "brought down," and the angry cloud dispersed. There was little chance of re-animating the debate : the election took place, and we "got a new editor." Egerton Ryerson was elected to that position.

Mr. Corson was re-appointed to *Dumfries* ; and, according

to the minutes, a powerful, energetic man, the Rev. William Coleman, was set down as his helper. Two such men, humanly speaking, ought to have accomplished much. But I surmise the Circuit had not the good fortune to retain Mr. Coleman; but some change was made, by which he was removed to a more responsible position, where his labours were more required. According to the usually accurate Cornish, a young New Brunswicker, late of the Long-Point country, was called out by the Chairman as Mr. Corson's helper, in the person of *Charles Gilbert*. Their labours were attended with good results. Mr. Corson says, "My salary for the two years was $400. Increase for two years, *fifty-one*;" making for the first, *twenty*; and for the last one, *thirty-one*. Mr. Chrysler says, "His farewell sermon was preached in Father Ellis's barn, assisted by Brother" (David) Wright," the then Chairman of the *London District*, in which this Circuit was comprised. The farewell sermon was looked to with expectation in olden times, and those were sometimes deeply affecting seasons.

1839, 1840.

We have come to the last year of the *fourth sub-division* of the second period into which I have divided the life of Mr. Corson; namely, the last one of the seven years of the first union, unless, indeed, we reckon the next year also up to the special Conference. The Conference which stood at the beginning of this year, was an anxious one; and though its proceedings, on the part of the majority, were largely taken with a view to stave off the disruption which loomed in the distance, they were ultimately in vain, if they did not aggravate the difficulty. The Rev. Dr. Alder had come over with the expectation of bringing the Conference and its organ, the

Guardian, more under the control of the British Conference, but when he arrived in Canada he found that prevailing popular opinion was against the views he represented. I need not, however, go into particulars at this time, as I have endeavoured to detail them with all possible candour and minuteness in another work. It is enough to say, that Mr. Corson and his fellow-labourers went about their work not without reason for feeling solicitude about the Ark of the Lord.

Our subject was appointed for the Conference year indicated above, to the charge of the old *Long-Point* Circuit which had been travelled by him during the third year of his itinerancy, now under a new name, that of THE SIMCOE CIRCUIT.

He was to remain there two years, although the last one of those two was to be principally under a new order of things. He was to have as his assistant, a devoted man, late of the British Army, and a bold "soldier of Jesus Christ," Hardie by name, and one who had learned to "endure hardness." Two more indefatigable workers never could have been pitted against each other, or more properly, associated, as there was none but a loving strife between them, if any,—no two were more equally matched yokefellows. True, Corson was lively but truly serious; and Hardie was grave, but yet quaint and genial.

The "Super's" own brief account of the matter for the two years is as follows :—"In 1839, I was appointed to Simcoe Circuit. I had an old bachelor for a colleague. I stopped the second year. The last year we had revivals. My salary for the two two years, $400. The increase for the two years, *sixty-one*." An *increase* is the exception with some ministers, who seem to give themselves but little trouble on that head ; on the contrary, Corson laboured for, and expected, numerical augmentation, and was surprised, if not distressed, when he did not witness it. Gain was the rule with him; loss was the rare exception.

About this time (continued for years afterwards) Mr. Corson began to write to me, year by year, on the subject of Connexional doings and prospects. I cannot say why it was: we had never been colleagues, and did not often meet, yet still he wrote me. It may have been because, like himself, I was a sort of middle man, against extreme and arbitrary measures, and desirous of peace and the restoration of those who had gone out from the main body. His letters, therefore, related to *increase*, or *decrease* in *numbers* and *funds*; and to the *movements*, prospects, and feelings of *other Methodist bodies*, likely to be rivals to ours. These characteristics of his letters were so prevalent that my good wife noticed it before I ever made any remarks thereon: she used to say that "Father Corson's letters are always about *numbers*, *funds*, and the *Episcopals!*" "Out of the abundance of the heart the mouth speaketh," and a man is known by his communication. The themes upon which he dwelt indicated that he "preferred" our Methodist "Zion to his chief joy." It is probable that during one or other of these two years at Simcoe, the occurrence at Woodhouse Church, already narrated, took place, and not at the earlier period, as first given.

The notable general increase for this Conference year, of *one thousand one hundred and sixty-four*, was a little like former days, and was proof that the Connexion stood well with the general public. Whenever our measures bore the aspect of liberality, our numbers went up; but when they were thought to be otherwise, we decreased numerically.

1840, 1841.

5. *The Seven Years of the interrupted Wesleyan Operations.*

If the Conference of 1839 was an anxious one, the one for 1840, held in *Belleville*, was still more so, began June 10th, and continued its sittings until the 20th of the same month. The unusual length of the session was an indication that this synod had to grapple with questions not of easy solution. I shall not go into details which may be found elsewhere: suffice it to say, that the British Conference, to secure what it thought a needful control of the Canada Connexion, made demands which involved TWO NEW CONDITIONS OF UNION, which if they had been concurred in, would have amounted to a surrender of its autonomy. These, however, were flatly refused by the majority of the Canadians; and it was decided to send a Delegation of two, who proved to be the Brothers William and Egerton Ryerson, to argue the matter with the British Conference. Mr. Corson, though candid and mild, might always be relied on by the majority of the original Conference to maintain its views and decisions; and with a determination to uphold it, and to advance its interests, he and the most of the brethren went about their work for another Conference year.

He was returned to SIMCOE for one more year, with *Brother Charles Gilbert*, once more, for his colleague. Although it was a stirring year for the Connexion, there is not much material at hand for illustrating his outward or inward life, or that of his family during the time.

It was while he was on this Circuit that he formed a closer intimacy with Colonel Neal, a veteran local minister who had planted one of the first societies in the province, that on the Niagara River. At the advanced age of 78 he rode around the Simcoe* Circuit in company with its superintendents, who received the old gentleman's experience of the Revolution, his conviction and conversion, his long experience as a Methodist and a preacher, especially in this country when it was new, and provincial Methodism was in its infancy, from his own lips; and had the rare honour of preaching the old hero's funeral sermon. From such men our evangelist embibed an attachment to Methodism which amounted to a passion.

But when the Conference year was only about four months transpired, the Delegates returned from England and convoked a "Special Conference," which came together in *Toronto*, on the 22nd of October, 1840, and continued its sessions seven days. The Delegates reported the *non placet* decision of the British Conference, whose representatives had begun to organize in the interests of the home connexion, even before the Canada preachers assembled: the Conference affirmed the doings of the Delegates, and resolved to appoint their own President, as they had a disciplinary right to do, the British Conference having failed to make an appointment. The venerable Thomas Whitehead was appointed President, and the Rev. John C. Davidson was elected Secretary. Eleven members of the Conference reported their adhesion to the British Conference, and were returned "Withdrawn," among whom was Mr. Corson's late colleague and much-loved friend, *Thomas Fawcett*—it was well that it was not to be a final estrangement. But as to the full details of all the then heart-wringing transactions of that memorable Conference, Behold are they not written in the Chronicles of "Case and his Cotemporaries," which record

* Probably when it was called the *Long-Point* Circuit, fifteen years before; for he died in 1839, aged 93.

obviates the necessity of reciting them here. So sudden and violent a disruption necessitated a good many changes in Circuits and among the preachers. As an example I will simply detail those of the LONDON DISTRICT, to which the Simcoe Circuit belonged, italicising, when I come to it, those that relate to that Circuit itself. The account is simply a paragraph from my History :

"THE LONDON DISTRICT, losing its former Chairman, E. Evans, receives Wm. Ryerson. The Grand River Mission, to which Mr. Ryerson had been appointed at the Conference in June, was placed under the care of the Brantford Superintendent, Mr. Bevitt, who had D. B. Madden sent to his assistance from the Academy, in the place of Mockridge, a probationer, who gave in his adhesion to the British Missionaries. Mr. Price, also, was brought from Walpole Mission to asssist in their extensive field : properly, Mr. Price took Mr. Mockridge's place. President Whitehead was a resident within this Circuit. *Simcoe took in the Walpole ground, which was supplied by its two former preachers, Corson and Gilbert.* Oxford retained its Superintendent, Kerr, but lost its second preacher, H. Byers, who must also be reckoned amongst the dissentients. I. B. Howard, like Madden, left his studies, and went to the assistance of Mr. Kerr. London Circuit had lost its Superintendent, Norris, but S. Rose went there in his place, retaining Wm. Coleman as his colleague. Hamilton, the first Circuit in that district instead of Manly, received McNab, and instead of H. Montgomery, G. R. Sanderson. There was also " one to be sent." Dumfries had lost Stoney, but that old warrior, Ferguson, sniffing the smell of battle, left his retirement, and again mounted his war-horse in that Circuit. His colleague was L. O. Rice. J. W. McCollum was appointed, but did not go. Thames retained

Williston, and J. Williams was his helper. St. Thomas lost Wm. Steer, but Montgomery, who did not leave till the year was out, went there in his place. Malahide suffered a cruel loss: Thomas Fawcett went away, and it received a chairman's supply. That supply we have since cause to believe was a good one—a located minister in the person of George Sovereign, already mentioned in these volumes, who resided in the Circuit. Guelph had 'one to be sent,' but pretty much passed out of the hands of the Canadian Conference for a time. Before the year was out Mr. Holtby was sent to take care of the Canada Conference adherents. The same remark might be made of Goderich. Muncey was supplied with Mr. Waldron, not by 'P. Jones;' Saugeen, by Wm. Herkermer, Indian preacher. Gosfield and Howard retained its ministers, Flummerfelt and Miles. Warwick and Adelaide had David Hardie."

It will be seen that the extension of their boundaries must have given the Simcoe preachers, at least, one-third more labour than they had had before, which I will venture to believe was itself quite enough. Between one and two thousand members declared their adhesion to the British cause, yet the division of Canadian Wesleyanism with which Mr. Corson stood connected had, after all, a net gain of *three hundred and forty-one*. It was the beginning of an upward tendency which showed itself for several years, until it was checked by a most deplorable occurrence.

1841, 1842.

The transition between the year 1840-41,—the year of controversy and disruption,—the year of unprecedented energy and effort, and we might add, of revival—and the

year 1841-42, was marked by the re-assembling of the
Canada Conference in *Toronto*. The time and place appointed by the regular session of that Conference in June,
1840—on the 18th of June, 1841. The assembly missed
some of those persons who had, either for many years
before, but especially for the last seven years, borne a
prominent part in its proceedings. Among the former, the
venerable Case was missed, and also E. Evans; and among
the latter, a Stinson, a Richey, a Lang, and others. The
Rev. Thomas Whitehead, the late temporary President,
opened the proceedings with devotional exercises; and he
was then replaced by the election of the Rev. William
Ryerson to the Presidental chair.

The Stationing Committee of the above-mentioned Conference appointed Mr. Corson to an important Circuit, but
which necessitated a long move. It was the NAPANEE
Circuit, where he was destined to remain two years, and to
experience sad changes in his attached and happy family.
His colleague for the first year was a man almost or quite
as old as himself, but not of such long standing in the
itinerancy, although he had been many years a local
preacher before going out. This was the Rev. Gilbert
Miller, who, while he excelled Mr. Corson in some things,
lacked other qualities in which his superintendent excelled.
They were both Canadians, not very dissimilar in tastes,
and they got on very smoothly together.

But first we must get him well on to his Circuit, and
show where his family lived; for in those days of very few
parsonages, preachers did not necessarily reside at the
reputed or nominal head of their Circuit. I avail myself
of the very interesting memoranda of Dr. William Corson:
"In 1841, father was transferred from Simcoe to Napanee.

As no railroads were then in existence, the moving of a family so long a distance was no light undertaking. So lately as that period, there were no furnished parsonages, and every household necessity had to be packed and unpacked. Mother and the children took the steamer at Hamilton for Kingston, while father and I" (a boy fourteen or fifteen) "made the journey by the carriage, which occupied us several days. We sang our way along the road, and arrived at our destination in due time."

"Before getting into our own home, while stopping at the house of a good brother, as mother was one day washing clothes by the river-side, she felt somewhat depressed; possibly thinking, too, that she had no home of her own, she gave way to a temporary feeling of despondency. At that moment she saw a turtle on the bank, and the thought occurred to her, that here was a creature of God that, like herself, had no home, but carried his habitation on his back, so to speak; and from that circumstance she gathered hope and courage."

We know who has said, "Speak to the earth and it shall teach thee." Earth is full of lessons to the observing, reflecting heart. Every reader is familiar with the heart and hope taken by Mungo Park, when, bereft of his horse, robbed, and left totally destitute in the solitudes of Central Africa, by casting his eye casually on a tiny delicate sprig of moss. He thought if the Omniscient, Ever present Creator and Provider took care for the maintenance and development of this minute specimen of vegetable life, he would not forget one of his higher creation, though apparently abandoned to perish. During the present rigorous winter I often go out and find the little sparrows about my premises, and feel sometimes inclined to indulge a feeling of extreme anxiety about them, until the words of Jesus recur to my recollection, "Nevertheless your Heavenly Father feedeth them."

Dr. William resumes, "The first year we lived near the village of Napanee, but the year following we removed to Newburg, where a large and most gracious revival took place, in the course of which two of the children were converted." But I must remand this witness for the present: he was about to narrate what was exceedingly touching, but it belongs more properly to the year following.

The husband and father's account of his appointment to Napanee, is in his usually brief and sententious style : "In 1841 I was appointed to Napanee, one of the oldest Circuits in the Province. I had a married man for my colleague. We had revivals in different places. Our increase for the two years was *sixty-two*. My salary for the two years was $640,"—$320 a year. Some advance on his early years in the ministry.

I am desirous to illustrate our Pioneer Preacher's disposition and doings by characteristic examples, some of which must be necessarily apparently trivial.

The following little incident indicates both good temper and tact. The honoured father of the Rev. John N. Lake, from whom I received the account, said that Mr. Corson was preaching on a very warm day in the old Switzer chapel, when the whole congregation, weary perhaps with the labours of the preceding week, became very drowsy, and finally the most of them fell fast asleep. The preacher knew that no benefit would accrue from preaching to sleepers ; yet he did not storm, or scold, but stopped altogether, till one after another, thinking the service over, aroused himself, and thought of leaving, when the preacher broke out with—"When the cradle stops rocking, the baby wakes up!" and went on and concluded his sermon to a more wakeful congregation. Each reader may inquire after the philosophy of the case for himself.

1842, 1843.

The Conference for 1842 recurred once more to Picton or Hallowell, after an interval of twenty years. That assemblage was pre-eminently Canadian : it was presided over by one who had gone forth into the work of the ministry from the same neighbourhood in which the Conference was held (*then* and *now*). This was the Rev. Anson Green, now D.D.,[*] who after the lapse of a score of years was among his old friends and neighbours, preferred to the highest office in the gift of his brethren. And he did not disappoint their confidence ; he made a good presiding officer for a deliberative assembly.

There was not much of the Conference proceedings that had any special relevancy to Mr. Corson's personal history, excepting barely two things :—First, his " standard-bearer," the last year's Chairman of his District, the Rev. John C. Davidson, joined those who were then the most efficient rivals of the Canada Conference, the " British Wesleyan Missionaries," as they were then distinguished—a change which, after the lapse of some years longer, was to be followed by the renunciation of Methodism altogether. Such things, however, did not move Robert Corson, who would have found it very hard to work in any thing but

[*] Alas, since departed.

Methodist harness—and that, too, of the old Canadian, or at least Anglo-Canadian, make.

To come to the second particular I had in mind, there was a change made (which proved only tentative and temporary at first), that involved a very considerable departure from the type of Methodism with which he first became familiar. This was the suspension of the Chairman's journeys around his District, in quarterly visits to the several Circuits. All Mr. Corson's original ideas of Methodism were Episcopal—that is, Presbyterio-Episcopal. He had a lively and pleasurable remembrance of the sermons and oversight of the *Episcopoi* who came in from the States in the days of yore. Nevertheless, though it is strange to say, our subject was one of the first who joined the movement to do away with the *Travelling* chairmanship. This agitation had existed more or less, from soon after the formation of the first Union, and now it was carried into effect, to the great satisfaction of Mr. Corson. Nor do I know, with all the changes on the subject, that he ever changed his mind as to the propriety of localizing the Chairmen. I think the reasons which influenced him were, the persuasion that the Presiding Elders were too expensive, or did not do enough for their pay, which required large drafts out of the slender resources of each Circuit to make up. And, in my humble opinion, the *Travelling* Chairmen were answerable for their own overthrow. There were too many of them who thought a couple of sermons in each Circuit once a quarter (and sometimes these were not given) was quite sufficient to entitle them to their claims on the several Circuits. Had all the Chairmen been like the late Rev. Henry Wilkinson—contriving to give a sermon on Friday night somewhere in the Circuit, on his way in to the place of the quarterly meeting; and then on Sunday night and Monday, on his way out, besides those of Saturday p.m. and Sunday forenoon—there would have been no demand for the change; or there would have been no potency in the demand when it was made. The loss of supervisal was an injury to the work in many ways. Such men as Corson needed no stirring up to labour it is true, albeit there were few as industrious as he; yet even he needed the supervisal and presidency of a Chairman in his official meetings, to counteract a loose and immethodical tendency in business and in smaller matters, to which he was prone. I do not write with any expectation of seeing the office restored; but think much might be done to compensate the want of the travelling overseers, if all the present stationed Chairmen were to show as much concern for their Districts, and as much activity and enterprise as some incumbents of the office I wot of, but whom, I suppose, it would not be proper to mention in this place.

At the Conference of 1842, Mr. Corson, as the reader will anticipate, was re-appointed to NAPANEE, exchanging one married colleague for another—giving up Mr. Miller, and taking *William Haw* in his place. This was a preacher of great volubility, not without eloquence; and if he had possessed his "Super's" humility, plodding industry, patient endurance, and steadfast adherence to the principles of Methodism and its itinerancy, he would have accomplished great things. Even as it was, he was ever and anon very successful in some great spasmodic movement for promoting revivals.

But this was a trying year for the precious Corson family. This is summarily referred to by himself. Speaking of Mr. Miller, his first year's colleague, he says, "The first year my colleague buried his wife; the second year I buried mine."

The reference to this sad bereavement by his son William is very touching, and all the particulars he details full of interest. Speaking of Newburg, he says, " Here, too, that saintly mother was called to her reward, under circumstances peculiarly trying and afflictive—she having been seized with an acute inflammation of the brain, causing loss of consciousness, and, in the course of two or three weeks, bringing to a termination her useful life." I suspend Dr. William's account to give some particulars furnished in her beautifully written obituary notice, published in the *Christian Guardian* soon after her death:—

"Several weeks before her death, she intimated to one or two friends, that she had an impression on her mind that she had not long to live. About a week before she was taken violently ill, she was forced abruptly to leave the class-meeting, which she always attended, on account of indisposition, and returned home and retired to bed. A few minutes after, one of the family softly approached the apartment, and, hearing a voice, stopped to listen. She was rejoicing and pouring forth ejaculatory praises upon her bed. After she was taken ill, she said to her husband, that she regretted that her sickness had prevented her from attending the love-feast held in the village at that time, as she had intended to discharge a neglected duty, in professing her enjoyment of entire sanctification, and that she felt that an unworthy timidity had prevented her from confessing Christ so fully as she ought to have done.

"In consequence of the nature of her complaint, she became permanently delirious, with scarcely a lucid interval, for several days before her death. Deeply afflicting as it was for her friends to see the mind prostrated before its clay tenement was, and they to be thus deprived of the opportunity of enjoying rational conversation with one whose death-bed testimony would otherwise doubtless have been full of holy joy and comfort. Yet it was an alleviation to think that she was thereby rendered unconscious of much severe suffering. The bereaved relatives must ever feel grateful for the unwearied kindness of numerous Christian friends, whose most indefatigable attentions were so freely bestowed during this mournful season of trying affliction.

"There was one incident connected with this death that was deeply affecting. A few weeks before her illness, several females living near her professed to find peace in believing, partly through the instrumentality of her pious conversation and prayers. Up to the time of her death the closest intimacy subsisted between this little circle and herself. They seemed, indeed, to regard her as a kind of common spiritual mother. During her illness they watched and wept over her with all the affection of children. Part of this devoted band remained almost constantly by her bed-side. Unitedly they offered up fervent prayers to Heaven that she might be spared to them a little longer. But they sought to stay

> 'A spirit ripe for heaven:
> And Mercy in her love refused,
> Most merciful, as oft when seeming least.
> The Angel of the Covenant
> Was come; and faithful to his promise stood
> Prepared to walk with her through death's dark vale!'"

About her funeral, her son William continues, "Our old

friend, Conrad Vandusen, happened to be in that vicinity, and officiated on that sad funeral occasion, taking for his text the words of the Psalmist, (lxxxviii. 18.) 'Lover and friend hast thou put far from me, and mine acquaintance into darkness!' While the coffin was being carried out of the old Switzer Chapel, the anthem, 'I heard a voice from heaven saying unto me, Blessed are the dead who die in the Lord,' &c., was sung. In the graveyard, close behind the pulpit, her body was buried. And, in the course of four years after, her son Robert, called after his father, " who died of typhus fever in 1847, prevalent in that year, was laid beside his mother's grave." Many a tender-hearted person will be grateful to Dr. William for so clearly indicating a spot to which, when opportunity offers, they will feel a mournful pleasure in making a pilgrimage. Let no one say that we have devoted too much time and space to one whose history is not an avowed subject of this book, at least whose name is not in the title-page. But Emma Freeland cannot be separated from Robert Corson without greatly marring his portrait. Doubtless she left the impress of her dignified, yet devoutly affectionate spirit, upon his character for good through the whole of his remaining days; but I have thought more than once that the Robert Corson of Emma's day, was, in some respects, a superior man to the Robert Corson the world knew after his angelic mentor and guardian had flown away from the rude storms of earth.

View the matter as you may, this death was a terrible blow to the Corson family. William sorrowfully says, "From the death of my mother, the family scattered, never to be re-united again on earth. The youngest son, Adam, was at this time only *four* years old, but was tenderly cared for by several families in succession, until father's second marriage, three years after the death of his first wife. Of course, with the loss of such an efficient co-labourer as she was, the ministerial success of my father suffered diminution." This is a just remark, and if there is any falling off henceforth in the cheering reports from "Father Corson," surprise must not be felt. The days of his widowhood were dreary years; after the enjoyment of a comfortable home so long, it was hard to be knocked about " from post to pillar," as single preachers were down even to that time.

1843, 1844.

Though Mr. Corson went to the Conference *at Hamilton,* this year, a sorrowing widower, the gathering was a hopeful one. There was one aspect of the cause in which he doubtless greatly rejoiced—the increase in the membership bordered on *four thousand,* that is to say, the noble gain of 3,833. There were many other particulars of great interest, but I know not that any more of them were in a direct line with our present inquiries.

Mr. Corson was not to move far, but was left where he could keep the younger members of his scattered little flock somewhat in sight : he was appointed to *Bath and the Isle of Tanti;* but, in several respects, it was a coming down. He was appointed under the superintendency of a minister a good many years his junior, the Rev. Cyrus R. Allison; and according to the absurd notions of pay-according-to-circumstances, he claimed only as a *single* man, which was $100, of which sum he received only *ninety.* It was before the existence of the children's fund, and he received nothing for the support of his little ones. No wonder they took to industries to support themselves, which, indeed, they so effectually plied, as to achieve both fame and fortune in the issue.

It is strange that the Conference was so slow to awake to the injustice of cutting a preacher, bereaved of his wife, down to a single man's allowance, almost as soon as the breath was out of her body, leaving him, at the moment his expenses were necessarily increased, with half the resources he had claimed before.

A year or two after that, two married ministers occupied the same Circuit, in a District over which I happened to preside. One of them, the superintendent, lost his wife about the middle of the year; his colleague insisted that for the balance of the time the quarterage must be divided, not *equally* as before, but as *two* to *one*, that is, that he should be paid *two-thirds* of the money in hand, and that his superintendent should receive but *one-third*, although he had rather the larger family of the two; and I was applied to to decide the matter. I endeavoured to persuade the junior to let the division go on as before, but he refused, and I was urged to define the law. Thus pressed, I could not but say that its letter favoured his claims; and this man exacted them. Thus, in the name of the law, I was the unwilling instrument in deciding against the claims of justice. I do not know that the exacting brother gained much in the end. He lost in popularity throughout the Circuit; and he gained little, if anything, in a pecuniary point of view. Many refused to pay at all in the regular way, but handed their contributions, in the form of *donations*, to the brother whose allowances were cut down. Mr. Corson says of this year, "Increase fifty in numbers; salary, ninety dollars."

1844, 1845.

In 1844 the Conference sat for the first time in the beautiful town of *Brockville;* and though the smallness of the place led some to predict that the members of Conference could not be entertained, they were entertained, and most comfortably provided for in every respect. At this Conference the travelling of the Chairmen was restored. I do not remember that Mr. Corson made any serious opposition to the return to the old method, but I do not think he ever changed his views of the inutility of the office. For my own part, at that time I confess I acted with those on his side : having made a change, I did not then see sufficient cause to reverse what had been done. But having once restored the travelling chairmanship, I am now sorry that that administrative measure was ever surrendered. It was an evil submitted to in 1847, to secure what its friends thought to be a greater good. When we get that far I may tell how it was brought about.

Mr. Corson says, "In 1844 I was appointed to *Consecon,* with a married man for my colleague." This was *John Sanderson* 1st. "We found a number of nominal members. We had small increase. Salary, $120." I have no means for illustrating the year any further.

1845, 1846.

The Conference for 1845 sat for the first time at *St. Catharines.* The Connexion was in some little anxiety. The Rev. Dr. Ryerson had seen fit to make a written, published defence of Sir Charles Metcalf against the accusations of his ministry. That side was unpopular with all the membership who retained their allegiance to the old Reform party. The discontent gave those who were desirous of organic changes of a radical kind in the Connexion occasion to agitate and to get up a paper in the interests of lay delegation; and there was the mournful decrease reported of 803, something which naturally saddened Mr. Corson's heart along with a good many others.

The state of things at that time was of a character to deepen the lesson which the Conference (at least its leading influences) were slow to learn, namely, that an interference with public, especially *political*, questions, is disturbing to the peace of religious bodies, particularly if the clergy are the governing authority. If Conferences will interfere with public questions then, in all reason and decency, the laity should have a representation in those bodies.

But the rank and file of the assembly went their way from the Conference determined to try and remedy the disaster, and regain their laurels. Among the rest was our widowed brother, who was appointed to an interior field of labour, by himself, the SHEFFIELD CIRCUIT. His own account is, " In 1845 I was appointed to Sheffield; stopped one year. But little revival. Salary, $120." For two years past there had been an increase of *twenty dollars* on his allowances.

I have no materials for illustrating our subject's doings and circumstances further for this year.

Only, I may say, I saw him once through the year: met him at a missionary meeting. He seemed cheerful, and his speech "brought down the house," or rather one of his stories, or his manner of telling it, did. With the care of his younger children his condition was peculiar and cheerless enough. Many of his friends urged him to marry again, among whom was his oldest son. Sundry friends also used their good offices to bring this about. Among these shall I be ashamed to confess that I was not wholly idle in that particular ‽ A maiden lady of my acquaintance declined to see him on such an errand, because some of us had detailed some of his rollicking sayings and doings, and familiarly, though fondly designated him as "Bobby Corson." A person may unwittingly injure a friend by a little too free use of his name. This person, however, would scarcely have suited him. I should have succeeded better with a comely, pious, gifted, well to-do widow, that resembled his lost one more than any other person I ever saw, who was far from listening to the matter with distaste, and would have married him, I verily believe, only that her two young daughters made an outcry at the idea of wandering about the world in the family of an itinerant minister; but it has so turned out that they have had scarcely less wandering than if their mother had become the wife of Parson Corson. I have introduced the above cases for the sake of a little gossip; and I am bound to say, that he and the persons referred to never met. The negotiations were at my own instance, and there is not more than one living mortal, besides myself, who knows who are referred to.

The preachers "laboured as in the very fire" to stay connexional decline, and to prevent impending disaster. Camp-meetings were held all over the country, and many souls were won; but in the mean time there was a spirit of distrust in some of our most prominent societies. No wonder, therefore, that there was a casting about for some new state of ecclesiastical existence; and many thought it would be wise to seek some composition with the British

Conference, by which one at least of our many impediments might be taken out of the way. This feeling reached its culminating point when the Conference assembled in *Kingston*, in June, 1846 : when the numbers were made up, and it was ascertained that the membership had decreased within twelve months to the amount of *one thousand three hundred and eighty nine*, which, joined to the eight hundred and thirty-three of the year before, amounted to *two thousand two hundred and twenty-two* in two years, it deepened the impression that something ought to be done to remedy the evils under which the connexion laboured. Several concurring circumstances rendering the matter hopeful, a deputation to the British Conference was decided on, consisting of the Revs. John Ryerson and Anson Green, who left in due time and succeeded in their mission. But I must not anticipate. I may barely say, however, that this mission of peace met with Mr. Corson's cordial approval, as did every measure at all times, to secure the harmony and unity of Methodism, he never allowing any pique or grudge to stand in the way of any such movement.

1846, 1847.

The Conference at which these decisions were come to, sat in the town of *Kingston.* At that Conference Mr. Corson was appointed so far west as *Warwick*, in the *London* District. That was the only time at which I ever knew of our good friend feeling injured by his appointment. The stations had been kept pretty close from the members of Conference by the Stationing Committee, and they were read off as the last act in the drama ; and pretty dramatic it proved. Mr. Haw remonstrated warmly at his removal from Brockville to Waterloo—Kingston; but Brother Corson seemed very much excited, and declaimed with vehement invective against the cruelty of sending an old widower like him, who had served the Connexion no less than twenty-four years, so far away from his motherless children, and to a new and poor field of labour besides.

But, hard as it was, I think it proved a good thing for him and his youngest child in the end. It decided him to ask a lady, who had been under consideration, to become his wife, who accepted him, and they started for his new Circuit in a very few days. But I will first allow him to tell the story, and then I will bring some other lights to bear on the subject:—

"In 1846, I was appointed to the *Adelaide* and *Warwick Mission*. I had not kept house since the death of my wife, not having any daughters. My oldest son was a physician in practice; two were learning trades; two were at college; and my youngest son, seven years old, I had to hire board for. After remaining single three years, I married an old maid. We were married early in the morning, and started for our new Circuit. Our journey 240 miles."

Dr. J. W. Corson, Father Corson's eldest son, a discerning, considerate man, and a physician, informed me near the time of his father's second marriage, that he had advised his honoured parent to marry, and not by any means to marry an old woman, but some person sufficiently young and active to be able to take care of him. The advice seems to have been judicious, and the old gentleman seems to have adopted it pretty much to the letter. Her maiden name was *Amy Lockwood*. She was born near Belleville, in 1814, so that she was aged 32 at the time of their marriage, and he was *fifty-three*, just 21 years her senior.

It is well known that the Methodist discipline contemplates a supervisal of ministers' marriages, as well as all other parts of their conduct. And among other things it is considered undesirable for elderly men to burden the Connexion with wives so young that they are likely to draw long on the funds after the decease of the husband; albeit, at that time the law was not in force which restricts the claims of widows to those "not more than *fifteen* years younger than their husbands." Notwithstanding, at the following District Meeting, when the question came up, "Who has married during the year; and Has the fourth of the 'Rules of a preacher been obeyed, which says, Take no steps towards marriage without first consulting your brethren?'" A quizzical sort of brother demanded to know the age of Brother Corson's new wife. That was a point of which the good old man felt disposed to "fight shy a little," and with a mixture of simplicity and shrewdness, he answered, "There is the same difference between the ages of me and my wife, that there was between Elder Case's first wife and himself." He presumed, dear man, that Elder Case's example might be followed without occasioning any challenge! Indeed, they might as well have spared their pother, for though he had started in the voyage of life in another century from the one in which his new wife was born, yet he was destined to survive her by some months, she getting into port before him.

But to return from this episode, I have the means of knowing that his children regarded his marriage as judicious and fortunate. Listen to the testimony of Dr. William Corson:—

"The virtues of the second wife are fairly stated in her obituary by the Rev. Wm. Willoughby. She was very prudent, very self-denying, willing to make any reasonable sacrifice for the sake of the children. She was a fond foster mother to the youngest of the boys; and erred, if at all, on the side of too much indulgence. Although she had not the superior mental endowments of the first wife, yet in justice to her it should be said she had many Christian virtues, which went far to compensate for the want of the high mental abilities which had shone with such lustre in the first. As a neighbour she was greatly beloved. I had this testimony from two of her nearest lady acquaintances, namely, that they, 'loved her more than their own mother. She was kind to the poor and the sick, and in a meek and unpretentious way fulfilled the will of her Master, whose mission on the earth was to go about doing good.'"

In the early summer of 1848 I was put in charge of the London District, in which the *Warwick* and *Adelaide* Mission was comprehended, and was often within its bounds during the space of three years. The year of my arrival was the one succeeding the removal of Mr. and Mrs. Corson, and I naturally heard something of both one and the other. The uniform testimony concerning the wife was, that she was quiet, unmeddlesome, and very industrious. Is it anything to her disgrace to tell that as she had been thrown early on her own resources, she had learned a skilled employment, by which she comfortably provided for herself for some years before marriage. So also now, after marriage, when domestic engagements were disposed of (and she was a tidy housekeeper) she thought it not beneath her dignity to ply her old occupation, when urged by the unprivileged people of that remote settlement, by which, to some extent, she helped to eke out the slender allowances received by her husband? I hope I have not many readers who think that labour is undignified, or that there is anything degrading in *any* one to *help himself*, when required by circumstances to do it, whatever his or her calling in life, especially with the example of St. Paul before them. I saw the second Mrs. Corson within two or three years after their marriage, as I also did many times after that again, when I was their privileged guest; and I always felt to rejoice, that little Adam and his father had fallen into the hands of a lady sizeable, strong, healthy, and industrious, who was so very able and willing to take care of them. Besides, she had lesser graces and recommendations: exemplarily plain in her attire, yet comely, indeed with a very pleasing countenance, and a lively, kindly eye, and modest, agreeable conversation.

Here is an entry I find in Mr. Corson's memoranda, laconic as usual, relative to "those women which had laboured together with him in the Gospel":—"*A few remarks in reference to my wives.* My first was quite above mediocrity, as a woman of talent and piety. My second wife has been a blessing to me and my children, and sets a good example worthy of imitation with regard to piety. She reads the scriptures and prays in the family in my absences. She is exemplary with regard to industry and plainness of dress."

But I must allow this untiring labourer to tell the rest of his tale relating to the *Adelaide Mission.*—"We arrived, but no house to go into." [A fine affair for a newly married couple! But did they despond, or complain? Hear what he says.] "However, we thanked the Lord and took courage. I had a colleague, a family man. We had hard work to get houses to live in, as the Circuit was new. I remained two years on the Circuit, and received $550. No increase."

The colleague, "a family man," he refers to was the *Rev. Thomas Williams*, then newly married himself, from whose facile and graphic pen I should have been glad to hear how they got on; and to have been informed of some of the unique sayings and doings of the ever lively Robert Corson. There is something abhorrent in a *dull* old man's getting married the second time, especially to a woman younger than himself; but I will venture to aver that the second Mrs. Corson found her husband as *young in heart* as herself, and that to the last.

Our subject was active in fulfilling District as well as Circuit responsibilities, albeit he did not believe in obtruding his services where they were taken at a discount—and I cannot say but he was right. The Rev. Richard Phelps tells a good story of Uncle Robert, which relates to one or other of the two years his name stood in connection with *Adelaide*,—the first I believe, while Mr. Corson was yet new in that part of the country. Mr. Phelps at that time was labouring on the *Gosfield* and *Amherstburg* Circuit. A large deputation had been appointed by connexional authority to hold the missionary meetings in the south-western part of our great Canadian Peninsula. There were two seniors on the Deputation, Messrs. Corson and Phelps, the rest were mere boys. The Deputation met for its first meeting at Wallaceburg, and, as usual, Father Corson was on time. Every-body knows that usually the later a speaker is brought on, the greater compliment it is considered to his ability to interest the audience, and to supply any defect in what has preceded; or he is as a reserve force, to repair any mistakes and disasters that may have been perpetrated in the early part of the missionary battle. Or otherwise, to have to go first, and to break the ice is the work of rougher men ; while the last brought forward is supposed to occupy the post of honor. So it was understood by the brethren assembled at that time. Whoever arranged the meeting, the old hero of a hundred battles was required to make the opening speech, and a rattling one it was. He, however, excused himself from going very much into details, "boy as he was of only *Twenty five* years ministerial experience, while there were so many venerable men to come after him, from whose able deliverances he would not detain the audience !" And, ever and anon, he would turn to the rear of the platform, make one of his irresistible bows, and with indescribably ludicrous expressions of countenane, speak of his "aged bretheren." This performance so completely brought down the house, that it was no easy matter for those who launched their boats after him, to paddle out of his wake. But the old gentleman's resentment did not end there ; for, to use the language of Brother Phelps, " The next morning, he 'put off, on a bee line' for his own Circuit, and we saw him no more." Perhaps some will be inclined to say, " Served them right !"

1847, 1848.

6. FROM THE RE-CONSTRUCTION OF THE UNION IN 1847, TO THE ADMISSION OF THE LOWER CANADA AND HUDSON BAY DISTRICTS INTO THE CANADA CONFERENCE IN 1854.

I have very little to say under the head of this Conference year, as the most of what relates to Mr. Corson and his Circuit has been anticipated, except it is to tell that an important event was accomplished, which had been pending for a year, namely, the restoration of the union between the British and Canadian Conferences; an event in which he greatly rejoiced, because of its bearing on the general interests of Provincial Methodism, with which he had been identified for thirty years; but also because it restored some intimate friendships which had been somewhat weakened for seven years. When such men as the Rev. Messrs. Case, Douse, Evans, and *Thomas Fawcett*, along with the whole of the Canada Western District meeting, came filing into the Conference, it greatly gladdened his heart; and when all the brethren, old and new, from both sides, joined in the season of weeping prayer and self-consecration which followed on the ratification of the Articles of the restored union, none wept more profusely or prayed more earnestly than Robert Corson. I need not give further particulars, as I have furnished the data and ample details elsewhere. If any one is anxious to be informed of the principles and particulars of that important transaction, they may be easily found.

Mr. Corson returned to *Warwick* and *Adelaide* for a second year, with the important task of uniting into one homogeneous whole the several societies of the two sorts of Wesleyans that had existed together on the ground—To meet the predilections of the British as well as Canadian side of the house, a brother who had been employed in a *quasi* relation to the travelling ministry among the former for the preceding four years was appointed as his colleague. This was *Rev. Thomas V. Constable*, a willing and efficient labourer. Though not yet ordained, he was married, or as Mr. Corson had it, "a family man," and his family had to be supported out of the slender resources of that then not very productive country and whatever the Missionary Fund could afford to give them. I believe the Canadian and the Englishman got on very happily together ; and I should have been glad if my appeal to Father Corson's former colleagues had drawn something from this survivor. They had the Rev. Wm. Ryerson for their visiting chairman.

I have nothing further to detain the reader concerning this first year after the union.

1848, 1849.

The Conference which sat in *Belleville* June, 1848, under the able Presidency of the distinguished Doctor Dixon, and was in all respects very important, appointed Mr. Corson to the centre of his old stamping ground of long years before, but under a new name, namely, to the *Norwich Circuit*, and arranged for him to labour alone.

He was now to be without the visits of a travelling chairman, which office was finally discontinued at the late Conference. Both the leading Canadian ministers and the Delegates from England at the Conference of 1847, wished to preserve the institution of a travelling chairman intact ; for both saw that its continuance was most important for the energetic and uniform administration of our Connexional system. But there was a large party in the Canada Conference who wanted the travelling part of the office discontinued. Another thing also is to be remembered, in order to a right understanding of the question. The Chairmen had, since 1828, been appointed by the Bishop, or President, by and with the advice of an Advisory Committee, elected by ballot, to counsel that officer. The party above referred wished to to have the Chairmen elective, especially if the union was to go into effect, else the British Conference, through the President whom it was to send out year by year, should have too much control in Canada Conference matters, particularly if the Chairmen thus appointed, should travel at large through their several districts. The most of those brethren, therefore, took a determined stand against the union, unless these two points were conceded, the appointment of the Chairmen by the President, and their itinerating through their several districts. The debates and pleadings were long, and passed over from one sederunt into another, until the hour of adjournment came one evening, with the understanding that this question should be the first thing in the order of the day on the following morning.

I was then stationed in the city of Toronto, as the *Canadian* Superintendent; and I was exceedingly desirous for the union to go into effect. Yet I knew two things very well: first, that the English representative would never concede or surrender the appointment of the Chairmen by the President; secondly, I was equally well persuaded that the *travelling* of the Chairmen (their coming and sharing the revenue of their several Circuits) was the principal ground of objection in the minds of the opposers. I gave the intervening hours between the evening and morning sessions very much to thought on this subject, not without some prayer also. I therefore decided on a certain course of action: I went early, and contrived to intercept Dr. Alder, accompanied by his associate, Rev. Enoch Wood, on his way to the Conference, and suggested the following expedient: " Go into the Conference said I," " And still continue the demand long enough to make them think that you regard both points as vital. When things are at something of a dead-lock, rise and offer a compromise: say *you* will concede the *travelling*, if *they* will concede the *manner* of their *appointment.*" Of course I gave him my reason for the probable success of this course of policy, and he agreed to resort to it, if nothing else would do. The Conference opened. A very considerable space of time was consumed in debate and haggling, till negotiations seemed at a stand-still, when the doctor arose and said that he had a compromise to offer—he would concede the point of localizing the chairmen, if the obstructionists would allow the manner of appointment to remain as it was. The leaders of the opposition caught at the proposal at once, and this article was carried in a few minutes; and the principal difficulty being out of the way, all the other proposals, as modified by the British Conference, were put and carried with great celerity, and the Union was consummated, by a majority of eighty-eight against eight. Further, there was sense enough left among all to concede that the travelling of the chairmen should be continued for one year, with a view to bring all the measures before the new quarterly meetings, and all the elements from both sides into a compact and homogeneous whole. This, to a great extent, was effected, and the whole period having transpired, the chairmen, instead of travelling, were stationed on Circuits. Brother Corson was rejoiced; but I, his friend, was sorry. And with all my respect for his memory, and my high appreciation of his zeal and diligence, I must say, if I am to be an honest biographer, that because of these very qualities—of impulse and push, he required a supervision at intervals to prevent his official matters from becoming somewhat confused, or at least a little higledy pigeldy. The presence of a Chairman would have greatly advanced his own interests

7*

and respectability. I shall have something to say on this subject a little farther on.

The loss of the Chairmen's visits were, in some measure, compensated for this year by its being arranged that the Rev. Dr. Richey, the Acting President, should travel through the Connexion. I know not, however, that he ever visited Brother Corson's Circuit.

Mr. Corson's entrance on the *Norwich* Circuit was not going to rest on a bed of roses, by any means. Certain difficulties are referred to in the following sentences from his "sketch":—"In 1848, I was appointed to *Norwich*. No colleague. My predecessor had left the church, and said hard things against us. He was a man of talent and influence. We had some trials. About ten left us; but we tried to pray, preach, and visit, and in a few months we could report an addition of *fifty* members. I stopped two years. Net increase, 43. "Salary" (for the two years) "$550,"—that is to say, $275 for each year.

Considering the times, the place, and the circumstances, Mr. Corson must have acted wisely and faithfully to succeed so well. There was a large radical element in that part of the country, always fearful of clerical tyranny and ecclesiastical centralization: to such, a return to an organic connection with the old conservative British Conference was viewed with apprehension. Then, the minister who had preceded the present incumbent, had not only sowed the seeds of discontent (perhaps undesignedly), but he remained to water the seed he had sown. His history will show that now he had taken a position of rivalry, he must have been a formidable opponent. He was, as Mr. Corson has told us, "a man of talent"—he possessed good powers of mind, and was very gifted as a speaker, and had, furthermore, acquired considerable learning. He was of German extraction, spoke that language, and, if I mistake not, had received a Menonite training, which would naturally predispose his mind to influences adverse to his being a thick and thin connexional Methodist. He had gone out to travel (at first under a Chairman) about the time the first Union was negotiated and consummated; and for a few years thereafter, had loyally co-operated, and did good service in the *Wesleyan* cause; but after a time, what with personal considerations, and his sensitiveness to the charge of "receiving Government money," consequent upon a financial connection with a controlling body which *had*, he became uneasy and dissatisfied—did not come forward for his examinations and reception into full connexion, but still stood in the relation of a probationer; and finally, after performing at least five or six years' circuit work with great efficiency, discontinued altogether, and went back to his farm. He dropped, however, into the local ranks, and preached with great ability as a layman. When the connection with the British Conference was severed, he felt more at home with the body he was in, the "Grants" during that time being suspended, and he began to extend the sphere of his evangelistic labours, and was made the instrument of some excellent revivals. About the year 1844 the Chairman sent him on a newly-opened Circuit, where his success was great. In 1845 he was received again on trial, and the following year he was ordained (1846). He had been two years at Norwich —one immediately before, and the other the year immediately after the reconstruction of the Union with the British Conference. His old feelings of discontent revived; and while he remained with us, it is not to be supposed that a pastor in such a state of mind could do much to advance and consolidate Conference Methodism. At the Conference of 1848 he sent in his resignation, and started a *Congregational* interest in the place where he had been labouring. He was superior to Mr. Corson in point of ability, and a grave, exemplary man withal, and was naturally, therefore, looked up to somewhat by the people. In view of all these facts, it is marvellous that his successor did not feel himself more embarrassed than he did; and that he (the decident) did not achieve more on his own chosen course than he did.

Yet, upon second thoughts, our hero was really just the agent to advance the interests of central Methodism under the worst circumstances. He was a man so good-natured and amiable, that it was a very difficult matter to commence a quarrel with him. Again, he was thoroughly informed in the history and principles of essential Methodism, and knew how to propound them so as to obviate objections. Furthermore, if it came to controversy, he was really skilful and adroit in that. Few could catch him napping; and very often he overturned his opponent's argument by an unexpected sally of wit and humour, which turned the laugh on the aggressor. I heard some instance of this, relating to that very place and time, which would have effectually confirmed and illustrated my present statement, but that they have eluded my recollection in their small particulars. Lastly, he was so tireless in labour, and so thoughtful of every family in his Circuit, none of whom he failed to see, that it was hard for any adverse movement to make headway against him and the cause he was labouring to build up.

The most untiring labours of from 180 to 200 agents, resorting to all sorts of extra means and expedients, resulted in only the moderate gain for the connexion, this year, of 426 members.

1849, 1850.

I do not know that the very interesting session of the Conference, which sat in *Hamilton* in the early summer of 1850, had much relevancy to the subject of our memoir, excepting that Mr. Corson was returned by it to *Norwich* for another year, during which matters were smoother for him than the first year.

In the course of the summer of 1850 I made a visit to a beloved brother of my own, who resided at Norwichville; and planned my visit, at Mr. Corson's request, so as to make it coincide with the celebration of his August Quarterly Meeting. Remaining several days, I had a good long visit with my old friend; and had an opportunity of obtaining some inside views of his family and his Circuit, besides observing somewhat the character of his administration.

On inquiry among those I met about their minister, there was a very general admission of his laboriousness and fidelity; but then, his very extra diligence, or the manner of exercising it, was made the subject of, I will not say sneering, but not very reverent criticism on the part of a few. Thus, they admitted that he was a thorough visitor, but then they made themselves merry at the notion of his sallying forth early in the morning, in his slippers, and his visiting ten or a dozen families before breakfast. But if he did, there was "method in his madness;" it was not done without a reason: he knew that he should find more of the family than after they were dispersed abroad for labour and for business; besides, he thought that a little pastoral admonition and prayer would give no ill direction to the operations of the day. He thought also, that to do it the first thing was to ensure its certain accomplishment. There are some who so much fear that their dignity will be compromised by directness and promptitude, that they seldom accomplish anything.

Then, there is little sympathy due to the damagers of the hard-earned fame of the working minister, who are in the habit of saying of God's servants, if they are somewhat elderly, or devoid of style, "Oh, yes, he's a good man—a very good man; but then he is so plain," or "odd," or "old-fashioned," or something else, that he is "not quite the thing for this place, you know." No, probably "not the thing for prophesying smooth things, and leaving people undisturbed in their lukewarmness and backslidings.

But, to return, on visiting Brother Corson's home and family I could not help thinking, on seeing the second Mrs. Corson for the first time, how fortunate he had been in obtaining a person so capable of keeping his house, causing the casual little dwelling in which they had taken up their abode (for there was no parsonage) to look so inviting; and to tidy up his own person which he was too prone to be forgetful of. And then, little chubby-faced Adam looked so neat and so happy—happy in his childish plays around the house; and apparently still more happy in the performance of the nameless little office (a child may perform) for his new mamma. The husband and father was much from home; but these two, both of them of a quiet temperament, seemed to be the counter-part of each other, and so very conducive to that noiseless happiness of which they were evidently the subjects.

I got an inkling of Mr. Corson's thoughtful endeavours to remedy evils, and to do direct and positive good by all available means. He and I had a friendly interview with the ministerial brother who had gone from us, certainly not of a character to leave him with a disposition to "lightly speak evil of us," or the cause we stood connected with.

There was a worthy couple who lived several miles from Norwichville, both of whom had been connected with central Methodism, first in the States, and then in Canada, a great many years, one of whom (the husband) had become depressed in mind, and withdrew his name from the Church-roll, although he was still friendly, and I think a supporter of the cause. He had taken the agitations and divisions of Methodism very much to heart; and he regarded the inevitable changes in minor matters as evidence of the hopeless deterioration of the Methodists. His wife was steadfast, and Brother Corson wished to encourage her; and hoped also that my conversation with the husband might lure him back into his old position. It was therefore projected that he and I should go and spend an afternoon and take tea with them. We did so. I found the good brother with a desponding look, but very friendly. Very kind consideration was given to all his querulous remarks and averments; and I thought all his objections were thoroughly met. But he was in a state of mind quite abnormal, which is often aggravated by an attempt to meet its cavils and complaints, rather than quieted thereby. We had, however, the satisfaction of trying to do good. I am not informed what was the individual's final course, but I have often thought that Mr. Corson's efforts to "lift up the hands that hung down," was a fine exemplification of the true pastoral spirit.

I think I gave them a sermon on the Saturday of the Quarterly Meeting, as in the olden time; at least I am sure

I met with his officials on that day, and I was struck with two things, the very great respectability of some of them, and the consideration they showed their pastor. There was a Brother VanNorman, a Brother Tilson, I think, and a Brother McDowell, a good local preacher; and yet another, either a Scotch gentleman or one who had resided in Scotland, a local preacher of great ability, who was one of the most acute in dealing with the peculiarities of Calvinism of any person I had ever met. I regret to have not thoroughly learned his name.

The services on Sunday were the usual ones, and I was to have conducted them; but I was not there early enough to suit the pastor's notions of punctuality, and he had opened the love-feast himself. There was a promptness, even to hurry, about his manner of conducting a service, which, I am obliged to confess, had rather a flurrying than a tranquilizing effect upon my own mind. I am compelled to think that he needed the softly staying, authoritative hand of his Emma all his days to abate the hurry of his manner, which sometimes defeated his own objects. I think there was not so much of that while his early mentor was with him.

The meeting was considered a good one. I preached both forenoon and afternoon, and I hope the services left a lasting impression. None of the rest of the materials at my disposal have any further reference to Norwich and the Conference year, 1849-50, I therefore pass on to the year—

1850, 1851.

This year dates its commencement from the second *Brockville* Conference, held in the month of June, 1850.

Two things were likely to impress the mind of Robert Corson: one was the visit of the Rev. Dr. Bangs, of New York, to the Conference; for, though an American by natural birth, the Doctor was a Canadian by spiritual birth and his introduction into the ministry; and the scene of his early religious and ministerial life was the Niagara Country, where Corson, when a boy, could not have failed to hear him. This meeting would impress the latter joyfully. The other circumstance was of a more pensive character, namely, the sudden death of two highly esteemed ministerial brethren, both of whom had commenced their ministry a little before he had, and would be the greater subjects of interest to him, both of whom died suddenly and alone, and abroad in the fields; one under the shimmering light of the stars of night, the other under the broad blaze of the full-day sun. The news of one death was reported to the Conference from his District Meeting; that of the other was telegraphed to the Conference, as having taken place since their assembling. These two men were, first, the genial, powerful, stalwart Healy; the other, the pure and pious, but gentlemanly Metcalf. The news produced a *Bokim* in the Conference, especially among the old Canadian preachers, but it affected none more touchingly than Robert Corson.

He went from this scene of solemnity to his far western home; but from thence he went still further west to the GOSFIELD CIRCUIT, to which he was appointed by the Conference. This region comprised a tract far to the west, between Lake Erie and the River Thames. The Circuit's boundaries had been circumscribed, and it was restricted to one preacher. Mr. Corson was alone, to whom it gave a large extent of travelling.

His own brief account of the matter is as follows:—" In 1850, I was appointed to the *Gosfield Circuit*. We found some good members, and a parsonage house" (if it was the one I saw the year before, it was a small, plain affair), " but a hard Circuit to travel. The increase was small. Salary $280. I was alone, and but one year on the Circuit."

The apostle says, "Who is weak, and I am not weak? Who is offended and I burn not?" An earnest minister, bent on building up the Church of God, must necessarily feel the influence of the commotions in civil society, all the neighborhood broils, and all the party strifes that agitate the general community coming within the sphere of his labours, for all these affect the Church in the way of disturbing and impeding. And in doing so, they greatly afflict the heart of him who "prefers Jerusalem to his chief joy," and who for Zion's sake is "hurt" and "black" with "astonishment" and "sorrow of heart." So it ever was with our pioneer preacher. During this year the question of "free schools" and taxation, or no taxation, to support common school education, was before the people within the bounds of Mr. Corson's Circuit; being a question appealing to the selfishness of those who had, and of those who had not, children to be educated, it avoke a considerable amount of embittered feeling, which had anything but a good religious effect on the minds and hearts of those whom the Shepherd wished to see live in peace and to be built up in holiness. But the manner in which their anxious pastor described the conflict at the breakfast table, at my boarding place, during a subsequent Conference at Kingston, when his toils and responsibilities for that year were passed, was so irresistibly ludicrous, without his intending it to be so, that it not only "set the table in a roar," but actually sent several from the table altogether for a time, to conceal their irrepressible laughter. But he was destined to be removed from the annoyances of the Gosfield Circuit.

1851, 1852.

The reader must now follow him to the *Toronto Conference* of 1851, which had nothing special with regard to him save that he was appointed to the CHIPPEWA, otherwise called the CROWLAND CIRCUIT. He states the matter thus: —" In 1851, I was appointed to *Crowland*. I had a young Irishman for my Colleague," that was true of both years, but not the same person both years. "An old Circuit—a few added to the Church. Salary $720," that is, for the two years, which would be $360 a year, the largest sum, I think, realized by him for one year up to that time.

The *Rev. Wm. Creighton*, a young preacher only a year or so from Ireland, was his colleague. He might have been a young man after Father Corson's own heart, so far as patient plodding labour was concerned, but no two could have been more unlike each other in temperament. Corson was lively, and playful to a degree; Creighton was sober almost to sadness. But I believe they agreed very well in all respects.

During the two years that Mr. Corson was at Chippewa, or Crowland, he was under my own chairmanship, as the Circuit was reckoned to the *Hamilton District*, and I was its Chairman, stationed at Hamilton itself. This relation brought me into closer and more frequent intercourse with him than I had ever had the pleasure of enjoying before; and I could not forbear remarking what an exceedingly respectful, pleasant old gentleman he was; and how very shrewd and well-informed he also seemed to be on all Methodist matters. He was a quick observer of any little matter that was unusual. During the District Meeting, held in St. Catharines, at the close of the first year of this relation between us, I was called upon by the minister of that Circuit, who arranged the religious exercises, to conduct one of the preaching services; and, as I always think it best in preaching to speak appropriately, if possible, I delivered a sermon in relation to ministerial obligations and duties. At the close of the service Brother Corson came forward in his own smiling manner, saying, it was "a long time since he had heard a Bishop's sermon" till mine, referring to the fact that the American Bishops always delivered something of the kind at our Annual Conferences in the days of yore.

1852, 1853.

The Conference for 1852 sat in *Kingston*. At that Conference he was returned to the same Circuit for another year, under a new name. It was *Chippewa* in the minutes the year before; this year it was changed to CROWLAND. This was a sensible change, Crowland being central, and the place where the parsonage was located. As a member of the Stationing Committee and Chairman of that District, I had the making of the appointments for Crowland as well as others on the District; and upon the supply of that Circuit hangs a tale.

However we may account for it, and how much soever we may deplore it, yet it cannot be denied that when preachers come into the neighbourhood of three score, no matter how strong, active, faithful, and, even vivacious they may be, they begin to be at a discount with many; and Mr. Corson, now at the age of *fifty-nine*, was no exception to the rule. The rising village, now town, of Welland, was in his Circuit; several influential members from that vicinity spoke to me at the District Meeting about a change of superintendent, on the ground that he was "old-fashioned," not observant of the lesser graces, and not adapted to command the respect of intelligent outsiders. I pleaded for the old gentleman—the injury to his feelings and the implied reflection on his character and doings, if he were sent away. As they had no objections to him on the score of fidelity, I persuaded them to accept of him another year, on condition that I would send along with him a popular young man who would make up for the "Super's" defects on the score of attractiveness. The next thing was to find such a young man; and then to embue him with such a state of mind as would take him there good naturedly. Pity such methods ever have to be resorted to! There was a young preacher of great preaching power, who had, however, all his days, been used to city life. Further, the only two appointments he had had before had been cities, namely, *Kingston* and *Hamilton*, in which latter place he had been my own colleague. That young preacher was *Richard Clarke*, who would have been very different from most young men under such circumstances, if he had not felt a shrinking from the country, and a clinging to the city; or if he had not felt a preference to the *Station* instead of the *Circuit*. However, when I talked the matter over with Brother Clarke, to his praise be it spoken, he consented to go; and to Father Corson's own praise it is to be set down, that he gave the young man with city habits a home in his own family. Although Brother Clarke had something to learn from his superintendent in the matter of systematic visiting, they were in most respects well adapted to each other. Clarke could help the old gentleman in what he was most defective in, penmanship and accounts; and then, so far as geniality, even to playfulness, they were very much alike. They both had the hearts of boys, and a life-long friendship was the result.

Having thus introduced him, I have great pleasure in laying before the reader a portraiture of Mr. Corson by this then young man, after the lapse of twenty-five years. Brother Clarke's letter shall be given *in extenso*, as furnishing all needful presentation of our subject during the time he was on the Crowland Circuit :—

"DEAR BROTHER,—At the Conference of 1852 I was appointed to what was then called the Crowland Mission, at that time in the Hamilton District, of which you were the Chairman, my Superintendent being the venerable Father Corson. I had therefore the opportunity of becoming acquainted with his character, gifts, habits, and labours. As it was my privilege to be a member of his family that year, I knew something of his life at *home*. He treated me with great respect and kindness, and was always ready to give me such advice and assistance as I required. In his family he was kind, genial, and happy. He was not remarkably gifted, and yet he possessed some gifts of rare excellence, one of which was *originality*. When you saw him, you saw Father Corson, and when you heard him preach, you were hearing no one else, living or dead. Some men possessing this gift are not very great; but without it a man is small. He was an early riser, and careful in the improvement of time. His reading was extensive, particularly in History and Methodist literature. These habits, together with a retentive memory, enabled him to collect a large amount of useful knowledge. In his way he was a diligent student, a faithful preacher, and a laborious pastor. In his time the Circuits were large, the work hard, and the salaries small. The fields in which he toiled were not those which modern Methodist Preachers speak of as the most desirable and the most worthy of their valuable services. What we now call *"a good Circuit,"* includes a wealthy and liberal people, little work, a long summer vacation, and a large salary. Such were not the Circuits of the early Methodist Itinerants in this and other lands. In those days of weakness, the Methodist Church was strong. Its preachers were heroes, and not a few of them were giants in the pulpit. Father Corson was a hero, if not a giant. Before he was a preacher, he was a hero in the service of his country. Many a time he delighted me, as he described the thrilling scenes of war connected with Stony Creek, Queenston Heights, Chippewa, and Lundy's Lane. Many a British soldier has been transformed into a valiant Methodist preacher. In travelling his large Circuits, doing his hard work, "enduring hardness as a good soldier of Jesus Christ," and receiving next to no pay, he was never sour, discontented, or given to complaining; but always cheerful, hopeful, and happy. He had the rare honour—now but little coveted—of preaching the Gospel to the poor. He was successful. In estimating the value of a minister, he always asked, "Is he successful?" I have often heard the older people, in different parts of the country, speak of him and his labours with great respect, affection, and gratitude. He was careful in the preparation of his sermons, though they were never called great pulpit efforts. He always wrote a brief outline of his discourse, and read all he could on the subject. Many a time he allowed me the privilege of reading his new manuscript, and often did he read one to me, much to the pleasure of master and scholar. His sermons were always short, seldom going beyond the fashionable length of twenty or thirty minutes in delivery. He could preach, and 'pray without ceasing.' I have known him to preach frequently four times on the Sabbath, and several times through the week, without weariness. He never tired holding prayer-meetings, class-meetings, and all kinds of religious services. He had a sound constitution, and always enjoyed good health. He was a loyal Methodist, sound in doctrine and strongly attached to the discipline of the Church. He thought it safer to bring the people up to the Discipline, than to bring the Discipline down to the people, though the latter is the easier method. He paid great attention to the duty of pastoral visitation. His visits were always short. Without spending much time in salutation and conversation on ordinary subjects, he would read a portion of Scripture, pray, perhaps sing a verse, and give a word of exhortation, and not unfrequently read a paragraph from some new book he was studying at the time. All this was done in a few minutes, and he left abruptly for the next house. Very frequently he remained from home over night, and was always as happy among the people as in his own house. He innocently thought his colleagues were hardly fit for the work if they did not keep up with him in reading, travelling, preaching, and visiting. He was very much afraid they would be destroyed by pride if they brushed the hair back from the forehead, did not tie the cravat in his fashion, and had not their garments cut according to his primitive simplicity. I believe he was always regarded as a man of genuine piety, wholly devoted to God's service. He was very successful in the government of his family. After spending many years of happy toil in the Itinerancy, he retired with great reluctance. Like a true Methodist preacher, he did not know when he was worn out, and would not believe those who assured him of the unwelcome fact. His choice would have been to 'cease at once to work and live.' In his retirement he spent his time and strength serving God and the Church, with great fidelity. To Father Corson, and the faithful men of his times, most of whom have finished their course, and are gone to their reward, this prosperous country, and the great Methodist Church owe more than they have yet acknowledged, or will ever repay.

"Affectionately yours,
"RICHARD CLARKE."

Brother Clarke, in the above testimonial to his old superintendent, which is as honourable to his own head and heart as to him to whom it is a just and fitting meed, mentions Father Corson's habit of often reading to the families he visited out of some profitable book. This was but the continuation of the practice of all the early preachers, who, in that way, made their visits agreeable and instructive, and brought the connexional works into notice, and promoted their sale to the great improvement of the people and to the advantage of connexional funds. He himself was a successful salesman of religious publications. He pursued the same plan with our connexional organ, the *Christian Guardian*, and with the same results.

During the Conference year 1847-48, the action of the joint meeting of the College Board and the Special Committee of the Conference on the then pending question of the Clergy Reserves and the Colleges, occasioned, through the influence of certain secular papers, considerable disturbance of the connexional mind; besides which, there were several other disturbing grounds of complaint put forward just then. On which account, as a person having had long acquaintance with our ecclesiastical proceedings, without ever having come prominently forward in any of the movements to which exception had been taken, I thought it well myself to address a long letter to the *Guardian* relative to the many allegations against the Conference and ministers in general, which the then Editor, Rev. G. R. Sanderson, now D.D., thought to be so adapted, from its kindness and candour, to have a good effect on the minds of the Methodists, that he gave it the post of honour, and placed it in his editorial columns in the place of the accustomed "leader." Mr. Corson (and he knew the Methodist mind as well as any one else) had the same opinion, and, as a consequence, I heard of his reading that letter to our dear friends in various places in his Circuit.

And, while I am in for matters of this kind, I may as well mention a curious proceeding by him, quite characteristic of the man. A gentleman of Scotch birth, classically educated, who had been some years a Wesleyan local preacher, came to this from another Province, while we were labouring separately from the British Conference, out of professed sympathy with our principles and position, —came as a visitor to us, and though a man of family, was taken on trial for our ministry, received ordination in advance of the time when he might have claimed it, and during the three years he laboured, was appointed to two of the very best city stations. Yet, though he had shown a great desire for the Union to be restored, when it was restored he soon found grounds of discontent with its details, or results. The issue was, at his own request he was first left without a Circuit, and then finally his name was discontinued from the Minutes. But the matter did not rest there. He thought proper (it may have been very sincerely, according to the very peculiar structure of his conscience) to commence a series of attacks, first on the administration of the Connexion, and, lastly, on the organization of Methodism itself, while yet claiming to be an Arminian. The letters had an annoying effect, yet no one saw proper to answer them. Father Corson, however, wrote a short rejoinder to all the accuser had said, in which he crippled each of the enemy's guns, yet he could not be persuaded to publish it; but in default of that, he carried the MS. with him, and whenever Mr. R's. allegations came up he pulled out his letter and read his answer to them; and it afforded a great deal of amusement, if it did no other good, for it was full of all sorts of "good hits." Only one do I remember. In parrying the assailant's thrusts at the Conference, in one place he replied: "In one case, I confess, the Conference has erred; it made a great mistake when it took you on so short an acquaintance, and ordained you before the proper time: the Scripture says, 'Lay hands suddenly on no man.'"

The next two years (from 1853 to 1854) Mr. Corson was continued in the *Hamilton District*, and as I remained in that city till the Conference of 1854, our relation to each other continued, much to our mutual satisfaction, a year longer after his leaving Crowland.

1853, 1854.

The Conference which sat in *Hamilton, June, 1853,* appointed Mr. Corson to the CAINSVILLE CIRCUIT, the head of which was near Brantford. This Circuit included a good many neighbourhoods comprehended in the old Dumfries Circuit, on which he had laboured four years, first and last, in the earlier part of his ministry; and it gave him an opportunity to renew his acquaintance with many old and endeared friends. He speaks himself thus of the appointment: "In 1853, I was appointed to CAINSVILLE. I had to build a house" (there being no Circuit parsonage, and it being difficult to find one to hire) "to live in. I remained two years on the Circuit. We had refreshing seasons among a warm-hearted people. Salary, $800"—$400 a year, the most he had ever received.

In going by private conveyance to London, in the autumn of 1853, attended by my little daughter, we took the residence of Mr. and Mrs. Corson in the way, with whom we lodged for the night, and were most hospitably received. His house was yet not quite furnished; yet, though I lodged in the loft, I slept most blissfully in the enticing bed prepared for me by my hostess. It was not, however, the last time I shared their hospitality.

Just before this, a young Scotch preacher formed the acquaintance of Mr. Corson. He has been impelled by fond remembrance to send me the subjoined letter, which will furnish me the best materials for illustrating that period of his life after he became elderly. The letter, as to authorship and everything else, may be allowed to speak for itself:—

Rev. John Carroll, D.D., Toronto.

"REV. AND DEAR BRO.,—I was pleased to observe in the *Guardian* a notice of your intention to publish at early date a 'Memorial Volume' of the late Rev. Robert Corson, and that you are now collecting materials for that purpose.

"'Father Corson,' as he was peculiarly called, was a worthy and useful Canadian itinerant minister in connection with our Church, who commenced his labours at an early period in the history of Methodism in this Province, and deserves more than an ordinary obituary notice. He had not the early educational advantages with which ministers in modern days are favoured, neither was he endowed with more than ordinary gifts. He could not be regarded as either eloquent or profound, and might perhaps be justly considered, intellectually, below mediocrity. Yet, being devoted to God and his work, and full of zeal for the cause of Christ, his self-denying labours were owned and blessed of God, and he was instrumental in bringing many to a saving knowledge of the truth, who subsequently became worthy and useful members of our Church in Canada, many of whom went before him to the better land, and will welcome him as their spiritual father when they that be wise shall shine as the brightness of the firmament; and they that turn many to righteousness as the stars for ever and ever.

"I first met with Father Corson in the winter of 1852. He was at that time stationed on the Crowland Mission (now Welland Circuit), on the old Hamilton District, of which you were Chairman. He came to attend the missionary services on the Glanford and Seneca Circuit, which was that year under the faithful and judicious superintendency of your old and intimate friend, the late Rev. S. Huntington, and I was the junior preacher. In those days missionary deputations, as you are aware, were much larger than is deemed necessary now. The following brethren were appointed by the Financial District Meeting as a deputation for the Glanford Circuit :—Revs. R. Corson, I. B. Howard, George (now Dr.) Young, J. Bredin, and Thomas Stobbs. Quite an array of talent. The senior member of the deputation, Father Corson, gave us some amusing incidents in connection with his early labours as a Methodist missionary in Canada, and his humorous addresses were listened to apparently with greater interest and attention than the more eloquent speeches of some of the other members of the deputation.

"In the fall of 1855, Father Corson, that year labouring on the Erin Mission, Guelph District, attended the Financial District Meeting, held that fall in the old Blenheim Church, county of Oxford. The old itinerant here met with a number of his former friends, and members of the church who had moved to Blenheim from the old Dumfries Circuit, where he had laboured years before. They all appeared delighted to meet with their old friend and pastor once more, and he was equally pleased to have another opportunity of seeing so many of his old parishioners. The children whom he had baptized had grown up to manhood and womanhood, and were glad to have a visit from the minister whose name was a household word in all that region of country. At the District meeting it was arranged to have service in the evening, and Father Corson was appointed to preach. There was, as you might expect, a large congregation, and the Blenheim Church was crowded. After going through with the preliminary exercises, in his own peculiar style, the preacher announced his text which was in John's Gospel, xxi. and 17, 'Feed my sheep.' In connection with his introductory remarks he stated that he was 'an old dispensation preacher,' whom it might be beneficial for them to hear occasionally, as a contrast to the more refined and polished preachers of the present day in Canada. He compared the past with the present, and referred to the superior educational advantages enjoyed by those who entered the Methodist ministry at the present day, when contrasted with the time when he entered the work. He then made a few appropriate observations in connection with the time when the memorable words of the text were addressed by Christ to Peter, 'Feed my sheep.' The following were his divisions: —1. The Shepherd; 2. The Sheep; 3. The Food. On dwelling on the last division he gave some advice suitable to the junior ministers and preachers who were present both with regard to preaching and pastoral visitation. The majority of us were young in the ministry, and the practical observations of this old experienced minister were both timely and beneficial. The sermon was unique and caused several to smile, but though quaint, made a good impression.

"The following winter I was appointed to attend the missionary meetings at Erin, Father Corson's Circuit, and was very kindly received and entertained by the Superintendent and his devoted wife. In connection with the reading of the Annual Missionary Report at the missionary meeting, a duty which generally falls to the lot of the Superintendent of the Circuit, the old Methodist itinerant related a few incidents in connection with his own fields of labour in this country. Take the following as a specimen : Once, on leaving home to attend an appointment in the old Newmarket Circuit, he was thrown from his horse and had to return home, and meeting his wife at the door of the parsonage told her what had happened, but assured her that he was not seriously hurt. She immediately exclaimed, 'My dear, do you know that your ear is off,' and putting his hand to the side of his head, he found that the ear was nearly gone. Turning the side of his head to the congregation at the missionary meeting, where he related the incident, he said, 'It is all right now, you can see I had the ear stitched on again.'

"In his farewell sermon on a Circuit, within the boundary of the old Toronto District, where he had laboured acceptably for two years, he called on an exhorter who was present, to close with prayer, and the brother gave thanks to the Giver of all Good, that, among many other inestimable blessings, he had heard Father Corson preach his farewell sermon, and made mention of the latter in particular as affording abundant cause for gratitude. In relating the above, Father Corson stated that there were a few evil-disposed persons present who put a wrong construction on the exhorter's words.

"When stationed on the Brighton Circuit some years ago, I frequently had an opportunity of both seeing and hearing the late Robert Corson at missionary and other meetings, and was always pleased to hear him relate from the platform incidents in connection with his early labours as an old Methodist itinerant,—many things which came under his own personal observation and related in his own quaint way. He laboured long and successfully in connection with our Church in Western Ontario, and took part in many interesting revivals of religion. In social conversation I received a good deal of information from him in reference to early Methodism in Canada, which I could not obtain even from the records of the historian. Many interesting facts, both with regard to ministers and Circuits, I learned from this well-informed aged minister.

"Although not a profound scholar or thinker, he was well-read and quite familiar with many valuable works. He read biography to good account, and was well-posted in all important matters connected with the history of Methodism generally, and with the Church in this country in particular. It may be truly said of this departed father in Israel that he has not lived in vain.

"Yours very truly,
"ANDREW A. SMITH.
" Cataraqui, December 17th, 1878."

1854, 1855.

7. *From 1854 to his Superannuation.*

The Conference of June, 1854, which sat in the town o. *Belleville*, was of a most harmonious character; and distinguished by two circumstances which would greatly gladden the old gentleman's heart, constituted as his was, surcharged with absorbing care for our Provincial Methodist Zion. The first was a reported increase in the membership of *two thousand seven hundred and thirty-five ;* and the other was the presence of a large and respectable deputation from the Canada East District Meeting, asking for affiliation with the Canada Conference, which went into effect immediately after the session of the ensuing British Wesleyan Conference, whose concurrence was required to give it final authorization. Father Corson always rejoiced in everything which contributed to increase and consolidate the interests of that form of Christianity to the interests of which he had devoted his life. This feeling was further heightened by the Hudson Bay Missions about this time being placed under the control and care of the Western Canada connection. This Conference received *Peter German*, one of the subjects of Mr. Corson's pastoral care in former days, into the ministry. The Stationing Committee re-appointed our old evangelist to CAINSVILLE, with regard to which, Mr. Corson's own account has been anticipated. In default of other materials for illustrating matters affecting Mr. Corson, I will here introduce some statements, incidentally made by his son, Dr. William, which relate to the place and time now under consideration. That affectionate, yet discriminating son, remarks: "From the time of my mother's death, in 1843, until the period of his settlement in Cainsville, a few years ago, I saw comparatively little of my father, making only occasional visits to him, as for instance at Norwich and Crowland, not having heard him preach for the last twenty-five years; but I learned from others that he rather improved with his advancing years, showing more animation and freshness, and more method and variety."

I was myself severed from him at the Conference of 1854, above referred to, having been one of the Western Canada preachers sent to Eastern Canada, upon its prospective transfer; and when that transfer was definitely consummated by the final action of the British Conference, I succeeded to the Chairmanship of the Montreal District, and was therefore separated by a very long intervening space from my old friend during this year, so that I am not able to say much about him, from personal knowledge, during the year 1854-55.

1855, 1856.

The Conference of *London*, in June 1855, brought us together once more; and it proved a memorable Conference to those of the old Canadian stock. The Revs. John Ryerson, Thomas Hurlburt, Robert Brooking, and Henry Steinhauer and Allan Salt (native ministers), went out from that Conference, or at least the Canada Church, about that time, to take possession of the Hudson Bay Missions in behalf of the Wesleyan Methodist Church in Canada. Also, at this Conference, by the request of the body, the venerable and REVEREND WILLIAM CASE, fifty years, with slight interruptions, a leading mind and agent in the councils and enterprizes of Canadian Methodism, preached his famous JUBILEE SERMON, preparatory, as it proved, to his "putting off the harness," and entering into his final rest and reward in heaven; which he did, not only before the Conference year was out, but before that civil year was ended.

At this Conference our subject was transferred to the *Guelph District*, and stationed at ERIN. How the transfer came to be made I do not now remember, and I think we have very little excepting Mr. Corson's own sententious notes to illustrate the year besides Mr. Smith's letter already given. His words are, "In 1855 I was appointed to Erin. A hard Circuit for an old man—long rides. A few conversions. I stopped one year. Salary, $400."

There was much to cheer the heart of so ardent a friend of the cause as this old itinerant. Every report made in the early part of the year, from any and every interest of the Church, was of an encouraging kind. Glowing statements appeared in the *Guardian* from the camp-meetings held east, west, north and south, for single Circuits, or for several, or for districts; from the many, the *Whites;* and the fewer, but not less interesting, the *Indians.*

One of the greatest revivals for this year was in my own station, *Belleville*, which resulted in a *net* increase of 265 members. This I should not have mentioned, as relating to myself, only that "thereby hangs a tale" relating to our our good old friend, Corson, himself. It will open the account of the next year.

1856, 1857.

The Conference at the opening of the above-mentioned year sat in *Brockville*, under the able Presidency of the Rev. Enoch Wood, now D.D., and with the *Rev. James Elliott, Secretary*. At that Conference I revived my intimacy with Father Corson. After the rise of the Conference, both he and I were delayed a day or so behind the others—myself to preach a funeral sermon for an old and highly-esteemed friend, of the Farmersville Circuit, Mrs. Ira Lewis; and he, I suspect, to see some friends, perhaps children, in the Bay Quinté country. I joined him on the Bay steamer at Kingston, or Bath, I forget which. It was Saturday, and he could not get back to his work by Sunday; and I, though I could get back to mine, did not feel in very good trim for going before my people in the pulpit, being very weary, and having been out of my study, of course, all the week. Aside, therefore, from the love of his company, and a wish to show him hospitality, I desired him to come home with me to the parsonage, and to help me with my work on Sunday. He consented, and became our guest. He was greatly delighted with what he heard and saw of the fruits of our most gracious ingathering. I asked him to take one of the services, and he consented; and I would have pledged him to conduct both, but for two things: first, I did not know but my people would exhibit a distaste to the homely ways and sayings of so plain a man. The other was, there was another strange preacher on the ground, a brother very fond of preaching; and while I secured "Father Corson" for the morning I pledged Brother R——k for the evening, and set my heart at rest from the necessity of preparing for the pulpit, and from the delivery of any sermon for one whole Sunday, a very rare thing for me in those days.

Sunday morning came; a great and earnest congregation assembled; at the proper hour my old friend mounted the pulpit, and turned his venerable, good-natured old face from side to side over the congregation, and seemed to regard them with paternal benignity; and the unsophisticated people seemed to be led by their pious instincts to respect and love him at once. He took for his text, Acts xi. 23, "And when he had come, and had seen the grace of God, he was glad; and he exhorted them all, that with purpose of heart they would cleave unto the Lord." It was a timely, well-conceived, and well-delivered sermon, attended by the unction of the Holy One. The "*Grace of God*"— the *manner in which grace manifests itself* to the eyes of observers—what there is in the manifestations of saving grace to "*gladden*" *the hearts of good men*—and the *appropriate counsels* to the recent recipients of grace, were points well handled, and well exemplified in his own expositions and advices. The sermon, though genial and kindly, was delivered with many tears, and it extorted tears profusely from his hearers' eyes. Indeed, smiles and tears chased each other through the service, like sunshine and shade; and, as he was not more than half-an-hour in delivering it, when he had closed the people, instead of "loathing," were "longing" for more—"sorry that he was done;" and wished to know if that dear old man would preach again in the evening.

Alas, I had to tell them that I had arranged with Mr. R——k to preach. Although I believe he was a good man, he was very dissimilar from Mr. Corson. Many would have thought, *primâ facie*, that all the dissimilarities were superiorities in Mr. R——k. Corson was without learning, and as artless as a child; but R——k was not only classically educated *thoroughly*, but pretentious to a degree, in short, as pedantic as pedantry could be. He used, not Mr. Corson's almost John-Bunyan-English, but the longest, the most thoroughly Latinized words he could find, even to technical terms, if he had to English them afterwards, as he often did. As a consequence, while Corson was brief to a fault, he was very long-winded, preaching an hour and a-half, which, from its wearisomeness, seemed more like three hours. The looks of the people were very much changed from what they had been in the morning. I was afraid to face them; and well I might have been, for, to use a homely, common saying, they were "ready to eat me up without a grain of salt." The popularity of Father Corson was unbounded; but the learned, lengthy preacher was dreaded exceedingly. The old gentleman's visit was talked of for several days.

At the Brockville Conference our old friend had been appointed to the KLINEBURG CIRCUIT, which, though it was in the Toronto District, was not a long move across the country from Erin. It takes its name from a pleasant country village at its head, in the township of Vaughan, I believe, situated on the Humber, which is here pretty in its meanderings, and agreeable from the Old Country associations with its name. His own account of his advent to, and residence at, Klineburg (albeit he seems to have lived a part of the time at *Teston*) I give in the next short paragraph:—

"In 1856 I was appointed to *Klineburg Circuit.* No colleague. A good people. Some revivals. We built a small house to live in." [The want of a parsonage and his having a little money, induced him to build.] "Remained two years. Salary, a *thousand dollars* for the two years— the largest salary I ever received during my whole itinerant life." As I have no materials for illustrating the year 1857-58, I will bring the account of the ACTIVE period of Mr. Corson's life to a close.

Just as I had closed the account of the year with the above short paragraph, I received a letter from a person signing himself *John Norris Harvey*, claiming to be a local preacher, living at Applegrove, within the original Klineburg Circuit; the letter embracing a number of reminiscences of Father Corson; the substance of the whole being, that his place of residence was, at least for a part of the time, in a neighbourhood now known as *Teston* ; that he was on terms of kindly, almost playful, familiarity with his people, who received these familiarities with the delight that children accept the caresses of their parents; that he took an interest in the budding efforts of his young local preachers, aiding the beginners with MS. plans of sermons for their guidance; and that the people cherish tender memories of his ministrations—this brother furnishing me with a memoranda of texts from which he had heard his aged pastor preach with profit and delight. He also mentions an awkward mishap which occurred to Brother Corson in the Newmarket Circuit, some years before, from the confusion of which I am sure no minister could extricate himself with less perturbation. This occurred from his kneeling hurriedly against a table loaded with dishes, which stood so slightly on its feet that it yielded to his pressure and overturned with all that was upon it; a mishap which I came very near having experienced myself more than once, but one, which, if it had occurred, I am certain I could not have out-faced like the guileless Corson.* The

* The mention of "tottlish" tables, chairs, &c., may be monitory to housekeepers and those answerable for the care of places of meeting, as well as to preachers. I could mention the battlement on the platform of a lecture room in a pretentious College, against which, when I came to kneel at the request of a "Professor," to lead in the accustomed daily devotions, I had nearly pitched headlong, along with the provoking piece of shiftlessness set up there to lure unwary strangers to their overthrow! I should like to know if that slipshod arrangement still obtains?

I feel inclined to add to the length of this note by referring to information obtained on a subject mentioned in the text, from another source. When in the *Simcoe* Circuit, having his eye on the possible usefulness of a youth not many months converted, he called him to take a seat by him on a log, and said, "Michael, do you think you could preach?" "No, I am sure I could not." "Come, let us see if you could not. Here is the text 'How shall we escape if we neglect so great salvation?' What could you do with that?" "I could do nothing." "But you could; let us try. The first thing is '*Salvation*,' what is that?" "It is *Deliverance*." "Very good, deliverance from *guilt*, and sin, and punishment. But it is '*Great*,' why? Because provided by a *Great God*, and from *a great evil*. But who are the '*Neglecters*' of it? The *Scribes and Pharisees*. All *unbelievers*. All the *careless*, the *lukewarm*, *backsliders*, *&c*. But what will they not '*escape*' from? *Accusations of guilty conscience here*, and the *punishment of sin and unbelief hereafter*." These were the sort of lessons in Homiletics by which the Rev. M. Fawcett was trained to be a preacher. No unprofitable theological student was he.

extraordinary incident to be given presently is affirmed by this writer, as it occurred in that region.

As Mr. Corson became older he was less observant of little matters of current interest, and also forgetful of many things, from day to day, which it is very important a minister in charge of a Circuit should recollect, and his brethren, both clerical and lay, began to think that although he had great strength and vitality, and that, though he might serve the interests of the cause of Christ in a local sphere, he ought to be released from the cares and toils of a Circuit—in short, that he ought to be "superannuated." He thought otherwise himself; his heart was young, his mind was active, and he believed he was physically as capable as most of the men who were yet young in years. This caused for a time a little uneasiness, until the die was cast.

An amusing instance, in which the two opinions and tendencies came in conflict, and which exhibited the original character of our unique brother, tenacious of life and labour, is thus detailed by those who witnessed the scene. At an official meeting where they were urging him to superannuate, on the grounds that he was *no longer physically equal to the toils of the Itinerancy*, he maintained that he was as competent as ever, so far as strength and activity were concerned, and much more so than many younger men. While this branch of the question was being considered, *pro* and *con*, he somewhat lost his patience, and his old Samson-like energy coming upon him afresh, he stepped out into the aisle, sprang into the air, as in the days of his boyhood, and rapped his feet three times together before he returned to the floor. "There!" said he with a look of scorn and defiance, "Are there any of you here that can do that?" What the weaklings said or did, deponent did not say.

Having come to the close of Mr. Corson's "effective" services in the Church, I think this the most appropriate place to present the analysis of his CHARACTER, most discriminatingly drawn up by his admiring son, *Dr. John Wesley Corson:*

"PEN PORTRAIT."

"Even as a matter of scientific enquiry, each trait of the body and mind of him who bore such a long and fearful strain becomes a matter of interest. We will try affectionately to sketch him by a familiar 'word painting.' He was so sternly honest, that with Cromwell he would have shouted to a cringing artist, '*Show me just as I am sir! Let me see that wart on my face.*' And so we will respect the memory and not flatter the picture. Yet to be true it must be radiant with sunlight, with scarcely a trace of shadow.

"Both Wesley and Asbury were moderate in size. Travellers long ago remarked, that the veterans who survived the campaign to Russia, to loiter about the Hotel or the Invalids in Paris, were nearly all compact little men. He whose likeness we are trying faithfully to give, was perhaps a trifle below medium in height. His shoulders were broad, surmounting a powerfully knit frame, incliniug to fulness. He had a sailor's swing of the arms, and, even in advanced age, a quick boyish step. Friends who used to see that veteran minister flitting about Brooklyn Heights, will understand the comparison, when we mention that his movements, and general appearance, strongly resembled those of the late Dr. Lyman Beecher. To use a homely phrase, both seemed tough. Perhaps his early habit of reading on horseback had given to our father a scholar's 'stoop of the neck.' Doubtless this was confirmed by his singular custom of hurriedly writing 'sketches of sermons' on his knee—just as a General might send off despatches in the heat of a battle. As he briskly walked the streets, this bend seemed rather increased. He leaned forward as it were in intense abstraction. Indeed, at times he was very 'absent,' and his eyes were then fixed upon the sidewalk as if, like Hugh Miller, he was profoundly studying the paving stones.

"When he awoke from this reverie, it was perhaps to greet heartily some old friend, and then his face, ruddy even in old age, would light up with a winning smile. Indeed, we may change the compliment from a fascinating Western Statesman, and say that the deceased was a model of a 'smiling' minister. Only with the latter the effort was perfectly sincere. He scorned pretence of every kind. It was the joy of a glad heart, flashing on the cheeks of a childlike Christian.

"His forehead was very broad above the eyes, as if the high massive brow of Sir Walter Scott had been pressed down a full inch, till it swelled around the ears—just to take out the romance. Below, it was fringed with thick eyebrows, and above, there floated carelessly about locks of hair, long of an iron grey. The eyes were blue, and had ever a merry twinkle. Probably to save the minutes he so valued in shaving, he wore plain side-whiskers. As if to set off the ready laugh that rolled in waves over his broad features, there was a deep dimple in the chin; but to temper this again, he had a massive, firm lower jaw, like that of General Grant, for beneath the sunny outside, there always lurked an iron will. The lips were liberal, as if made to speak easily.

"When young Henry Brougham, afterwards himself a Lord, thundered at the Bar of the House of Lords, in defence of Queen Caroline, the end of his long nose was said to twist and twirl like a finger of scorn; but in the present case the nasal projection was strictly modest and peaceful.

"Youthful Americans, years ago, will remember a queer phrase of the students of the Latin Quarter in Paris, who used to jeer at their then countrymen, the half Germans of Metz and Strasburg, as 'Square heads.' The worthy subject of this notice had the full round visage of a German Professor who thoroughly enjoys life, and not only studies, but feeds well.

"Outside of the sacred desk and in the family circle, as we have before hinted, irresistible mirthfulness bubbled up as a part of his very life. One might as well have attempted to choke an Artesian well, or the Geysers of Iceland. Yet these outbursts were often changed in an instant, as by a current of strong religious feeling. His prayers abounded in praises, and he loved to sing snatches of happy hymns as he rode through the dark woods.

"This irrepressible cheerfulness was doubtless the charm that rendered him so welcome in hundreds of rural homes—for he made countless pastoral visits. It was his special pleasure to seek out 'neglected' people. As a pious lady once said, he was always 'hunting for souls.' Sometimes his zeal led him to attack the enemy 'without orders.' He would suddenly leave his Circuit with a temporary supply, and plunge into the nearest wilderness in search of poor immigrants who were hungering for the Bread of Life. He flew from house to house, and from farm to farm, like the famous Wandering Jew of the Poet Beranger. He was ever in a hurry, and in his haste, at times, his joys and devotions were curiously mingled. While a broad smile was yet on every face, he would say quickly, "Let us pray!' and then he would drop suddenly on his knees, and utter a brief prayer so full of mighty faith, and yet so simple and touching that all would rise in tears.*

"Frequently, on a week day, he would tell comical stories, like those of Abraham Lincoln, to the very door of a log school-house, but the moment he entered all was changed. The converted wit that had kept the garrison on Burlington Heights in a roar for months, was now an Ambassador of Christ. Once in the pulpit, not a jest escaped his lips. Trifles in youth often fix the tastes of a life-time. Had he not marched in a clean 'British uniform' to service long years before, on many a Sabbath morn? Did he not then join in the responses of that gift of the martyrs of the Reformation, the English Liturgy? For even Christians who prefer extemporaneous prayers,

* In illustration and confirmation of what Dr. John says in the above sentence, I was informed, many years ago, on the Bath Circuit, where, the reader will remember, Mr. Corson once laboured, that he was visiting one day on the Isle of Tanti, and "going into every house in order," as the Discipline directs; pursuing which course, he came to the dwelling of a Roman Catholic, with whom he had some friendly conversation on general subjects: when, all at once, he said to him, "You are a Roman Catholic?" "Yes." "Well, I'm a Methodist; Now, what if we pray together for once!" And, before the man had time to object, or indeed reply, he said, "Let us pray!" And, falling on his knees, poured out a subduing prayer, though short, which left the Romanist with no disposition to cavil, and, indeed, profitably impressed.—ED.

can admire a book so full of gems from the Bible for the masses,—gathered when the sacred volume was very costly.

"He was now a 'Soldier of the Cross,' and he was reverently neat in his clerical wardrobe. The black coat for Sunday must be of the finest broadcloth, 'piously' single-breasted,—something between an ancient 'continental' and a modern 'dress,'—and gracefully curved in front like the wings of a dove, and his cravat gave the contrast of dazzling whiteness.

"As he entered the pulpit and sat down, his face wore a peculiarly sweet and solemn expression. Sometimes it brightened suddenly, as if from a happy thought within. An English historian, describing the wild dash of the French Zouaves, as they came to the rescue of his countrymen at Inkermann, said: 'They came with the light of the battle on their faces.' So the countenance of the departed shone at times with the radiance of the Holy War.

"One of the grand accomplishments of a backwoods preacher, in those primitive days, was a thundering voice. With happy memories of the playful sallies of him whom we are trying to portray, we may venture to remark, that like a church bell, it summoned all the neighbours. It echoed through the trees, till it made sinners tremble as the horns of the Israelites shook the walls of Jericho, and then it silenced even the scoffers on the outskirts of a camp-meeting.

"Seriously, it was a gift too useful to be neglected by the fortunate owner. The worthy subject of this sketch, in the prime of his manhood, spoke not only in stentorian tones, but his words flowed rapidly, like a mighty torrent. Those who have listened to the famous evangelist, Mr. Moody, hurriedly addressing a vast multitude, will understand his impassioned manner. The body swayed to and fro, and the broad chest heaved mightily. His sermons were brief, clear, and forcible. His 'divisions' were natural.

"The great German linguist, Grimm, has predicted that English, from its simple brevity and convenience in trade, is destined in the future to be the leading language of the world. It certainly has singular power in the pulpit. The deceased always preferred its short, telling words. He would call a spade a *spade*. It was not an 'agricultural implement.' We may illustrate his plain taste by quoting a discussion in a prayer-meeting in which the speaker, himself a proficient in several tongues, asserted that in no other form could that delightful assurance in the Twenty-third Psalm be so well and briefly expressed as in the four Saxon words '*I shall not want.*' The closing thoughts of the subject of this narrative were always given with much solemnity and force. He threw his whole strength into the 'Application.'

"As he grew grey, and began to be called more frequently 'Father Corson,' he gradually lost the fervent declamation which tradition assigns to St. Peter, and melted gently into the tender style of St. John. His cadences grew more soft, and his sentences more deliberate and finished. This last improvement an intimate friend playfully attributed to the 'piles of books that he read.' In fact to a very late period he plodded through a great many volumes in a year.

"The truth that he so loved, compels us to say that in a high artistic sense he could hardly be called a prodigy in eloquence. Yet there were grand occasions when the magnetism of his utter sincerity told wonderfully upon an audience. In early days his efforts were singularly blessed in extensive revivals; and he was mercifully spared to commune with many aged Christians, whom, as Andrew led Peter, he first brought to Jesus.

"Doubtless the chief element of his success as a revivalist was his overmastering *earnestness*. We remember a few years since reading a touching tribute from the few survivors, to the powerful appeal of the Rev. Mr. Draper, of Australia, as he pleaded with his fellow passengers on the deck till the waves chocked his voice and he perished with the wreck of the steamer *London* in the Bay of Biscay. And he whose portrait we are trying to paint, commonly preached as if it might be his last sermon on earth.

"He was so pure and upright as a man, and so prayerful and exemplary as a Christian, that his very cheerful temperament did not seem in the least to lessen his influence as a minister. Those frank, easy ways of his disarmed all criticism. His 'merry heart' soon came to be regarded as a part of his nature, as much as the width of his forehead or the colour of his hair. His witty sayings, too, were often in exchange for unmeasured Christian hospitalities. The 'young converts' in the log cabins in the thick woods of forty and fifty years before, were now, to use a favourite expression of his, 'Prospering for both worlds.' Spacious farm houses, great barns and orchards, and golden harvests had come to cover the hillsides. And they had a still richer inheritance in the fair land beyond Jordan. They lavished tokens of regard upon their early friend, sometimes hurrying to the very gate to meet him. Paul, with the chain of a Roman prisoner upon his arm, awaiting sentence from Nero, was so moved with gratitude that he could write the 'most joyous of his Epistles,' thanking the ever faithful Philippians for those generous gifts which followed him everywhere even to his death. And the key note of that martyr song of triumph was, 'For me to live is Christ, but to die is gain.' Thus this aged 'Evangelist,' welcome in hundreds of Canadian homes, in his own peculiar way, only obeyed the exhortation of the heroic apostle, 'Again I say rejoice.'

"We who now mourn his loss may gratefully recognize in this buoyancy of spirit, one of the most potent influences in prolonging his useful life; but here we may doubtless recognize another agency equally powerful. It was his unceasing toil. He abhorred idleness even in extreme old age. His active brain was never palsied for want of use. Writing to one of his sons at eighty-four, he said, 'I have preached seventy sermons during the past year.' He was ever seeking Christian work, and he enjoyed it to the last. He especially delighted to preach, as he termed it, to his 'old friends.' Recently he wrote, 'last Sabbath I spoke to the people with whom I laboured just fifty years ago.'

"As we have remarked before, his transitions from smiling to weeping were sometimes sudden. Even in middle life he was occasionally interrupted by deep emotion in the pulpit, which, with a mighty effort, he would restrain for a time, until at last both speaker and hearers were ready to weep together. As years passed on he 'melted down' more frequently.

"More than a quarter of a century since, one of his sons rose with the crowd in Exeter Hall, London, at the first great meeting of the Evangelical Alliance, to do homage to a little old man bent with years, with broad shoulders, shaggy eyebrows, and a full round face—almost the image of his own father. He too had been a pastor fifty years. He seemed overjoyed at the sight of those gathered tribes of the Israel of God. His lips moved, but there came no sound; then he burst into tears and sat down. It was William Jay. So he whose memory we now revere, lived often to weep with joy with multitudes of his spiritual children—lived to sing praises at the wonderful gospel triumphs of the Church he so loved, all over his native land—till he could say with Simeon, 'Now, Lord, lettest thou thy servant depart in peace,' 'For mine eyes have seen Thy salvation.'"

III. FROM MR. CORSON'S SUPERANNUATION TO HIS DEATH : OR FROM 1858 TO 1878.

The Conference at which our subject received a superannuated relation sat, for the first time after the incorporation of the Canada East District with the Canada Conference, in the city of *Montreal*, that great commercial emporium ; and the laying of this active-minded man on the shelf just at the moment he had a chance of seeing how our borders were enlarging, and new doors of usefulness were opening to us, must have been the more trying to his ardent heart. He pleaded to be allowed to continue, as he felt himself quite equal to Circuit work physically, saying that "he could still preach three times on Sunday; meet three classes; and be so fresh on Monday, that, if required, he could jump up and strike his feet together three times before he came down." The Conference was almost too dignified an assembly for him to make the scene of an actual exemplification of his agility as he did before the select officials in the Klineburg Circuit. The only reference to this crisis in his history in his "sketch" is as follows: "In 1858 I superannuated. Located in Cobourg. Built a small framed house, and kept boarders for those who were attending college; and educated my youngest son, Adam Clarke."

1. *From his settlement in Cobourg, to his removal to his house in Cainsville, a period of fifteen years.*

At the Conference of 1859, which sat in *Hamilton*, the enterprising old gentleman made application for restoration to the effective ranks, but his brethren thought that all he was capable of now doing could be best achieved in a retired sphere and in connection with "a local habitation." This fact will explain some allusions in the following sketch.

It was while Father Corson was standing up in the Conference, stating and defending his own case, that I took the idea of writing the "CONFERENCE CRAYONS." He was accordingly the first one portrayed, and placed at the head of the list. The book is now out of print and inaccessible to most; and, as many have expressed a desire to see that sketch, who have otherwise no opportunity of seeing it; and as it will conduce to the objects of this volume, I have decided to reproduce it, and in this connection :—

"CRAYON FIRST."

"Having resolved to try and hit off, in an easy manner, a few of the more prominent members of the Canadian Wesleyan Conference, I begin with one of the oldest, one who was superannuated last year, but who still thinks himself effective, as he has applied for restoration to the active work. We have heard somewhere, that British soldiers never know when they are beaten. In this respect as in all others, FATHER CORSON is a true Briton. He thinks he is as capable of circuit work as he ever was; and physically, I think he is nearly so. But, alas for the dear old man! he, like some others of us are, is behind the times,—though like most others in a similar predicament, he does not know it. He never was distinguished for very great intellectual power, although a shrewd man; and his early education was defective, a defect which he never greatly remedied by private study, although he has been one of the most voluminous readers in the Conference. Even yet, he reads more books through in a year than almost any man we wot of. Furthermore, he has an excellent memory for the *historical* parts of what he reads. He is a sort of standing table of reference for *facts* and *dates* relating to American Methodism. Notwithstanding the drawbacks above mentioned, he has done good service for the Lord in the woods and wilds of Canada, during the last thirty-five years. We remember our first sight of him at a camp-meeting thirty years ago, when his word was like electric fire among the people. And if he is not highly educated himself, he has raised up a family of educated sons, who are an honour to him, while they bear traces of the intellectual superiority of a good and dignified mother. Our hero never filled a City appointment, but he has traversed and re-traversed nearly all the rural parts of the Province, from Kingston to Sarnia, and from Lakes Ontario and Erie to Huron and Simcoe. For preaching *often*, and *visiting* he has no equal. He has been known to preach *forty* times in the month, and to visit a dozen families before breakfast. He has never filled any office in the connexion higher than that of Superintendent of a Circuit, and has never received any particular mark of his brethren's appreciation, although he lives in the affections of every brother's heart. We know not that he ever published anything beyond a letter in a newspaper, but we once knew him to have written what we wish he had published.

"No person ever bore toil and lack of honour better. He has sometimes made humorous allusions to his great abilities and high position. *Humour* is his forte. His is of the most broad and grotesque, yet genial and pious character. How he has "brought down the house," (for be it known he is a celebrated Conference debater) all acquainted with the deliberations of the Conference very well know. In this respect he has answered a valuable purpose in our ecclesiastical discussions, often dissipating the acrimonious feelings engendered by a stormy debate, by one of his irresistibly ludicrous speeches. Though ludicrous they are not trifling; he is often most laughable when most in earnest. Father C. holds very decided opinions on all questions, and is not afraid to express them either. He often does the latter by very sound arguments, which would be really weighty and convincing, if it were not for the odd and humorous way in which they are put. To see him rise in Conference is the signal for a titter of delight to run through the assembly, while significant nods, and winks, and smiles, amount to saying, 'now for some innocent amusement.' The make of his tawny, good-natured face, is comical; and his nod, when he addresses 'Mr. President,' is formed on the most approved school-boy model of other days, when the urchin was expected to bring down his head to every passing stranger, in the use of the strictly enjoined 'bow' with a jerk that was dangerous to the vertebræ of the neck. But if our hero's arguments are not telling in the ordinary sense, he often makes very lucky hits, which do good without hurting much. We have two of these in our remembrance, which were decidedly rich, but hesitate a little for the present in publishing them.*

* I have at length given them in the pages of this memoir.

"Still it must not be forgotten, that though Father Corson often provokes a laugh, he frequently beguiles the people of their tears, as he is by no means parsimonious of his own. Nor are they crocodile tears either; he has a warm, tender, and pious heart.

"The old-fashioned itinerant, by an odd juxtaposition, has settled himself at Cobourg, where our rising Ministry are receiving the polish of a liberal education. They may very profitably take some leaves out of this book.

"May God in his mercy give him 'a serene old age,' and the happy death of a 'good soldier of Jesus Christ,' such as he is! Amen."

Of the time our venerable friend spent in Cobourg, he says in his usual summary way, "I remained fifteen years in Cobourg. During that time I preached *fifteen hundred* sermons and read *five hundred* books. I was planned both in town and country. I was blessed with friends both in and out of the college;" and he might have added in and out of the Church.

There are many retired ministers who would, perhaps, be ashamed to have it said, that they, as Father Corson did and avowed it, "kept a boarding house" (calling, as he always did, a spade a spade), albeit I have no sympathy with such squeamishness. They seem not to have adopted the maxim of John Wesley, the Founder of our Methodism, namely, "Be ashamed of nothing but sin." Let it be remembered, moreover, that Mr. Corson was of an active, industrious temperament, and he had been an industrious man all his days; and it was impossible for him to be idle—to have enforced idleness upon him would have been to kill him before his time. Besides, let it be recollected that he was naturally a shrewd man of business, a man who would have made a fortune if he had not been a Methodist preacher, presenting "his life, his blood," for the honour of God and the good of the Church. He had no absolute need of doing anything to make money, for he would have had a small competency at any rate; he had a higher motive than money. But if he had been impelled by no more elevated object, there would have been nothing derogatory to a retired minister's dignity in doing it. William Anson, a fascinating preacher, and the first appointed to *Yonge-street* Circuit, including *York*, had to do the same thing in his old days, to support himself and family. If Mr. Corson netted any gains, which is very doubtful, he made a good use of them: his habitual generosity, and the position of respectability and usefulnes in which he placed his sons, is sufficient to answer all cavils on that subject.

But he had a higher motive, and he realized it. His first motive in going to Cobourg was to have facilities for giving his youngest son a liberal education. To bring it more within the compass of his means, he invested his little disposable resources in a house of his own, in preference to paying rent. Then, he had many friends through the country, who had sons to send to college, who desired to have those youths under the care of the old minister in preference to anyone else.* He kept a good table, furnished good beds, his terms

* Father Corson's extensive acquaintance with the heads of Methodist households in the country was a great source of influence for good among their descendants. Rev. John B. Clarkson, the old gentleman's last pastor, who had known him at Cobourg while passing through college, remarked, in preaching the crowned-warrior's funeral sermon, that Father Corson would say to this, that, and the other student, whom he met at the Institution, "I married your father and mother." "I took your father and mother into the Church," with sundry other pleasant remembrances of their parents and friends respectively.

were very reasonable, and he was not exacting about the pay weekly, if, in some instances, he were paid at all. There was another class who had a natural affinity for the genial old preacher; these were the "Conference students"—young preachers who had preached one or more years and were allowed to attend college; these found the complement for their youth and inexperience in this old hero of a hundred battles. These naturally went to his hospice; they counselled him about the treatment of the text they were endeavouring to master, and he gave them suggestions, often writing them an outline for them to fill up. And let no one smile at the idea of *his* outline, as some pretentious ones may be inclined to do. Corson was a natural sermonizer, much better than some who were rated higher. Furthermore, there were indigent young men, who could not have sustained themselves at college at all, if he had not given them easy terms and long credit: he knew the hardships of the struggling poor, and showed practical sympathy. I have heard no complaints from him or his family, but I am morally certain, that, in some cases at least, among these persons there was neither pay nor much after gratitude. It was a a kind of business and a sphere of usefulness into which he was providentially led; and, although it was an unusual line of operation, he had penetration enough to see that it embraced a pleasant employment, one in which his paternal heart could find congenial occupation, and he had simplicity and moral courage enough to pursue it, without going around to ask, "What will the world think?" It was the substitution of a more comprehensive sphere for fulfilling his ministry to that of the direct, personal ministry of the word as a Circuit preacher.

He might have defended his occupation by the same line

of argument that Dr. Chalmers did in answer to the remonstrance of an humble but pious co-labourer. Everyone knows what extensive schemes of parochial usefulness the Doctor was employed in when he received an election to a Professorship in the newly-constituted Free Church Theological College, which he saw fit to accept. When his devoted lay assistant, or city missionary, Sandy Patterson, heard of it, he, not having any very high opinion of the necessity for systematic training, compared with direct and apparent results, went to his minister and expostulated with him for giving up such direct and certain opportunity of serving the interests of souls, for one which to him appeared only indirect, if not uncertain. The Doctor heard him patiently, for he had a great regard for this truly original and very useful man, and answered him by a question: "Sandy, which do you think is the most useful man, the man that salts the pig, or the man that makes the salt that salts all the pigs?" The quick-witted helper was not slow to see the point, or to acknowledge the force of the argument, and responded at once, "Oh; if it comes to that, the sooner you are in the salt pans the bether." This will apply to Father Corson's work; for if he did not "salt" the animals, he did that without which the salt of theological lore would have been of little avail, he *fed them:* something which goes before the *salting.* (See Talmage's doctrine of beef-steak.)

His residence in what might be called a Collegiate town, and his constantly presiding at the head of a table full of genteel young men whose manners he had to mould, contributed to rub off any rusticity of deportment he may have acquired in his rural circuits, and to polish his own manners; for he was an improving man to the last. Insomuch so that some of his early acquaintances remarked to his children, "How

9*

exceedingly urbane and polite your father has become." It was not, however, that false refinement which makes its possessor stiff and formal; something Father Corson could never be.

Besides, he did not preach prospectively or by proxy alone, through those whom he aided in acquiring qualifications for that sublime and important work, but he still laboured in word and doctrine, as he has told us—" in town," and in a wide area of country all round. In preaching *fifteen hundred* sermons in fifteen years, he preached what was equivalent to *one hundred* sermons a year for each year he was there. Pretty good for a superannuate. And this work was done under circumstances of great fatigue and hardship. Since I sat down to write this part of his life, a mutual friend, the Rev. Charles Silvester, who knew the facts, informed me that one of the old gentleman's Sabbath day's excursions embraced a horseback ride of nine miles to his forenoon appointment, ten to his afternoon service, and several miles (the exact number I do not remember) to his appointment at night. My informant did not know but that he may have gone to the first place on Saturday evening, and may have returned to his home not till Monday, and, of course, I do not know. But even admitting that, a horseback journey of eighteen or twenty miles and three sermons (and if there were classes, I will venture to say he did not turn his back on them) was a great exploit for an old man of approaching eighty years, with as long a journey to go to, and return from, his first and last appointments, besides the actual travel on Sunday.

I have been furnished with several characteristic and amusing stories, illustrative of his life and labours during his sojourn within the shadow of our great Connexional

University, some of which I will give. The first one of these was furnished by a senior minister who laboured in that vicinity at the time. It illustrates Father Corson's zeal, laboriousness, and punctuality, as also his disregard of what the world calls "appearances," when he was called to overcome obstacles which conflicted with what he thought the punctual performance of his duty; while it shows how much use he made of suggestions produced by passing occurrences on his mind.

I have the authority of the Rev. Wm. McCullough for the following, and I give it in his own words, to secure accuracy, and because of the neat and agreeable manner in which it is narrated :—

"On a certain occasion 'Father Corson' preached in a village east of Cobourg, in the forenoon of Sabbath, at half-past ten o'clock. He had also an appointment in a certain neighbourhood some miles distant, at half-past two o'clock p.m. After the morning service he went to the house of the R. S., Mr. A. H., to get some dinner for himself and 'Old Sal,' his mare. He had a 'good time' in preaching as he usually had, and was in fine spirits. But when he went to his friend's house his spirits fell several degrees, for the dinner was not ready, nor likely soon to be, and he feared being late for his other service. But he was not often at a loss to know what to do. He went to the cooking stove to ascertain the state of culinary affairs, and to his joy found a pot of sweet corn boiled to perfection. He at once filled his pockets with corn, mounted "Old Sal," ate his corn with as much satisfaction as if he had been at the 'Feast of Tabernacles,' and went on his way singing with a glad and thankful heart, and preparing his afternoon sermon. He went into the church, entered the pulpit, took down the Bible, and selected for his text, 'And the disciples plucked the ears of corn.' I could give you many quaint anecdotes of 'Father Corson,' but the above is sufficient, for you are likely to receive thousands from his numerous friends, 'lay and clerical.'"

There is another from the same source, and it relates to the period of his residence at Cobourg, and is so characteristic of the dear old man and the pleasant manner of his intercourse with his "troops of friends," that I give it now, and without abridgement or change.

"When the writer of this short notice lived in the village of M——, his next-door neighbour was a worthy son of 'Father Corson,' and, like the rest of his noble sons, was shrewd and intelligent. He was the proprietor and editor of a respectable newspaper,—*The Economist*—and his wife the sister of an Hon. Senator of the Dominion of Canada. He was not yet a member of the Church, but a regular hearer of the Word, and Father Corson visited this son more frequently than some others, because of his parental anxiety for the salvation of the only son out of the fold of Christ. During one of those paternal visits he put his horse in my stable for the night, and he felt free to do this, for we had been acquainted for years, and he knew that even his horse was welcome. The next morning I had occasion to make an early start for Toronto, and about 5 a.m. I went out to the stable to feed my horse, and to my surprise found Father Corson there, who had fed my horse and his own also. I asked him why he was up so early, and said, 'Does your conscience trouble you about anything, so that you cannot sleep?' He replied, 'Do you call this early? Why, I have spent some time in secret prayer for my poor son, and I have read the two Books of Chronicles through and through besides.' 'Why, Father Corson! Would you not have received more good from one chapter in the book of John than from the reading of the Chronicles of the Kings of Israel?' He replied, 'My duty is to read the whole of the sacred Scriptures, besides it was a good thing for Israel that King Ahasuerus had read to him, when he could not sleep, the chronicles of the kingdom.' 'But what did you do with the hard names in the first ten or eleven chapters?' Why, I just looked at them, and bid them good morning, and then passed on to the next. But brother,' he said, 'you must not be too critical.' 'Good morning Father Corson, I must leave you and go to Toronto.' 'Good morning brother,' he said, 'I must leave you and go to Cobourg, and when you come my way you will find an empty stall for your horse, and a welcome for yourself.' 'Father Corson, I do not want an empty stall for my horse, I want something in it for him to eat.' 'Ah, brother, you will disclose the country you hail from. I will pray for you, brother.' 'Father Corson, your prayers are by far too short, the Lord has hardly time to hear them until you are through.' 'Short or long, my brother, the good Lord always answers them.' 'Well, Father Corson, I must be off, good morning, but do pray for me.' 'I will, indeed, for you need some one to pray for you, I am sure,' and he laughed heartily. Father Corson was pure-minded, and perfectly transparent. He was an Israelite, indeed, in whom there was no guile. He was a man of strong faith, and his life was spotless and consistent."

Myself and others have spoken of Father Corson's readiness to lend a hand to help his ministerial brethren in their work, in the vicinity of Cobourg. These preaching excursions were extended to more than a day's travel from his home. From 1861 to 1864 I was stationed in the town of Peterboro', of which I have very pleasant remembrances. The Society was very large, and the communicants therefore numerous, and a quarterly Sacramental occasion was a somewhat onerous affair. I was consequently always glad of the company and assistance of a brother minister,—an advantage, however, I seldom enjoyed. I often thought, remembering the visit at Belleville, what a luxury it would be to have Father Corson with us, for at least once. Arrangements were at length matured that he should come; but unhappily for him, it chanced to be the November Quarterly Meeting, and not very early in the month either, but far on towards the close. It happened also that the weather was more than usually severe for the season; but Father Corson came, not by the comfortable, though, roundabout, expensive way and means of the cars, namely, *via* Port Hope, Millbrook, &c., but across the country in his old rickety buggy and ancient white horse, whose pace, at the best, did not exceed four miles an hour. This without expense to any one. He must therefore have had to leave home pretty early on Friday, yet he was in Peterboro' timely on Saturday. Despite the raw weather, the services were well attended, and the meeting a good one. I have not been able to recall his subjects, but his efforts were happy and well received. Here he met his old friends, Mr. and Mrs. Alexander Morrow, whom he had known when he laboured on the Whitby Circuit the first time. This worthy couple informed my wife that they could remember when they thought it was the greatest treat to "go and spend a day with Brother and Sister Corson," despite the distance between Hope and Darlington. Monday, after our Quarterly Meeting, proved cold and stormy, in fact, a very dreary day, and we wished to retain our lively and agreeable guest; but no, he "had engagements, and must be home." If the worst came to the worst, he "could stop in Cavan," and off he went. And our hearts ached to see the poor old gentleman, with nothing but a thin cloak around him, clamber into his buggy, poorly provided with wraps, and whip off his unwilling old horse on his toilsome journey.

The Rev. Alexander Hardie, A.M., Moral Governor of the Stanstead Wesleyan College, was an inmate in Father Corson's family during the whole of his collegiate course, and had enjoyed the maternal care of Mrs. Corson the while. I had often heard him and his brother Robert, now a legal practitioner in the United States, tell stories by the hour, during their vacation visits at their father's house, of their student life at " Father Corson's." Stories, by the way, which showed that with the characteristic mischievousness of youth, the young men sometimes played practical jokes on the dear, simple-minded, unsuspecting old gentleman, more, I could believe, out of fond familiarity with him than anything else, knowing how forgiving and boylike he was himself. I say, because of this, I wrote Mr. Hardie for some reminiscences of that period. Unhappily my letter overtook him from home, whence he had been banished for months by the stern necessity of canvassing for subscriptions to discharge a most burdensome debt on the institution with which he stands connected, and, therefore, having neither leisure nor conveniences for recalling and writing out the memories of those privileged and happy days as he could have desired, still, what I will give of his letter will be most pertinent to the object I have in view.

Mr. Hardie says, "I am sorry I cannot take the time to give an outline of dear Father Corson's character as it was seen by us. He was a man of great physical and mental vigour, and possessed a strong emotional nature. He acted upon the apostolic injunction, 'Not slothful in business, fervent in spirit, serving the Lord.' * * * * His prayers were exceedingly brief, but comprehensive. He often used these words, 'O Lord, help us to get good, to be good, and to do good.'"*

"As a rapid reader he had few superiors. His knowledge of books was somewhat extensive. He was well up on the old Calvinistic contentions. He never wearied in explaining to us the five points of difference between us and our Presbyterian brethren. His knowledge of Methodist theology was both extensive and accurate for one of his opportunities.

"He wasted no time. Diligence was, I think, the most prominent feature in his character. He was a remarkable man. In his case, 'the fly in the pot of ointment' was his apparent avidity for small gains.

"Of course you have heard about his sermon on 'Feed my lambs,' the characteristic feature of which was the contrast between the hog and the sheep, the amusing point being: The swine when he goes to rest at night, just rolls over and goes to sleep; but the sheep goes down upon his knees before he goes to rest!

* The brevity and comprehensiveness of his prayers were often exemplified when called upon to open or close the Conference with prayer; while often, in doing the latter, he has raised a smile upon the countenances of his brethren, by falling suddenly on his knees, and hurriedly uttering the prayer, "O Lord, forgive our sins! Bless the President! Bless the Conference! Bless the Queen! Bless and save us all, for Jesus Christ's sake! Amen."—ED.

"He took a great interest in young preachers. His heart really yearned towards us. He would do almost anything for us. For our benefit he spared no pains in writing out outlines of sermons. These were liberally bestowed upon young preachers. * * * * * *

"Of Father Corson I must say that he feared neither storms, nor hard journeys, nor hard fare, nor hard service for the cause of Christ. He was grandly loyal to the Church. He was willing to stand at any post on the walls of our Methodist Zion. He was shrewd, and yet possessed a vast amount of courage. I saw him only in his old age. I am sure that in his prime he was a princely man, and belonged to the flying artillery of the Church. He was by nature a frontier man."

There are some preachers, I am sure, who will smile at the idea of Father Corson being a teacher of Homiletics to students who had enjoyed liberal advantages, and I was quite inclined to do the same, till I opened and perused two of the old preacher's MS. sermon books, or rather outlines of sermons which have fallen into my hands with other relics of him, upon the perusal of which I was struck with the happy selection of texts and their just analysis by him. Some, if not all of these, I will furnish in an appendix, if the publisher can afford me space. They are in the old-fashioned *Methodical* style, and demonstrate that the "Illiterate Methodist Preachers," as they were once derisively called, knew "whereof they affirmed."

Father Corson was a very ready man. It was impossible to take him at a disadvantage for an impromptu speech on the platform of a popular meeting for any imaginable subject, among ourselves or other denominations. Some of these latter were of the number of our "small friends;"

but among them Father Corson never feared to lift up his head, and he always gave them, *very good naturedly*, "tit" for any "tats" they had dealt out to the Methodists, whether overt or covert ones. The students at the college knew his readiness, and the usually amusing character of his spontaneous sallies; and it was a very common thing for them to call for "Father Corson" after an audience had been satisfied to repletion with the elaborate orations of men of high reputation, and he never failed to bring down the house. And, unlike most old men, he never wearied by prolixity—five, or ten minutes, at the longest, was all he ever occupied, and sometimes not more than two or three. He gave them as much in that time as they ever got in their lives from anybody else, I will be bound for it. Shall I give only one specimen that occurs to me? When called upon late at a Missionary Meeting, he said, "Mr. Chairman, in one of my Circuits, I went one day to a house, and found one of the children with his head tied up. I said to his mother, What is the matter with Billy? 'Ob,' says she, 'he has got the information in his eyes!' Now, Mr. Chairman, we have had a good deal of *information* to-night, and you will not need much more from me, &c." But the *information* he gave, although in tit-bits, was always interesting and valuable.

I do not think there was a person in Cobourg but what esteemed and loved Father Corson. A highly cultivated gentleman, who lived in his immediate vicinity in that town, though declining to write anything at large about him, on the ground of not being enough acquainted with him, albeit he is a most accomplished writer, says, "I knew him as a good, simple-hearted, eccentric man, whom I held in respect for his abundant labours in the service of Christ."

During his long residence of fifteen years at Cobourg, Father Corson ever and anon dropped a letter to the *Guardian*, informing us of his whereabouts, his doings (how many sermons he had preached, how many books he had read, &c.), his views of our Connexional prospects, and his great interest therein. These, if we had time to make the search for them, would be found of great interest and value, too, in illustrating our theme. In default of this, I venture to present a letter from the old pilgrim directed to myself, and interesting to me as the last I ever received from him. It is dated Cobourg, March 22, 1873, and bears the usual impress of his letters. It will speak for itself in all respects :—

"DEAR BROTHER,—In writing to you I may not be able to help your book, but I can give information that will cheer your heart. We have been nearly fifteen years in Cobourg. It was here our youngest son finished his education, and subsequently got his profession.

"As I keep a short journal, I will give you a few items, embracing my ministerial labours since I have been in Cobourg :—Preached 480 sermons, read 500 books, wrote 300 sketches, and 600 letters, and made 2,000 religious visits.

"The improvements on the Cobourg District are as follows :—Built thirty-two churches and parsonages. We have succeeded in sweeping off the debt on the college, and in getting $90,000 subscribed as an endowment. All this has been done within the last fifteen years. And lastly, but not least, we are blessed with a gracious revival of religion in Cobourg. Thank God, it is getting into the college! Our Conference students work well.

"Yours as ever,

"ROBERT CORSON."

One of his last letters to the *Guardian*, given below, will furnish all the information required relative to the period we are now illustrating.—It was written so lately as November 20, 1864. It is now laid before the reader. In addressing the Editor of the *Guardian*, he says:—

"DEAR BRO.,—Some six months since I decided to go to New York and Philadelphia. In so doing I could see my sons in New York, and attend the General Conference in Philadelphia. If you think proper you can give publicity to the following narrative; you are at liberty to make any alteration you may deem necessary.

"It was in May last I left Cobourg for New York. While waiting for the boat, an aged man wished to give me some information in reference to the expenses in crossing the lake; in doing so, he took the name of God in vain; when I reproved him he made an apology and offered up a short prayer for me.

"At 5 p.m. we were in the United States. We took the cars and arrived at Albany next morning. We then took the boat, as we could have more reading, observation, and conversation. I soon got into conversation with a lady from Kentucky. She was a member of the Baptist Church, but a strong believer in slavery. She said they owned a number of slaves, and they were good, as they were Methodists; the arguments she brought to prove her doctrine were, first, we read of hewers of wood and drawers of water; secondly, the little white children would always drive little negroes. I asked her if she had read Uncle Tom's Cabin; she said it was a miserable affair.

"I had a conversation with a Baptist Elder from Vermont; he was a man of extensive information, a strong abolitionist, and had been favoured with a good revival in his church.

We arrived at New York. Soon found myself in East Broadway. Met Dr. William with a smiling face, glad to see his father. I had but little opportunity of talking to him, he had so many calls to visit the sick; next morning I took the cars for Philadelphia. In passing through New Jersey I had some serious reflections: my parents had their birth and education there; came to this country more than seventy years ago, when Canada was a wilderness; in Canada they ended their days; only five of their children out of twelve survive.

"In passing through Pennsylvania I got into conversation with an aged Quaker; he said the war was an extraordinary war, and the Quakers *did fight in this war*, as they were abolitionists. I soon found myself in a comfortable hotel among a lot of Methodist preachers, who were members of the General Conference. In a few minutes I was in the midst of a large body of ministers assembled at their General Conference; they were fine in their appearance, plain in their dress, and quite above mediocrity in talent; I was glad to hear the old veterans contend for the ancient landmarks. As a body of ministers, I found them loyal to their country, and friends of the oppressed. I arrived at Philadelphia on Wednesday, the same evening I heard Bishop J. T. Peck, D.D., preach a powerful sermon. On Thursday I attended the General Conference in the forenoon, in the afternoon I was invited to attend a class-meeting; it was a refreshing time. I learned that the Methodists were much the largest body in Philadelphia, it is said that they number forty congregations. On Friday I left for New York; arrived safe in the evening. I found my youngest son, Adam Clark, who had arrived safe from Canada. I also met Dr. Kennedy and Rev. John Keagy, from Canada. On

Saturday Dr. William requested Adam to take his horse and carriage and give his father a drive through the great city. On Sabbath morning Adam accompanied me to the following places of worship: First, to Brooklyn to hear the celebrated Ward Beecher. He is a great man; calls a great congregation, and I trust is doing a great amount of good. At 3 p.m. I attended a Methodist congregation in Allen-street, the Rev. Mr. Roach, the minister. Bro. Roach requested me to preach, but I refused, as I had a desire to hear a New York preacher; he preached a plain, practical sermon. I called on Dr. and Mrs. Palmer; they were not long from England. Mrs. Palmer brought a cloak formerly worn by Mrs. Fletcher, presented to Mrs. Palmer as a token of respect. We rejoiced and wept together, prayed and parted. I had a desire to go to John-street Church, where the first Methodist Society was formed in America. I was a little late; the pastor had commenced giving out the first hymn; a gentleman ascended the pulpit and spoke to the preacher in a low tone of voice; the preacher came to me and asked me if I were a minister. I said I was an old Wesleyan from Canada; he then asked me to preach for him; I consented and had a pretty good time; at the close a number shook me by the hand. On Monday morning Dr. Adam accompanied me to the cars; I gave him a dollar and a little good advice, and we parted.* On Wednesday I was in Cobourg, and found all well.

"I stopped at home a few days; worked in my garden; planted five bushels of potatoes, and then made my way to Conference. Here I met my old brethren who laboured with me when roads were bad, rides long, and

* In making the change, Adam was found in debt a dollar; and the father in his simplicity gave it him.

little pay. We met Brother Whiting; we succeeded in getting him into the work some thirty-eight years ago. He has been faithful and successful in winning souls to Christ. Bro. W. retired from the work of an itinerant. There is a great contrast between this Conference and the one we attended forty years ago. Our itinerants then numbered thirty-six, now more than five hundred. We have a number of young men who bid fair to be useful and successful ministers. At this Conference I met W. Musgrove, who boarded with me two years; he has been bereft of his parents; His father was an old minister, and died at his post. William has the charge of the surviving family; he is also Superintendent of a Circuit, and stands high as a preacher and pastor.

"I remained at home a short time. We made an effort to get to Newburgh, as Mrs. C. had a desire to see her aged parents. We stopped at Frankford with Mr. Jenkins, where we enjoyed the society of our grand-daughter. The next day arrived at Napanee; here we stopped for a night with an old friend and Brother, Dr. Grange. We took him into the Church some twenty years ago, then an orphan boy; now he is an acceptable local preacher, and has a good practice as a physician.

"On Saturday we arrived at Newburgh; I was quite ill; a little better on Sabbath; tried to preach to my old friends. We returned to Cobourg—remained a few days— took the cars, and found myself at the Peterboro' camp-meeting; here I found old friends; the ground was well prepared; the order good; a notice as we entered the ground 'no smoking or talking in time of service.' I found a home at Brother W's. At this camp-meeting we found a chapel, parsonage, splendid tents, and lamps hung by the side of the trees which lighted the encampment. At this meeting I had a conversation with J. R. Armstrong, Esq., formerly a merchant in Toronto. At his house the preachers had a home. I asked him his age; he said seventy-seven, and a member of the Methodist Church more than sixty-five years. I was glad to see him in the prayer-meetings encouraging poor sinners to seek salvation through Christ. At this meeting I heard seven sermons; I also heard poor sinners cry for mercy; they did not cry in vain. After remaining a part of four days I returned to Cobourg, and commenced a journey to Prince Albert. We arrived at our son's on Saturday; preached on Sabbath morning; heard W. Washington in the evening; he is a young man of promise. Thirty-six years are gone since I came to this place as a Missionary. The amount of inhabitants was then small, some four families of whites, and a hundred Indians; the Indians are removed, and the population in the same locality is two thousand, embracing four villages; there are four churches, the Wesleyans the largest.

"When I commenced my labours in the township of Reach, thirty-six years ago, I found a home at Bro. A. Hurd's, and his house is a home for the ministers at the present; he is now in his seventy-fifth year; has held the offices of leader and steward more than thirty-six years. We returned home by the way of Markham; stopped a night with our daughter-in-law, Nancy Corson; her husband has gone to the land of gold.

"We found ourselves again in Cobourg; I remained in Cobourg a few days, attended some appointments, and again commenced my journey for Cainsville, a village near Brantford. I stopped at Bro. Keagey's near Dundas, here I have had a home for years, and here is a family of orphans, they have been bereft of both parents; they have plenty of the world, and the six surviving children are pious; their eldest brother is a graduate of Victoria College, and is in the work of the ministery, and a sister is married to a Wesleyan minister. It was Saturday in the afternoon when I stopped; they pressed me to stop over Sabbath. I made a special effort and arrived at Brother Isaac Horning's late in the evening. Sister Horning is the daughter of Father Howell who was virtually the founder of Methodism in Jersey Settlement some sixty years since. It is said that more than sixty of his children and grand children are members of the Wesleyan Church. On Sunday morning I heard Bro. Kennedy Creighton preach a stirring sermon in Jerseyville in their new brick church. I had to preach in the evening. Some forty years ago I was appointed to preach to the people in this locality; here my family resided, and in this place we found many warm frinds.

"On Monday I passed through Cainsville. Attended a little business matter with Bro. Pearson. Passed through Harrisburg. Called on Joseph Larison, who is a first cousin and an old Methodist, I also called on J. Larison who was very ill; he was trying to trust in Christ for salvation. I tarried over night with C. Nixon—his wife is my niece; they are both members of the Methodist Church.

"Tuesday, passed through Preston; dined with my old, tried friend, Adam Snider. On Tuesday evening stopped in Guelph with Brother Kelly; here I felt at home. We had the privilege of attending Brother Carroll's first lovefeast. This love-feast was profitable, and called to mind the first time I saw Brother Carroll, nearly forty years ago at a camp-meeting on Yonge-street. He was then called 'the praying-boy.' At nineteen he took the field as an itinerant,

10

and I am glad to learn that he is labouring faithfully and successfully in Guelph.

"Wednesday, I passed through Circuits where I had laboured in former years; I arrived at Brampton in the evening. Stopped over night with my eldest son, John Wesley; here I formed a small society some thirty-three years ago. Some have joined the Church above; others are on their way to heaven. Dr. John had a number of calls during my short stay. I learn he is an acceptable local preacher; my prayer is that he may do well. On Thursday I dined with Brother Morrow, and tarried for the night with my old friend Thomas Lackey, near the city.

"On Friday I passed through Toronto, purchased a few books; preached in Canton Circuit; found myself in Cobourg on Monday, August 24th. Four of my old friends are to board with me while attending college; a few more arrived, and our family enlarged.

"On the 21st of September I received a telegram from my son, William Corson, of New York, the words are as follow: 'Adam ill, recovery improbable, come immediately!' We felt the shock—wept and prayed, took the boat for Rochester, the following morning arrived at New York. Adam had succeeded in getting a situation in a military hospital; was succeding well, but was caught in a shower of rain, took cold and was taken with typhoid fever. The hospital was located some nine miles from the city. His brother attended him night and day; two of the best physicians in New York were called; but his brother, Dr. William, was discouraged and exhausted. However, Adam was better both in mind and body. Brother Hubler, the pastor of Forsyth-street had just left, Adam spoke of his visit in high terms. I stopped a night and part of a day;

my son gave me leave to return home. They seemed glad to see their father in time of trouble.

"On Saturday I arrived safe in Cobourg, and attended a camp-meeting in Percy. It commenced the 1st of October. It was rather wet, but the friends had erected noble tents, and the meeting was attended with a great amount of good.

"I will now give you a short account of my labours for the last six months past:—

"Travelled 2,000 miles by railroad, and 2,000 with my own conveyance; preached fifty-one sermons; read sixteen books; wrote thirty letters and four sketches. I am in the seventy-eighth year of my age.

"I remain yours as ever,
"ROBERT CORSON."

One thing must strike every person who reads the above letter and all other journals of his travels, namely, how much he kept to the old method of conveyance to the last. Instead of availing himself of stage and steamboat, and railways, he drove his own old horse and rode in his own carriage, taking short-cuts across the country, making "stages" from one friend's house to another, stopping for breakfast, dinner, tea, or lodging, as the case required, and to "bate" his horse, as in the early days, reading, singing, and praying at every place, and very likely preaching at night. Thus it was that the first itinerants of the country were constantly exercising their ministry and doing good. And, as far as possible, why should not their successors continue to do the same?

I do not know that I can command any more material to illustrate his manner of life at Cobourg, or that any more is required. One day was the pattern of another. They were all formed on the model of Wesley's hymn:

"Our days are spent in doing good,
Our nights in praise and prayer."

I have not been directly informed of the reason, but I suspect increasing age and infirmity were the causes, for his leaving Cobourg. His son Adam had got his profession and was practising in the United States. He felt no doubt that neither he nor his wife were any longer equal to that unwearied service of others which had employed them for the previous fifteen years.

2. *From his return to Cainsville till the death of his second wife, in 1877.*

The reader will remember that Mr. Corson acquired a little property while labouring on the Cainsville Circuit, built a house and located in that village, which he seems to have considered as pre-eminently his *home*, especially since his son, Dr. William C. Corson, who regarded his father most affectionately, had gone to reside in the adjacent town, now city, of Brantford. He alludes to the transition in the few following words:—"In 1872, we removed to Cainsville. We found old friends, as this was one of our former Circuits. But my health failed, and I made my will and prepared to die. My son William attended me, and succeeded in arresting my disease."

It was a merciful providence that just at that time he should have had so near him one able to render medical skill with filial assiduity and tenderness. But the above was not his only attack, for he was forced to make another entry in his "sketch" similar to the one given above. He resumes, "In

1875 I was again brought low with inflammation of the lungs; but I am now quite better, and enabled to visit and preach a little." That entry was made after 1875, when he must have been eighty-two or eighty-three years of age. Yet he felt it his duty still to "visit and preach," and seems to have been disappointed that he could not do it as aforetime.

Since writing the above, I find Father Corson did perform considerable labour after going to Cainsville, and for a little time as a regular supply. Dr. William, in a letter received the other day, gives me the following particulars:—
"Father was uncommonly active and laborious in preaching up to the time of his last sickness—the last year of his life. About three years before his death, the junior preacher of the Cainsville Circuit was obliged by failure in health to leave his work, and father immediately took up his appointments, preaching with much of the animation of his earlier years in the ministry. In his humorous way, he gave it out that he was 'the young preacher on the circuit,' though at the time he had passed four score years! The Rev. Mr. Willoughby, his last pastor, mentioned, only a day or two ago, his fidelity in attendance on prayer and class-meetings, &c."

His periods of enforced inactivity left his still active mind leisure to work; and he employed that leisure in transferring to paper, for the good of others, memories and reflections of a most interesting character. They are in his usual sententious style, and as follows:—

"I will now give a sketch of our Methodist Church in Canada for the *fifty-seven* years," he must mean of its separate existence, since dismemberment from the parent Church in the States. "Our Methodism was planted in

Canada by preachers from the United States, and we were distinguished as Episcopals. When I united with the Methodists there were only *twelve* chapels, some *fifteen* itinerants, and a little more than *three thousand* members in the Province.

"In 1824 we had our first Canadian Annual Conference. It was afterwards decided that we should ask the General Conference of the United States to let us off as an Independent Connexion. In 1828 we became independent. We engaged" (only by implication) "to retain our name and usages as Episcopal Methodists. We elected *five* different ministers to become Bishop,* viz., Hedding, Bangs, Cookman, Stratton, and Fisk, but they all refused. We then made an offer to join the British Conference, as this was a British Province and our English Methodists the oldest. This union was ratified in 1833. We had then some sixty preachers in the Conference, and only one voted against the union.

"In getting our union with the British Conference, we adopted their usage with regard to local preachers. No more local preachers were to be ordained. This made dissatisfaction among some of our local brethren and their friends. We were also charged with changing our politics and becoming Tories. In 1835 a superannuated preacher and three local elders met and set apart a local elder by imposition of hands, to presid over their body as a General Superintendent or Bishop. Thus it was said the old church was resuscitated. There was trouble: both churches claimed the chapels. Lawsuit succeeded lawsuit, and some of our preachers were curtailed in their allowances.

"In 1840 there was a misunderstanding between the

* I suppose not more than three of these came to the actual ballot, Bangs, Fisk and Stratton.

English Conference and ours. The English thought it would be better to dissolve the union; and dissolved it was. We were in hopes that the Episcopals would unite again with us; but they were partial to their Church government, and we had become partial to ours.

"In 1846 we sent a delegation to England. The English Conference gave us a better union than the first. It was felt and seen there were too many bodies of Methodists to prosper. In 1847 our union went into operation. We put Presiding Elders on Circuits and Stations; and, in 1858, we made the office of chairman elective. Since our re-union with the English Conference, we have had a great measure of prosperity. Our net increase for the last twenty-seven years is more than 50,000 Church members, and our country is studded with churches.

"Since our union has worked so well, there has been an effort to unite all the Methodist bodies in one. However, the union between us and the English Conference has been dissolved, but with the best of feelings on both sides. Our Conference became so large we could not manage it; and we anticipated a union with the New Connexion. Our hopes have been realized. Some 7,000 Church members and more than 100 itinerants have united with us and we with them. The union, thus far, has been a success. Our total number of members in three Conferences: namely, *London*, *Toronto*, and *Montreal*, is 85,779.

"The other Methodist bodies number as follows:—

Episcopal Methodists	23,012
Primitive Methodists, (say)	7,000
Bible Christians, (say)	4,000
The German Methodists, (say)	6,000
Coloured Methodists, (say)	1,000
Making the smaller bodies, in all	41,012

"We have formed a union with our Wesleyan brethren in the Eastern Provinces. We adopted the American system in the matter of Annual Conferences, with a General Conference once in four YEARS.

"*I will now make a few brief remarks on our Methodism in 1817, and our Methodism in 1875.*

"Our old Methodism was a great success. The preachers were plain, self-denying men; their salaries small, their labours hard (some twelve appointments a week), the preacher always meeting the class after preaching.

"There was not as much anxiety manifested about salary then, as now. I remember *Isaac B. Smith*, a great preacher,—we have no greater now. He only received $50 for the year—had a large family,* and had to ride fifty miles to get to see that family. Then we had but little time to study. I have read on horseback, to my comfort.

"*Their manner in preaching* was to name the text, a short introduction, mention their divisions, and preach forty-five or fifty minutes, speaking louder and louder to the close, the congregation often weeping in every part of the house, especially in times of revival.

"Yet we had more Church trials" (courts of inquiry, he means) "in those days. A preacher who united with us knew our Rules, as they were read in public, and remarks made thereon. We had no special services as we have at the present,"—there being no time to hold them.

"*The preaching at the present time* is more like reading an essay—divisions are not named—but little weeping—a

---

* Strange that sons who witnessed such hardships should have adopted their father's calling; but they did, *four*, if not six of them, becoming preachers, and a daughter a preacher's wife.

long prayer. At times the preacher speaks loud, and then so low that a part of the congregation cannot hear him. But we have at the present time some powerful preachers, holy men, who are successful—ministers that labour night and day to win souls.

"The special services are a great blessing to the Church. Young preachers are heard, and old preachers are revived. Our lay brethren take a fresh start for the Kingdom.

"Then, our Sabbath Schools and Bible Classes are an acquisition to our Church.

"The cause of Temperance has been advanced by our ministry. Our President" (the Rev. Dr. J. A. Williams, then President of the London Annual Conference) "is a great Temperance preacher.

"*I will now make a few remarks in reference to my labours:—*

"The *first eight years:* My first Circuit, *Westminster*. No chapels. Our salaries, only $250 for two preachers with families. Now we have eleven Circuits, and six Stations within the bounds of the old Circuit.

"My next Circuit was *Dumfries*. This was a two weeks' Circuit for one preacher. Now we have *nine* Circuits within the limits of the old Circuit.

The next Circuit I shall name is *Long-Point*. Two preachers with families. Salary for both, $300. Now there are *sixteen* Circuits within the bounds of the old Long-Point Circuit.

"The next I shall name is *Whitby*. No chapel. One preacher. Now ten Circuits. The above-named Circuits are in connection with our Canadian Church.

"Other bodies of Methodists have Circuits organized in the same localities. My average amount of salary during

10*

the *thirty-six* years of my itinerant life was $252 per annum. This embraced children's allowance, table expenses, horse-keep, and fuel," as well as quarterage.

There are many, perhaps, who will think that the above details are dry and prosaic; but I think there are many who rightly judge them to be of great interest and significance. They embody memories and lessons for the collective ministry of the Church, and the whole Church itself, of great value; but they are adapted to set forth the man we have sought to portray as most laborious and self-denying through the whole of his active life, and active-minded and thoughtful when no longer capable of much bodily activity. And they are interesting for the artlessness of the style, and as being the last work of his preserved to us.

I am glad I have the means of presenting, at least, one scene adapted to present the position and feelings of the old patriarch in the midst of the people among whom he had chosen to end his days.

There is a gifted, devoted local preacher, as tireless in every good word and work, as Mr. Corson was, residing at Brantford, who has been in the habit of going to Cainsville, from time to time, to preach. He had the thoughtful kindness to address a letter to me relative to a certain interview between himself and Father Corson in the place of the latter's residence :—

"Brantford, Dec. 30th, 1878.

"MY DEAR DR. CARROLL,—I perceive from the *Guardian* that you are writing a memoir of the late Father Corson; and you request any one to write you what they may know about him. Please just allow me to say: the last five or six times in my appointments at Cainsville he sat at my left hand. The last time, the 17th of March,

1878. My subject on that morning was Hezekiah's sickness and recovery; my text 38th chap. Isaiah, verses 18, 19. In winding up my subject I observed a number of aged persons in the congregation. In addressing them I said, God requires of us, my aged friends, that we consider the past; hence to Israel, he said, 'Thou shalt remember all the way which the Lord thy God led thee these forty years in the wilderness,' &c. Permit me to ask how have you filled up your days? What have you done worthy of life? What have you tried to do? Is the world better for your having lived in it? The Bible says, 'The hoary head is a crown of glory if it be found in the way of righteousness;' if not, as Jay says, 'Instead of a crown it will be a fools' cap.' 'The wicked will rise to shame and everlasting contempt.' And then pointing to Father Corson I said, 'Look at my venerable friend, his hoary head is a crown of glory, it is found in the way of righteousness.' And then addressing him I said, Your salvation is nearer than when you first believed; and God says, 'I remember thee, the kindness of thy youth, the love of thine espousals when thou wentest after me in the wilderness. Israel was then holiness to the Lord, and the first fruits of his increase.' And then, stepping to him and laying my hand on his head I said, 'Permit me to bless you my friend, I gaze upon you with deep interest, you will soon see the King in his beauty, and rest in the quiet of the skies; and then, following the example of Billy Dawson with Mr. Lessey, I repeated the following stanza:—

> Through all the changing scenes of life,
> Thy servant, Lord, attend;
> And oh, his life of mercy crown
> With a triumphant end!'

And the congregation said, 'Amen!' He, referring to this service afterwards, said, 'It was a second ordination.' Well, his end you know was quietness and assurance forever. Well Dr., time is shaking us by the hand, and we shall have to put off this our tabernacle. What a mercy to have the hope of the Gospel that when absent from the body, we may be present with the Lord—we must needs die—'We are to the margin come and we expect to die.' May our end be glorious through our Lord, Jesus Christ! Amen.

"I am, affectionately yours,

"WM. BELLAMY."

3. *From the death of the second Mrs. Corson in 1877, to his own death in 1878.*

The loss of his second partner was a serious blow to Father Corson. A more than usually strong and painstaking woman, a score of years younger than himself, and without any children of her own to occupy her time and attention, and without any children of any ones, after his son Adam grew up and went forth to do for himself. She devoted her undivided care to make the old age of her husband comfortable. But, young and strong as she was compared with him, she failed and fell before her much-loved husband, going before, from the evils to come, and escaping the loneliness of widowhood.

I have no other means of illustrating this crisis in his history than that of furnishing the well-written obituary of Mrs. Corson, composed by the Rev. Wm. Willoughby, the pastor of both husband and wife at the time.

"AMY CORSON."

"Mrs. Corson, the beloved wife of Rev. Robert Corson (or, as he is usually called, 'Father Corson'), was born near

Belleville, 1814, and died at Cainsville, December 19th, 1877. Under the faithful ministry of the word, by the late Rev. Cyrus R. Allison, she was enabled to 'believe with a heart unto righteousness,' or justification, in 1840, and having obtained help of the Lord, she was enabled to walk henceforth in the fear of God and the light of his countenance. She was united in marriage to Rev. R. Corson in 1846, and on the morning of their marriage started for their new Circuit, about two hundred miles distant, in the west, leaving the home of her youth, and all the cherished associations of early life, to enter upon the arduous and self-denying duties of an itinerant Methodist preacher's wife, with all its responsibilities and cares. What rendered the situation still more peculiar, she was Mr. Corson's second wife, and had immediate charge of his dear little Adam, then four years old; and the next eldest, who was absent at school most of his time, was equally cared for and loved by their adopted mother, on his periodical visits, in times of vacation and holidays. This was William, who is now Dr. Corson of Brantford. Thus did she with a mother's care, devotion, and love, labour to train up in the 'nurture and admonition of the Lord' those over whom the providence of God had placed her, whose own mother was a saint in heaven. In the absence of her husband in his long rounds of Circuit work, she never neglected the family altar, nor any of the duties of a godly household. Thus did she live and labour to train her youthful charge for heaven, and cherish in their young hearts those principles of piety and godliness which had been previously sown there, by her who was now at home with God. Nor was she disappointed, as she had ample satisfaction of witnessing the developing of upright prin-

ciple, grow to healthy and vigorous Christian manhood in
those who were the subjects of her early charge. The elder
of these is Dr. William Corson of Brantford, who holds a
highly respectable position there in the medical profession,
nor is he ashamed to be the son of an old-fashioned Methodist preacher, nor to be a loyal and devoted member of the
Methodist Church, and an office-bearer in connection with
the Wellington St. Methodist Church in Brantford. The
younger, who was the late Dr. A. Clarke Corson, of New
York, who won his way to high position and affluence by
earnest and successful study, and by exalted uprightness
of moral character, 'died in the Lord' some two or three
years ago, and is now, in Abraham's bosom.' Mrs. Corson
was in this place (Cainsville) a universal favourite: she
was loved by all, young and old, both in the Church and
outside of it. Seldom have we known an instance of any
who have won the hearts of all as she did. And she
had the comfort of having many of those friends with her
in her protracted and severe suffering, especially her own
sister, Mrs. Phillips, who with true sisterly love, lingered
around her bed like a guardian angel, doing everything that
love could suggest for the comfort of the dear sufferer till
released by the messenger that called her home. The
constant attention of Dr. and Mrs. Corson, his estimable
wife, their sympathy and solicitude for their suffering relative, was just what it ought to be in sanctified humanity;
like the Master's it was lovely, touching, and beautiful.
Our dear sister bore her protracted and severe sufferings
with unfaltering patience; she had learned the doctrine of
St. James, 'Let patience have her perfect work that ye
may be perfect and entire, wanting nothing;' and with
unwavering faith she had given her case into the hands of

her precious Redeemer. In the midst of intense suffering she could say, 'My Father's will be done.' 'He is too wise to err, and too good to be unkind.' The only wish she had to live was for the sake of her aged and venerable husband, that she might be permitted to smooth his path, and solace his heart in his downward passage to the tomb. But it pleased the good Master to take her first, while he still lingers on the shore, waiting with confident and joyous hope for the King to say, 'Come up higher,' 'Enter into my joy, and sit down on my throne.' As the pilgrimage of life drew near its close, she looked forward with intense interest and delight to her heavenly home, and sometimes she feared she was too anxious to see the struggle ended. But she could fully adopt the Christian poet's theme,—

"'Close by thy side still may I keep,
Howe'er life's varying current flow;
With steadfast eye mark every step,
And follow thee where'er thou go.'

"A short time before her decease she anxiously desired to receive the Lord's Supper, which she did with her aged husband and sister, and a few select friends, when a hallowed influence rested on all present, while her soul seemed to be filled with peace and love divine. She felt indeed that nothing could separate her from the love of her Saviour. She felt that perfect love could cast out all fear, and banish every doubt and cloud from her mind forever. Thus the love of life and dread of death were entirey removed, and joyously could she say,—

"'Tis love that drives my chariot-wheels
And death must yield to love.'

"At length the hour of release came, and calm, clear,

and beautiful was the triumph of her faith: death was conquered and 'mortality swallowed up of life.' A few moments before she passed away she whispered to her weeping sister, 'I'm near home now.' Farewell. Fare thee well, sweet spirit, thou art safe at home, ' to be forever with the Lord.'

> "' O ! that is a world of changeless bliss,
> Inviting our flight from the woes of this:
> Where saints shall possess a glorious share,
> Then, O my God, I long to be there.'
> "W. WILLOUGHBY."

After his second wife was decently under the ground he left his now solitary home, and accompanied his excellent and reverentially affectionate son, Dr. W. C. Corson, to his comfortable residence in the city of Brantford, where Mrs. Dr. Corson received him and waited on him during the almost a year which intervened between the time he laid his Amy in the dust until he himself "returned to the dust as it was." His happiness, even to playfulness, was greatly promoted by the presence and playful attentions and companionship of his two beautiful and affectionate grandchildren, girl and boy, of that family. He and they seemed to find the complements of themselves in each other. Indeed it was hard to say which was the more childishly sportive, they or he. He entered into all their playful liberties with him (dressing him up in fantastic forms) with all the innocent glee of a child. The attentions he received from surrounding friends, both old and new, were at once honourable to them and very grateful to his own feelings and those of his children, dotingly fond as they were of their dear honoured parent.

He had never missed a Conference a single year since 1824 to 1877, that is for fifth-three long laborious years; and he looked forward with fond anticipation to the session of the *London Annual Conference* to be holden in the town of St. Thomas in the month of June, 1878, to commence on the first Wednesday, and prepared for it as usual, by providing himself with another suit of black clothes, that he might be in beseeming clerical attire. But his son and physician, with all his other friends, dissuaded him from it, perceiving that his weakness and infirmities disqualified him for the undertaking. To this conclusion he was at last forced to come himself, and he reluctantly gave up the fondly cherished project, and had to content himself with a fraternal message to his brethren. To a person so active in mind and body as he always had been, and so devotedly absorbed in Connexional interests and doings, this was, no doubt, a great sacrifice and a great trial: to be "laid by for God," as the Rev. Joseph Alien phrases it, being so much harder than being "employed for him," to any Christian person, especially to one constituted as he was. But he found the grace, when needed, which made him in all things "more than conqueror through him that loved him, and gave himself for him." He was buried in the unworn suit. I am glad that I can furnish an accurate and appreciative account of his LAST HOURS from one who was at once his *son*, his *physician*, and his *host*, all in one. Dr. William Case Corson writes on that subject as follows:—

"Towards the end of life our good father exemplified the patience and cheerfulness in affliction which a faith that leans hourly upon Christ only can bestow. When perceiving that his earthly course was nearly run, he contemplated the close of life with a serenity and composure worthy of a Christian hero who had fought and won many victories in the service of his Master. For days, and sometimes for weeks together, when his mind wandered and ideas became confused, his thoughts travelled back into his life work, and in imagination he was engaged in ministerial duties. No matter how much his mind wandered he always led, however, in our family devotions with willingness and fervour. At other times he sank into a drowsy stupor from which he would emerge like one raised from death to life to give expression to some unusually quaint and happy thoughts like the fitful gleam of an expiring flame. It was in one of these states of lethargy one bright day in October, 1878, that he sank into that last sleep which knows no waking, while his redeemed spirit soared to that world of unclouded splendour about which he had thought and talked so much while on earth. His brethren in the ministry, most of whom had known and revered him for long years, assembled at his funeral, and with loving hands bore his remains to their final resting place in the old cemetery in Brantford, where they lie peacefully only a few rods from the grave of one who had been many years previously his colleague, the Rev. Thomas Fawcett. 'They were lovely and pleasant in their lives, and in death they were not divided.'

"On the following Sabbath evening the Rev. J. B. Clarkson, who had visited and prayed with him in his last illness, preached a memorial discourse in which his life and labours were touchingly reviewed.

"A memorial granite shaft has been placed over his grave by his grateful children, the simple inscription upon which concludes with the memorable words of St. Paul, 'IN

LABOURS MORE ABUNDANT.'" The precise date of his death was October 8th, 1878.

N.B.—Anything else which may arrive in relation to the dear departed, or anything now available, the product of his own mind, for which the covers of the book may afford space, will have to be relegated to an *Addenda* or *Appendix*.

FINIS.

APPENDIX.

"OUR MOTHER."

It is said that the last word most frequently whispered by dying soldiers in hospital, or on the battle field, is "Mother." And there is a reason. More than any earthly being, she stamps upon them the noblest qualities to prepare them for being honoured in both worlds. If they are either brave, or gentle, or good, they probably owe it to her whose memory is so dear. And the children of a Christian mother like ours, after mourning her loss for long years, may easily invest her likeness with beauties which strangers could never see. Yet we will try to be both loving and truthful. The "Pen Portrait," which we have elsewhere given of our father, would hardly be complete without a corresponding sketch of the faithful partner who, for the first twenty years of his ministry, shared in all his sufferings and joys:—

In the backwoods of Canada, in those days, an efficient "minister's wife" was a real treasure. Her trials and labours were very great. In a quiet way, she tried to keep one end of an immense Circuit alive, while her husband travelled over the rest. There is a story told of a New York merchant, who lived so far from the city, that he concluded to move to a point nearer, that, as he said, he might "get acquainted with his wife and children." Our father had a like experience. On his earliest Circuit, as we sadly remember, he managed, by travelling half the last night, to see his family at first for two, and finally for four, days in four weeks.

A woman who could worthily occupy a Methodist parsonage was in special demand. She needed to be a sympathizing companion, a tidy housekeeper, a gentle peacemaker, a prudent counsellor, and a general female evangelist. Her mission had a wide range. Not only did she mend the clothes of her children, but she meekly tried to repair the losses in the congregation. She must have what Mrs. Stowe calls "Faculty." If, as in the case of our mother, she happened to sing and pray with wonderful acceptance, she became, so to speak, a perpetual revivalist. Many precious souls were converted in the fervent prayer and class-meetings of that day. Indeed the early settlers were famishing for the Bread of Life. They travelled, perhaps for miles, through the woods to worship God. And they were not hard to please. Sometimes a woman's prayer kindled the spark that spread into an extensive conflagration. Great numbers were in this way added to the Church.

The excellent women who thus aided their toiling husbands in this field, might well be classed with those whom St. Paul affectionately remembers as "Fellow Labourers." With the sick and their own sex, their influence was very great. And in the exemplary performance of all these duties, her grateful child, perhaps, may be pardoned, for believing that he has never seen the superior of his sainted mother.

Methodist usage, even in those days, gave large scope to

the energies of woman. It was a revival religion. In the attempt to convert the world, she could not be spared. Others might not so need her aid. But the Methodists could not fail to remember that Susannah Wesley and Barbara Heck stood high among the founders of their denomination.

It is not proposed here to discuss that delicate question about which Christians naturally differ, the proper sphere of woman in the work of the Church. We are only writing history. Yet we cannot but feel that the religious world " moves." It was true that Mrs. Judson was then known to have braved death to feed her husband in prison in Burmah, but Miss Rankin had not yet been besieged by insurgent soldiers as the heroic pioneer missionary to Mexico. At that time the most timid Methodist was not offended if a gifted sister " led the class," addressed a revival meeting, or thrilled a multitude at a camp-meeting love-feast.

Success in oratory often depends on what is familiarly termed " personal magnetism." In this, as a rule, women are richly endowed. We need not wonder that the famous speech of the Empress Maria Theresa, with her child in her arms, took by storm the nobles of Hungary.

Although our mother had a rare command of choice words, and her cadences were very musical, it was mainly the air of " goodness " that melted the throngs around her. Both are now with the " Saints in Light." We may record the popular verdict that she quite equalled our father in eloquence.

It is but just to mention that she bore her honours with singular meekness. Her custom was not to speak in any large assembly except by invitation. With true delicacy, she gave no sign that she knew her power. We may illustrate her modest bearing by the case of an early friend. He was a class-leader, a plain farmer, whose prayers were so child-like and faulty in grammar, as often to excite the smiles of the neighbours who listened. One day we found him greatly excited over a letter. It had crossed the Atlantic and come four thousand miles from an English soldier on the Rock of Gibraltar. In the joy of his conversion, he had written to his former employer, to thank him for the daily family prayer, in that distant Canadian home. It had awakened his first religious impressions, that had never ceased, till he had found the Saviour. With tears rolling down his cheeks our friend exclaimed, "Why I never dreamed that I prayed anything extra!" Nor had he. It was the blessed Comforter that Christ so lovingly promised His disciples that had given his lips the charm to melt a human heart.

The Stationing Committee at the Conference not only enquired of the Presiding Elder about the gifts of the preacher they were to send, but they sought to know the graces of his "Better Half." Did she gossip more than she prayed? "Was she a hindrance or a help?" The female members of the expectant flock went even a step farther. They whispered, perhaps, "Does she wear bright ribbons in her bonnet?" "Has she ruffles or furbelows to her dress?" Let not the reader smile. They were nobly sincere. The self-denying Methodists of those times had inherited the simple tastes of their religious ancestors, the Moravians. They bore the "Cross" even in their plain attire. Railroads, intercourse with cities, and general worldly prosperity, have since vastly changed the habits of even earnest Christians. But the strict views of her neighbours then required that the wife of an "Itinerant" should in her apparel appear as a sort of compromise between a saint and a "Quakeress." There is a tradition that gaudy parasols were once forbidden. We may illustrate by referring to a custom, long since abandoned. With a slight change in the poetry, we may describe the sensation of the ancient door-keeper to a love-feast, who shook his head at young ladies with too many adornments, with the thought—

"Too gay—ye cannot enter there.

We sometimes meet, with persons who fail to impress us at first, but who on further acquaintance gradually unfold qualities which make them very attractive. Our mother thus grew upon you. She lived before the age of the photograph. There remains of her no good likeness. It falls to the lot of one of her children to give an outline of her appearance, from faint "word-painting." As a slender girl, she had been called a beauty. When she developed into womanhood she was moderately tall, elegant in figure, and graceful in all her movements. Her face had a sincere childlike expression. Though not so exquisitely moulded as some, it was wonderfully pure. In fact it was a perfect mirror of her thoughts. Many of our readers will remember a master-piece, by Guido, in the Barberini Palace at Rome, representing the beautiful Beatrice Cenci, gently turning her head to look back, on the morning of her execution. It reminded her child at least, of our mother's parting glance, as she left for a moment his sick room. Yet she ever showed more smiles than tears. She seemed born to cheer others. Just as the sunlight flashes all the more brightly on a green forest below, when it is seen from a mountain-top in springtime, if it is now and then shaded by fleecy clouds; so the

11*

flitting shadows seemed only by contrast to heighten the prevailing gladness of her Christian life.

Those who have visited Hamburg and the German shore or the Baltic, will recollect that if a fog veils the sun, it also protects the delicate waxen features of woman. She had brought from foggy New Brunswick, a clear red and white complexion. This was afterwards slightly clouded by a fever in middle life.

Her abundant brown hair helped to conceal a high poetical forehead. Her eyes were soft hazel; her nose was Grecian, and her teeth were white and faultless, and seemed to shine like pearls as she smiled. Her lips and chin were delicately fashioned, and her cheeks were faintly rosy even to her death. But these attractions were nothing compared to her wondrous gift for sympathetic conversation. She charmed everybody. With ready, womanly tact she drew you out. She knew just when to listen and when to speak. Gray-haired men and timid men alike sought her counsel.

With the natural associations among the early immigrants on these outposts of civilization, it seemed always a mystery how she could be so refined and lady-like, with an ease that gave no offence,—for she was generally beloved. Doubtless most men and women who rise to distinction, adopt in childhood some ideal model of excellence. It is thus that the good live in generations to come. Even white children stolen by the Indians on western plains, are said to retain for years traces of their gentle training. Could it be that our mother carried to the wilds of Canada a passion to imitate the graces of her early friend, Emma Carleton?

This feminine gentleness was strangely mingled with the loftiest courage.

With his exemplary devotion to his work, and his untiring industry, our father had fits of extreme prudence. There was one thing he mortally dreaded, and that was *debt.* His honourable caution in finances was the secret of much of his success in life. If the expenses of reaching a new distant Circuit were likely to exceed his slender means he would despond for days. But he was blessed with a wife equal to any emergency. They were happily mated. Each had some rare quality in excess. If he was wisely cautious, she was ever hopeful. She never quailed a moment at any danger. There could scarcely be a nobler gift from the Father of mercies to the wife of a frontier missionary than this lofty heroism. If our space allowed we could give many incidents to illustrate her bravery. Once in her girlhood in the war of 1812, a drunken Indian raised the musket to fire at her. As coolly as if she were his chief she said, "put down that gun!" and then quickly quieted him with food. An insurgent captain in the Mackenzie Rebellion who wished to force her tender boy early one morning against his will, into the ranks, was compelled gradually to give way to her womanly strategy. "Leave him Captain," said she, " or I must march with your company to take care of him." "Really you don't take women, do you?" "Oh no," said he laughing. But what could one loyal woman do with a company of armed men? She looked at the hungry crowd and said in her graceful way, "Gentlemen, I fear you have not had your breakfast. Help yourselves to all you can find in the house." They cleaned out the cellar, and generously left her boy behind. She was in fact the resolute enterprising member of the "Firm" that quietly ruled the parsonage. At the tender age of fifteen her eldest son utterly broke down in tears at his father's refusal to sanction what he sincerely deemed an extravagant plan to study medicine. He was very properly reminded there were six sons to be educated. His mother softly followed her sobbing boy to his room, laid her hand tenderly on his head, and said lovingly, "Never mind my child, you can do *anything* that you think you can. Then remember that I will always be your friend." These electric words turned the scale; they made him a future physician. He looks in the glass as he writes this. Grey locks cluster around his face, and tears of gratitude roll down his cheeks. More than forty years have passed since he heard that sentence. Yet even now he seems to to hear the silvery ring of that magic word, "*Anything !*"

She nobly kept her promise. Possibly it may cheer some desponding woman who knows not her power, to finish the story. Partly to gratify her extreme fondness for poetry, he had just been reading with his mother an English translation of Homer's Iliad. He was slightly heroic. When his tears were dried, he went back to his father with a little speech. It amounted to about this: "Father, I will not ask you for a dollar. You need all your salary to educate my younger brothers, let me help you all. You know that the Greeks took Troy in just ten years. I will work like a slave night and day, (to be a doctor) for ten years to come." His father shook his head in doubt, but at last said: "Well, you may try !" That last word stung him, "Try." Indeed, I will, murmured the choking boy. Perhaps he was too sensitive.

He then recollected that his father was an enthusiast over "hard work." While the latter was absent on a distant mission, the former, under safe maternal advice, contrived a pleasant surprise. He took a contract requiring severe manual labour for weeks. His hands were delicate and soft. He had never been accustomed to rough "out door" work. His task was really quite beyond his strength, for he was pale, thin, and "small for his age," at fifteen. Yet he managed to toil steadily, week after week, from dawn till dark. He felt that loving eyes were watching every step. As he groped his way homeward at night, all weary and worn, with his hands bleeding and blistered, he would often meet his mother far out in the fields, coming to take his arm. And as he lay half dreaming near the blazing fire, he would hear her whispering softly, "Children, be still. Let him sleep. That is the boy that *works!*"

There came a staunch friend to her rescue. He was a neighbour,—"Father Gardner," of Toronto township, living like a patriarch among a tribe of honoured sons and daughters. When our father returned, this friend said to him, tenderly, "You must never discourage that boy again!" From that time all were agreed. The son went on toiling, but with the blessing of his father.

Just here we may mention another precious friendship during that dark period, it was that of J. R. Armstrong, Esq., of Toronto, a model "Christian merchant" of that day.

The phrase, "ten years," seemed afterwards like prophecy. In just ten years from that month, a grown-up young man of twenty-five grasped a roll of parchment, which said he was a physician, and it was all the more precious to him from the secret thought that it was earned by his own hands and brains. No, he was mistaken, it came mainly through the inspiration of one "ministering spirit." In the wards of the hospital, in the weariness of the dissecting room, or as he sat listening in the crowd to the lectures in the college theatre, he was cheered by her gentle influence. During all that chapter of early struggles, her wise foresight, her excellent judgment, her lofty resolution, and her strong sympathy never failed him. He was thankful that she lived to see the battle won.

If we were asked to name the quality in which our mother excelled above all others, our prompt reply would be, "In the pious education of her infant children," that, as our commercial friends would say, 'twas her "specialty." Her gentleness and tact in developing the cluster of little ones, that like flowers blossomed at her feet, were really wonderful, in proof we may add a few details.

Not from any foolish personal vanity, but simply as a convenient way of illustrating her virtues by actual facts, we continue our narrative, and what she did to one, she tried to do to all her children. But an early misfortune happened to give to the writer rare opportunities to study her domestic character. He was a frail, sickly child, born just after the loss of an infant elder brother. Family tradition says he cried more than all his six younger brothers put together. He wailed all day as steadily as the Scottish Piper at Waterloo. She who was bereaved redoubled her attention to quiet the little "crying machine," that kept the house in uproar. It was all in vain,—as if to fix more deeply her affections, he remained a delicate lad for years. When he could fairly speak, she laid her hand gently on his head, and taught him the prayer, "Now I lay me down to sleep," and soon after came, "Our Father who art in heaven,"

After he had learned to read, he would spend hours at her feet, looking up into her face, and conning over his story books, for she was both his playmate and mother. She wisely nourished his taste for history. Sometimes she seemed to go back to the merry days of her own childhood. She made witty remarks about the tales that he read. The "Man Friday," in Robinson Crusoe, came "just in the nick of time." Munchausen's dog, with two feet up and two feet down, "never got tired." She was only planning for his good. These playful indulgences won his young heart, to prepare him for better things.

"Was it not curious that the great load should roll off the back of Christian, in Pilgrim's Progress, just as he first saw the Cross?" The child grew fond of tender themes. One day he brought her, as he sighed deeply, that beautiful description, by Mrs. Hemans, of the faithful little son of the dead Admiral at the battle of the Nile, who awaited orders from his father, till he too perished:

> "The boy stood on the burning deck,
> Whence all but he had fled;
> The flames that lit the battle's wreck
> Shone round him o'er the dead.
>
> * * * * * *
>
> There came a burst of thunder sound,
> The boy, Oh where was he?
> Ask of the winds that far around
> With fragments strewed the sea.
>
> With mast and helm and pennon fair,
> That well had borne their part,
> The noblest thing that perished there
> Was that young faithful heart."

He asked her whether the boy should not have left the burning ship. Her exact words in reply are forgotten; but the sense was, "Poor boy, he did not know then that his father was dead. It may be, my child," she added, "that you would have been just as brave and as true as Casabianca." Thus she ever encouraged the noblest sentiments.

At his urgent request she would sometimes relate the story of her travels. We merely give the substance from memory. New Brunswick was damp and chilly,* but it had many good things, the pastures were green, the streams were clear, the potatoes and fish were delicious, and the people had rosy faces, and were very kind. Beyond the upper branches of the St. John's River the journey was fearfully hard. When their company of emigrants came to the Gulf of St. Lawrence they saw a broad sheet of water like the ocean. They could not see across. The place where Wolfe and his army climbed up at Quebec, was as a great high wall, reaching towards the sky. Above Montreal the St. Lawrence was a mighty river, like the Mississippi or the Amazon, only it was very unruly. It twisted and turned just as it pleased. Often it was clear as a mirror, and then again it flashed and rolled like a sea of buttermilk. There were miles of white rapids dashing, foaming, and surging, just as if the Niagara Falls tapered all the way down to Queenstown. The Thousand Islands were scattered here and there as far as the eye could reach, as in a broad crystal river that ran through a paradise of green islets, all covered with trees and flowers. Those French boatmen toiled all day, and then danced around the fire and sang sweet songs at night. She had caught even their Norman accent of a few familiar French words. "What

---

* We suspect Dr. Corson is in error about the interior of New Brunswick being "damp and chilly;" this may be true of the seaboard, but not of the neighbourhood of Frederickton, where Emma Freeland was brought up, and where the skies are as sunny as is our own Italian-like sky.—ED.

did they sing about?" asked her eager child. "Oh! I cannot remember all," she would say with a patient smile. "Some, I suppose, were like the boat-song of Moore:"

"Row, brothers row, the stream rolls fast,
The rapids are near and the daylight's past."

The child soon learned that she most enjoyed his reading at her feet, as she was sewing all day, of "pretty stories" from the Bible, and he loved to please her. He would turn over the leaves, perhaps, till he came to the history of Joseph, or the night assault of Gideon, the triumph of Deborah, the duel between David and Goliath, the deliverance of David, or the shipwreck of St. Paul at Malta.

We have told the story of her shaping the worldly fortunes of her eldest son; her sway over his spiritual destiny was even greater. At the age of nineteen he found himself far from home amid ent're strangers, pursuing his preparatory classical studies at Cazenovia Seminary, in central New York. He had previously read some sceptical books that had filled his mind secretly with terrible doubts. He was indeed sorely tempted; but there always came a reply to these evil whisperings as if from the voice of the Comforter: "Remember the sweet religious life of your mother!" It was a lesson of surpassing beauty. In all the years of close observation, from his earliest childhood, he had never known an act or word of hers inconsistent with the purest Christian faith. It was a sermon that he could not forget.

At last, in the midst of a "student's revival," a committee of three young acquaintances rooming near him, rapped at his door to enquire tenderly "Why he was

11*

not a Christian?" He had never before told the secret of his wrestling with infidel speculations. He now confessed all. When they were gone, he went to his trunk, and found a beautiful pocket Bible inscribed, "A Mother's Gift." He burst into tears. He fancied that he could hear her silvery voice in prayer for his conversion. Soon after, at a student's prayer-meeting, to his great joy he found peace in his Saviour.

Her influence over the youth in leading them to Christ was always very great. When in the lovely month of June, of "forty-three," she was gently sinking in death, at Newburg, on the banks of the Napanee River, it is said that no less than six young ladies, who had been led by her to the fold, were seen kneeling in prayer at her dying bed.

Her voice was what musicians call a "contralto." Unconsciously, to her, as it seemed, its lower notes rolled out and quivered with rare sweetness in her prayers. Her choicest petitions were uttered in the absence of her husband, in her unfailing night and morning devotions, for many years in the midst of her group of children, and these last were never forgotten. Her pleadings were singularly rich in figures from the Psalms. One of her frequent requests was, "Take me to the Rock that is higher than I." And the beautiful ninety-first Psalm in particular, seemed like a mirror in her "life of trust." One of her sons, remembering this, wrote not long since, a little poetical commentary on this Psalm, published in the "Sailor's Magazine," and dedicated to "Christian seamen." It is set to a soft Italian melody with an unmusical English name. The fourth stanza refers specially to her "voice," and the dreams of her child for years after her death.

TRUST.

A HYMN.—BY J. W. O.

"In Him will I trust."—Psa. 91 : 2. 11.

Air, "Dennis."

LORD, teach me as thy child,
 Unfailing trust to gain;
The faith to bear each tempest wild,
 Let me till death maintain.

Come in the darkest night,
 When seas as mountains roll;
Shine in the storm—my beacon-light—
 With joy to fill my soul.

My bark will surely fail
 To reach that happy shore,
Unless thy hand shall trim my sail,
 And guide me safely o'er.

A voice, that childhood's prayer,
 At twilight taught me well,
In dreamy slumber, calls me there—
 Like sound of signal-bell.

When earth-worn, I would sleep
 To waken with the blest,
Oh Saviour, let thine angels keep,
 And take me to thy rest.

HARDSHIPS.

THE PARTING.

THE first cry of Saul of Tarsus, as he rose from the blinding vision on the plain of Damascus, a loving disciple, was, "Lord, what wilt thou have me to do?" He sighed for action. Providence, in strange mercy, thus prompts human hands and lips to convey the Gospel. Every true Christian, in the joy of his conversion, has felt this missionary *thrill*. He has longed to do something for the Master. It was perfectly natural that Andrew should hasten to tell the great discovery of his life to his brother Peter, and that he should walk all the way by his side to Jesus. George Muller gives a touching tale of a poor sempstress in his flock, who was suddenly left a fortune. She never changed even her calico dress, but began to give like a princess. When reproached by careful friends for her lavish benevolence, she replied, "Did not my Saviour shed the last drop of blood in his veins for me?" We can fancy that Pilgrim, when he found that the City of Destruction and the Slough of Despond were behind him, that the great load had actually rolled off, and he was surely marching towards the Beautiful Gate—was quite overwhelmed with gratitude. The young convert sighs to be serving his Lord. He longs to be "doing good." Like the Roman freedman, once a slave, he is now the "heir" of a great estate. He is "looking unto Jesus." There are longings for the Land of Gold, beyond this vale of tears. And he cares little for earth. Motives like these, doubtless, led our father to take a step at that dark hour, which seemed utterly at variance with the dictates of worldly prudence.

Sickly, "petted" children are often more precocious and observant than others. When the writer was a little turned four years of age, he noticed that good " Elder Case," then in the prime of his young manhood, with his gentlemanly, " winning ways," his mild, dark eyes, and his handsome face, was a frequent visitor at our home. Something was going on. Both father and mother sang and prayed more than usual. There were whisperings and midnight consultations. Were those *sobs* that he heard? There is a story told of a young poet, who was also a tailor; when he was reproached for his careless stitches, his defence was, that he " had a soul above buttons." Our father, before so frugal and industrious, began to neglect our beautiful farm. His heart was elsewhere. Unconsciously, as he bent forwards, he would walk, as he dreamed, by the wayside past his own home.

There lay before him, as if to tempt him from his lofty purpose, two hundred broad acres, that were his own, in the fertile township of Oxford. They were close to the Harris settlement, and a little more than two miles from Ingersoll. The land rose gently to a ridge in the centre, like the back of a buffalo; a barn stood on the shoulders, while the head was represented by a comfortable frame house, surrounded by a large orchard of choice fruit trees. The road, in front, was fringed by a little brook, crossed by a bridge. But what were the lowing of herds or the ripening of harvests now to that enchanted young farmer? Nothing. He had once armed for the fray, as an earthly soldier. The great Captain had now sent an officer of his staff to summon him to a nobler conflict. That was the mission of Elder Case.

The principle of "Probation" in the Methodist economy is a "triumph of genius" in perhaps the greatest "organizer" of the modern Church—John Wesley. Both members and ministers must be thoroughly "*tried*" before they are finally accepted. As we afterwards learned, our father was preparing to be sent out "on trial" by the Presiding Elder. He was invited to leave his beautiful farm, his devoted wife, and his tender little ones, and to plunge into the forest— for four weeks at a time—to preach the Gospel to the perishing souls in the wilderness around him. He obeyed. One day a young man, just turned thirty, led his horse up to that gate. He tenderly folded his arms around the neck of his wife; and the tears fell from both like rain. Then he hastily rode away, as if he dared not look back. Homer's dream of Hector parting with Andromache at the Scæan gate, was not more tender.

When the horseman had disappeared, his wife led her boy back to the house, asked him to kneel down by her side, with his face towards that gate, and prayed—as he fancied he had never heard mortal plead before. That kneeling seemed to last a whole hour. He lived afterwards to stand in the courtyard of the great Orphan House at Halle, on the very spot where that pious German, Herman Francke, was carried to make his dying prayer for the two thousand orphans he had gathered there. And was not the parting petition of that wife for her missionary husband possibly just as beautiful.

DANGERS

In sections of that country the wolves yet howled, and pursued the traveller at night. Swamps were crossed by the "corduroy bridge," made of small sticks of timber a little longer than railroad ties, and often unsafe. The roads were frequently mere waggon-tracks, winding among thick woods. In great floods the close ricketty bridges sometimes floated away, so that the horse must wade; or if the stream was large, he must swim. A friend writes, that his relatives used to conduct our father "through the woods by the marks on the 'blazed trees,' with torches," to a night appointment.

When the horse happened to mire in a morass, and turned back, there was a singular Methodist invention, by which the rider could tie his beast to a tree, and then, like the stream in Tennyson's "Song of the Brook," he could still "go on." For the unconverted, awaiting him in the neat log schoolhouse, must, in some desperate way, be reached. The English in India are said sometimes to frighten the savages among the hills by a little cannon, carried on the back of a pack animal, called a mountain howitzer. So the Methodist "itinerant" of that day, if his horse mired, walked on with a supply of Gospel ammunition on his arm, concealed in a leathern bag holding about a bushel. This he tenderly took from the back of the jaded beast. It had pouches at each end like the receptacle of the Australian kangaroo. It became famous in the early struggles for religious liberty in Canada as the "saddlebag." The term was sometimes used in the plural; but in memory of its distinguished services, both to religion and freedom, we prefer the more delicate singular.

Seriously, we may here indulge in a little historical episode, throwing light on one of the darkest conflicts in the early career of Methodism in "Upper Canada." In 1827, the whole province was convulsed by a cool attempt of one set of politicians to disfranchise the other side, in the famous "Alien Bill." It created quite as much commotion as did the blow at the Dissenters, proposed by Lord Sidmouth in England. An eloquent and utterly fearless young Methodist minister seemed to be raised up for the occasion. It was Egerton Ryerson.* He will doubtless be better known to future generations of his countrymen by his peaceful labours as the founder of the comprehensive and excellent system of schools for Canada. But in the struggle of which we speak, he wrote a series of public letters which roused the whole country. His eloquent missives and the petitions against the obnoxious "Alien Bill" were both carried largely in Methodist saddlebags. The home Government in England nobly came to the rescue, and vetoed the measure. And in the elections of 1828 the Methodists and their friends of other churches triumphed, and elected what their opponents called the "Saddlebag Parliament."

We gladly seize this occasion to record our sacred obligations to an accomplished and faithful teacher who seemed to wield a wonderful influence for good over all his pupils. George Hughes, Esq., was then the Principal of a flourishing "select school" in the town of Port Hope. Just previous to the usual day for writing "compositions," a loved companion of ours, the son of a greatly respected

---

* I think Dr. Corson is slightly in error. E. Ryerson first drew his pen to vindicate the character of the Methodists from the attack on them, made by the Rev. Dr. Strahan, in his funeral sermon for Bishop Mountain, published July, 1826.—ED.

member of Parliament, playfully proposed that we "fire up" on opposite sides of this exciting question. The writer, then a lad of thirteen, accepted the friendly challenge, as the "son of a saddlebag."

Our two essays convulsed the whole school. The beloved Principal was a sincere "High Church Episcopalian," and a strong "Conservative." But he was also as generous as a prince. The most valued literary compliment that the writer has ever received, was amid the cheers of his fellow pupils as he felt the fatherly touch of his teacher's hand, with the tender words, "Well done my little saddlebag."

But let us return to our story of dangers. Our father's saddlebag once nearly cost him his life. It did not explode. No, it was an accident of another kind. Just at this period considerable "war losses" had been paid throughout the province in packages of silver. The wise and generous policy of the British Government towards the Indians had rendered them, as a rule, quite peaceable and inoffensive. But there were a few rough exceptions. Our father was creeping along homeward at a slow pace at midnight, just beyond Ingersoll, when he observed an Indian at a distance first staggering as if he were drunk, and then walking rapidly as if to overtake him. He saw in a moment that the drunken gait was a sham, and quickly spurred his noble beast. As soon as the savage saw that his game was escaping, he brandished a huge knife, and shouted in a rage, "give me money! you got dollars in dat ledder bag!"

When our father had gained a few rods on his pursuer he turned and said, "No money here! only Methodist books!" But the unbelieving Indian chased him for a full half mile, and finished with his loudest "war-whoop." Our father rode home as if a whole tribe of Indians were at his heels, at a pace like that of Tam O'Shanter escaping from the witches. And the spirited mare lost not even a hair of her tail. Had the Indian captured the saddlebag he would have been woefully disappointed. One end was spiritual, and the other temporal. The first contained, perhaps, Wesley's sermons, the Preacher's Manual, Fletcher's Checks, and a Bible and hymn-book. The other end was very "worldly," and swelled out probably with a change of linen, and, we may as well confess it, with provisions for the minister's family. We remember being once puzzled in surveying the Catacombs at Rome as to how the millions of Christians who hid themselves there were fed. It was doubtless a mystery to many in the privations of early Methodism how the ministers and their wives and little ones lived. We here venture to give a single hint. Their hungry children always eagerly watched the opening of the saddlebag.

JOYS IN TRIALS.

WE shall devote this closing sketch of our father's "hardships" partly by presenting two traits in his character, which helped to cheer him in these toils to the very last. They were the rainbows that followed his storms. The first we shall notice immediately. But the second we shall reserve for the end of this paper.

There have been passing allusions elsewhere to his unfailing cheerfulness. But it entered so largely into his daily life that it deserved a more careful analysis. It rang out in joyous laughter; it twinkled in his blue eyes, and it sparkled in his inexhaustible fund of merry anecdotes. It is said that the martyred Lincoln was wonderfully solaced during the long agonies of the civil war by the practice of telling mirthful stories. Of these our good father had a full assortment for every possible occasion. He could, in a comical way, "illustrate" any earthly subject. Sometimes his wit took the form of quick repartee. At others it was more narrative.

Even in the solemnities of Conference he was utterly fearless in his playful sallies. In the history of the largest Methodist body in Canada to which he always adhered, there were frequent separations and alliances, and often grave, honest differences of opinion. Debates were naturally at times quite exciting. In the midst of a storm he would pour oil on the troubled waters by a speech full of drollery. For at heart he was always a peacemaker. He dreaded violent extremes of any kind. As Shakespeare says of madness, there was always "method" in his fun. His object was to soothe. And he generally managed to leave all parties in a roar. It seemed that even his wit became consecrated. He loved best to tell stories illustrative of his dearly cherished Methodism. We select a few specimens from his large collection.

A young farmer on the Dumfries Circuit, once wittily complimented his Methodist "earnestness." On his return from a missionary tour to the destitute back townships, our ever watchful mother discovered that he wriggled and twisted something like a boy with the St. Vitus' dance. He had the peculiar motion of the elbows common to a certain affection of the skin known in Scotland as the "Fiddle, Fiddle." Our good mother was always energetic. She had treated him with sulphur, as a humorous patient once said, "outside, inside, and every side." Our father had a familiar way of joining any farmer in his work. It was in hot July. He began to "cradle" in the harvest field. All at once his friend stood still, and snuffed the air audibly with his nostrils two or three times. Then he said with mock gravity, "Mr. Corson, you have been chasing the devil very hard; you have got a little of his SMELL."

He had had another story about Earnestnes. A wealthy retired "High Church" minister, a good Episcopalian, was so genial and kindly that any of his high-born associates dared to ask him the most familiar questions. He lived in a splendid mansion in the midst of a garden in a certain city, opposite a very noisy Methodist Church. At the hour of prayer, winter or summer, you might hear a chorus of amens and hallelujahs. At last a jovial friend asked him how he stood the Methodist thunder over the way. "Oh," said he, laughing, "they keep up such a singing and praying that my hens have stopped laying eggs."

Our Father was fond of noticing children. To a bright little boy he would sometimes relate a tale of his eldest son —how the latter once escaped a lecture, or some kind of punishment, by being able to " quote scripture."

The boy, a thoughtless urchin of fifteen, had inherited his father's early fondness for wrestling. One moonlight Saturday evening he wrestled with his young friends until ten o'clock. As he was on his way to bed his father arrested him with "stop my son! Are you not ashamed, as a minister's child, to be wrestling so late at night?" Quick as thought the lad replied, "Why, father, Jacob and the angel wrestled all night till daylight in the morning, and what good people they were." " You may go to bed, my boy," said our father, laughing in forgiveness.

Many of his playful reminiscences were of his ministerial

brethren. An eloquent colleague had brought not only his wit but just a faint trace of gentlemanly "brogue" from the ever green Island. One Sabbath as he rode through the woods in the maple sugar season, he was grieved to see the smoke of many camp-fires. His sermon at the next log school-house was about the heroic prophet Daniel. He dared to pray three times a day. "So he did," said the speaker. "He faced the lions themselves." At last, raising his voice to a shrill pitch, he shouted, "And Daniel never boiled sugar on Sunday!" The hit fell like a bomb-shell in the crowd. One stricken sinner jumped to his feet and said trembling, "I suppose you mean me." "Oh, no," said the faithful preacher, "I mean you all." But he added sharply, "If the coat fits *anybody* he can wear it."

A witty clerical friend of our father was dozing late at night near him in the "Preacher's tent" at camp-meeting. There was a very worldly brother, a tall layman, whose chief religious accomplishment was a powerful, clear, stentorian voice. He was quite conscious of this. Like the thirsty land of Egypt, he needed to be annually revived with a camp-meeting inundation sweeping over him like the river Nile. Then he would make the very trees tremble with his far-reaching voice. On the night in question he became hoarse and speechless, and with mistaken taste disturbed the dozing ministers. "What shall I do for my hoarseness," he said. "My brother," said my father's companion, waking up in mercy for the emergency, "You have got what is called a 'Methodist cold.' There is only one cure. Take a small piece of salt pork, and tie a string around it, then swallow it and pull it up as you would a little fish several times." There was a general explosion, and the patient in haste retreated.

We have not deemed it proper to occupy too much of the space so generously offered by our valued friend, the editor. It would be easy to add largely to our few examples of "hardships." We may close with a single additional illustration.

In the autumn of 1827, as we were again happy in the abundance of our home on the Oxford farm, our father was suddenly ordered to move one hundred and fifty miles eastward, in the cold and muddy month of November. He was assigned to the Whitby Circuit and the adjoining Scugog Indian mission. It was awful. The "personal effects" and furniture were to be sold for a song, or given away. A wife and five children, and the little comforts it could carry, were to be packed into a single lumber waggon, covered with a white cloth. It was a regular gipsy looking affair. But a staunch Methodist, the venerable Daniel Harris, the father of a noble family of sons, was to be the safe driver. Our father, like the mounted guard to a diligence in Italy, rode ahead with his trusty horse, and the inevitable "saddlebag." Young as the writer then was he enjoyed the excitement. Methodists along the road, like the early Christians, fed and warmly greeted the family. There was a large lunch basket with cold chicken and other tempting things which was often replenished. We bought a salmon in crossing the River Credit. In Toronto, then "York," we were hospitably entertained at a Methodist home. The day that we left York and crossed the River Don was made more dreary from the fact that a young printer named French, was to be hanged for what many thought was justifiable homicide. The town was very gloomy.

When we arrived at Whitby Circuit, it was found that it

was reduced by Church dissensions to six appointments and a little mission. The wheat crop had been extensively stricken with the "rust." It was almost a famine year. Flour was very dear. Our father's means had been exhausted by an unexpected long journey. We were thrust into a deserted log house, through the crevices of which we could see the stars. It was just in the outskirts of the present town of Whitby. Our bread failed. We were reduced to small potatoes. At midnight the writer heard his mother weeping and saying, "Husband, what shall we feed the children to-morrow?" Next morning the boy went to his mother and, without telling her what he had overheard, said tenderly, "How sweet those little potatoes are." Our trials were soon over. Members of other Churches and the few straggling Methodists soon rallied round the new comers. One of the first to bring supplies to the famished wife and children was a young man, since honoured in political life as James Willson, Esq.

The second solace in his trials that we would mention now came to cheer our anxious father. It was what our Episcopalian friends call the "*communion of saints.*" He was always extremely liberal towards "All who love the Saviour." He was very fond of "union services." The little Methodist classes in the sparse, new settlements were often peacefully gathered from all the leading sects. They met on the broad "platform" of John Wesley, and included all who desired "*to flee from the wrath to come.*"

Our father's genial temperament led him all his life to court fraternal relations with the different branches of Methodists, and with all evangelical Churches. Yet he was strongly attached to his own spiritual home.

Just at this time he accepted an invitation from Baptist

friends, to join them in special revival services in the frame church below Whitby. Many conversions followed. Methodism soon rallied to a prosperous condition. His social relations were delightful. Few spots have ever had so warm a place in his memories in after years as Whitby Circuit.

The Union sentiments to which we have alluded grew stronger as he neared the heavenly land. In extreme old age he promptly accepted the hospitalities tendered him by Presbyterian, Baptist, Congregational, and other friends; and frequently appeared in their festive gatherings to make pleasant speeches, as "Father Corson."

Doubtless children are often indebted to pious parents for their religious thoughts. Knowing that it would please him, one of his sons sent him, a few months before his death, the following hymn and its history:—

PRAYER FOR CHRISTIAN UNION.

A HYMN.*—BY J. W. C.

"That they all may be one."—John 17. 21.

Air, "Arlington."

THAT precious gift, Thy parting prayer,
That we may all be one,
Blest Saviour, help us now to share,
And breathe, "Thy will be done."

One home above to faith appears—
One path by millions trod ;
One Cross lights up this vale of tears,
To all the saints of God.

---

* Let me briefly tell the story of this hymn. I happen—as then a very young member—to be one of the few survivors of the first general meeting of the Evangelical Alliance, in London, in 1846. It came in the hour of sore spiritual need.

With those that gazed from Tabor's height,
   Let love unite our throng;
May "Jesus only," fill our sight,
   And echo in our song.

Our pains, and toils, and conflicts here—
   E'en Jordan rolling past,
Will be as dreams, when pressing near
   The Throne, we meet at last.

Fade earthly shrines, and altars fair,
   And names, and temples old,
If, Lord, Thou wilt but claim us there,
   And count us in Thy fold.

Reign in our hearts, Thou Lamb Divine!
   And make us one in Thee,
Bring us, with all the host of Thine,
   Thy glorious face to see.

I was depressed in my religious feelings, from close confinement for many months previous, in my studies as a young physician, among the narrow lanes, crowded hospitals, and gay Sabbaths of the "Students' Quarter" in Paris. And the contrast of that hallowed vacation of fourteen days among the venerable Christians in London, seemed almost heavenly.

The leading spirits in that gathering are nearly all now with the "Saints in Light." Tholuck, Adolphe Monod, Eardley, Bickersteth, Norman McLeod, Candlish, Bunting, Burns, Angell James, Lyman Beecher, Baird, Peck, Emory, and a host of others, have all gone home.

The sainted Bickersteth, with his pale, sweet face lit up with emotion, stopped to weep as he attempted to give out the opening hymn. And we all choked with tears at the first stanza, as, to the tune of Luther's Old Hundred, we commenced to sing, in English and other tongues, "Before Jehovah's Awful Throne."

But the suspense was only for a moment. Soon there swelled, from more than a thousand voices, a mighty chorus, like the sound of a battle hymn sung by the Swedes and Germans before an engagement in the Thirty Years' War. I then sighed for more Union hymns. You have the fruit before you.—J. W. O.

SKETCHES OF SERMONS.

Two moderate sized MS. books of skeletons of Mr. Corson's sermons, and a few on detached papers, have come into my hands. One of the books, labelled " III.," was filled up while the writer's hand was yet firm, and may have been written in middle life. The sermons in the second book, marked " IV.," were written after his hand had become tremulous with age.

These plans are interesting on several accounts ; 1st, as showing the style of sermonizing in vogue in the Canadian Methodist ministry at the time our pioneer's method was acquired ; 2nd, as indicating his own comprehension of mind and habits of thought, both in the noon and evening of life ; 3rd, as comprising, in a miscellaneous way, much like the manner in which truth is taught in the Holy Scriptures, the range of his own theological system ; and 4th, they indicate how much, or how little, reputedly extempore preachers committed to writing in those days.

But I further hold that these germs of thought are really valuable, as well as curious. They are instructive, or at least helpful to thought. They do not exhaust their several subjects-matter, 'tis true, but they rather suggest ideas. Suggestive writing is better for a beginner than exhaustive writing. Instead of superseding thought and invention, it is helpful both to one and the other. These outlines may be pondered with profit by lay preachers, who have not much time for original research, and also by young ministers, who yet hardly begin to know how to direct their researches. Their very defects may lead to an inquiry after thoughts more profound and exhaustive, and forms of expression and illustration superior to those here employed.

I intended, at first, to classify them, either in the order in which their texts occur in the Bible, or according to the sequence and relation of their several subjects to each other; but upon second thought have decided to leave them in all their tangled negligence, with the aroma of the fields upon them, like the fragrant brush-wood through which he rode to his early appointments, by the bridle-paths, along which they had been thought out and filled up, on the horse's back, after having been outlined, pencil in hand, upon his knee, as was his wont.

I pray that these once "hot-shot," after being heated to white-heat in the furness of prayerful meditation, once more may be fired off with such skill and precision as to shatter the enemy's ramparts and to explode his magazines! Even so, Amen!

I.

THE DIVINELY COMMISSIONED AND WILLING MESSENGER.

Isaiah vi. 8.—" And I heard the voice of the Lord, saying, Whom shall I send, and who will go for us? Then said I, Here am I; send me."

We have sublime truths embraced in our text—God—Christ—and angels. Man also is alluded to as being unclean. But a remedy is provided and applied.

First, we may consider these truths, and *Secondly*, the improvement of them.

I. In Isaiah's Vision we have Important Truths.

1. *They refer to the Saviour of the world.*—His divinity presented in the words of the text. He is the "Lord," which signifies Jehovah. He is the "Mighty God, the Everlasting Father, and the Prince of Peace."

2. *Our fallen state is also alluded to.*—Isaiah acknowledges that he is "a man of unclean lips, and dwells among a people of unclean lips."

3. *A remedy is provided.*—An angel flies to the altar and applies a coal to Isaiah's lips and tongue, and his "iniquity is purged," and his sin is taken away. God provides a remedy through the sacrifice made by Christ; but the Holy Ghost, who is the Comforter, applies the blessing of pardon and peace.

4. *A call from God to men.*—"Who will go for us?" Only one responds, "Here am I; send me!"

II. We must Improve this Subject. It teaches us sundry lessons.

1. *Humility.*—Angels veil their faces before the great I am, who is seated on the throne.

2. *The work of angels.*—To fly at the command of their Lord. We ought to imitate angels, who humble themselves, and fly as "ministering spirits."

3. *God has a work for us to do.*—We ought to be willing to fly at the command of God: "Here am I; send me."

4. *None can forgive sins but God only.*—Yet man may be a messenger of salvation.

II.
THE NATIVITY OF CHRIST.

Isaiah ix. 6.—" For unto us a child is born, unto us a son is given; and the government shall be upon his shoulder: and his name shall be called Wonderful, Counsellor, the mighty God, the everlasting Father, and the Prince of Peace."

In this chapter we have a description of a battle-field. The King of kings is described, and his lofty titles are alluded to in our text.

First, we may consider Christ as *human* and *divine*; *Secondly,* we may consider him as the "Wonderful, Counsellor, and the Prince of Peace."

I. CHRIST'S DIVINITY AND HUMANITY.

1. *His advent was anticipated.*—Predicted by prophets. The wise men of the East enquired after him.

2. *He is born of a virgin,* and is a *man*—the "child born,"—the "son given."

3. *His supreme divinity is sufficiently plain*: as he is the "mighty God" and "everlasting Father." He is "the great God and (*even*) our Saviour;" and "the true God and eternal life."

II. CONSIDER HIM AS THE "WONDERFUL COUNSELLOR AND THE PRINCE OF PEACE.

1. *We need a Counsellor,* one in all respects competent. Christ is that Counsellor, and his counsels will stand.

2. *He is the Prince of Peace.*—Man has fallen and become wicked, but Christ has proclaimed peace—by angels—and "he will speak peace to his people," as he did to his disciples when he met them alone after his resurrection. He has also bequeathed peace to all his followers.

III.
READING AND SEEKING OUT OF THE BOOK OF THE LAW.

Isaiah xxxiv. 16.—" Seek ye out of the Book of the Law, and read."

No people are more happy and blessed than those who live in a land of Bibles. Yet how many have the sacred book in their houses and neglect to read it.

We may pursue this subject in the following order :—

First, ask why the Bible may be called "The Book of the Law;" and *Secondly,* How we are to " seek out of this book and read."

I. WHY THE BIBLE MAY BE CALLED THE BOOK OF THE LAW OF THE LORD.

1. *It was written by men inspired of God*, as they were " moved by the Holy Ghost" to write the Scriptures.

2. *The Scriptures lead us to the Lord,* as the refuge to the prodigal. He is pointed out as the way of return to his heavenly Father.

3. *They treat of the Lord.*—From the Bible we learn that he is a Holy Being. His mercy is also exhibited, and salvation is proclaimed through this medium.

4. *The Scriptures are sanctioned by the Lord.*—" They went and preached everywhere, the Lord working with them, confirming the word with signs following." And Paul has declared that " The Gospel is the power of God unto salvation."

II. HOW WE SHOULD SEEK OUT OF THE BOOK OF THE LAW AND READ.

1. *We should do it sincerely and humbly.*

2. *With attention and perseverance.*
3. *We ought to read and seek in order to obtain good to our souls.*

IV.

THE REWARD OF THE RIGHTEOUS, AND PUNISHMENT OF THE WICKED.

Isaiah iii. 10, 11.—" Say ye to the righteous that it shall be well with him: for they shall eat of the fruit of their doings.

Woe unto the wicked! it shall be ill with him: for the reward of his hands shall be given him."

There are diversities of gifts in the Church, all of which we ought to appreciate. But in the Church we have lukewarm professors, hypocrites, and backsliders. Out of the Church the great majority are sinners of the deepest dye. In fact two characters embrace the whole human family: these are denominated " righteous " and " wicked."

We shall *describe these two characters; and consider what God has said concerning them in the text.*

I. WE ARE TO DESCRIBE THE TWO CHARACTERS.

 1. *The Righteous are—*
  (1) Sincere.
  (2) Humble at the feet of Christ.
  (3) They have faith in the atonement.
  (4) They bring forth good fruit.

 2. *The wicked are—*
  (1) "Like the troubled sea," that can have "no rest."
  (2) They have "wicked and deceitful hearts."
  (3) Their whole course is unbelieving.

Finally. They disobey God, break his commandments, and live to themselves.

II. CONSIDER WHAT GOD HAS SAID CONCERNING THEM.
1. He says, "*It shall be well with the Righteous.*"
   (1) In this *life*—they have peace in their hearts—love one another—and God loves them.
   (2) They have their peace made with God—they glorify him here with their bodies and spirits—and consequently, *heaven is their eternal home.* And, therefore, it will be well with them in the *other world.* And when called to stand before the bar of God, it will be well with them: they will hear it said, "Come ye blessed of my Father, inherit the kingdom prepared for you from the foundation of the world."

2. *It is otherwise with the wicked.*—There is a "woe" pronounced against them.
   (1) In *this world* they are unhappy.
   "In pain they travel all their days, to reach eternal woe."
   (2) They must die; and, as they are unpardoned, they will be lost.

We may *learn* from these words—
1. That God looks at the heart; and that a bad heart brings forth evil fruit, and will end in death.
2. God has manifested himself to his believing people in mercy and in blessings.
3. We ought to examine ourselves and see who is our Master, and what is our hope.
4. The righteous have a blessed promise: "It shall be well with him; he shall eat of the fruit of his doings" —participate in gospel blessings.

V.
THE FOUNDATION STONE LAID IN ZION.

Isaiah xxviii. 16.—" Behold, I lay in Zion for a foundation a stone, a tried stone, a precious corner stone, a sure foundation : he that believeth shall not make haste.

Many titles have been given to Christ. He is called a vine, a sun, a door, a rock, a stone, a shepherd, a king, and our Redeemer. In the words of our text he is spoken of under the emblem of " *a stone, a sure foundation.*"

We may consider *Christ*—the *Church*—the *Believer*.

I. CHRIST. He is the one presented under the idea of " a tried stone."
  1. "*Tried by his Father*," and then acknowledged as his " Beloved Son, in whom he is well pleased."
  2. " Tried," by thousands of his humble followers. And many here present have tried him ; and it has been unto them according to their faith.
  3. *He is a sure foundation.*—The rock on which all must build who would have a just anticipation of the eternal salvation.
  4. " *A precious corner stone.*"—As the corner unites the two walls of a building, so all nations, tongues, and peoples may be united to him.

II. CONSIDER THE CHURCH OF CHRIST.
  1. *They are redeemed by the blood of Christ.*
  2. *Christ is their foundation*, the rock on which they build.
  3. *They are united in him*, as stones in a building, and find him " precious " to their souls.

III. WHAT IS SAID OF THE BELIEVER.
  1. *They* " *shall not be confounded.*"—God has been their portion, and they have stood firm in the trying hour.

2. *It is said they shall "not be ashamed."*—Their faith is well grounded, and they do not feel disposed to disown him or his followers. Christ has been rejected of men, and crucified as a malefactor, but we "glory in his cross."

3. *They shall not make haste*; shall abide his time; await the unfolding of his purposes; but trusting in God, we resign ourselves to him.

VI.
THE TURNING AWAY OF GOD'S ANGER AND THE RESULTS.

Isaiah xii. 1.—" In that day thou shalt say, O Lord, I will praise thee: though thou wast angry with me, thine anger is turned away, and thou comfordedst me."

This is the language of every converted man and woman; and many of us have occasion to adopt it, and praise the Lord, the God of all our mercies.

We may consider:—1. The nature of his "anger;" 2. How it is turned away; and 3. How we are to praise God.

I. THE NATURE OF GOD'S ANGER.

1. *God is holy;* and his anger is constrained by his holiness. He is too pure to behold sin with allowance.

2. *His anger has been manifested at different times, and in diverse ways.*—Th.. destruction of the old world, of Sodom and Gomorrah, the Canaanites, and the judgments on the Jewish nation at different successive periods attest this.

3. *God is angry with the wicked every day*; and " the

Great Day of his wrath will come;" and then "Who shall be able to stand."

4. *Every unbeliever is condemned*, and " the wrath of God abideth upon him."

II. CONSIDER HOW HIS ANGER IS TURNED AWAY.

1. *This is through Christ the atoning lamb*, " Whose blood speaketh better things than the blood of Abel."
2. *Repentance is absolutely necessary.*
3. *We must come to Christ and believe on him*, "with a heart unto righteousness."

III. HOW ARE WE TO PRAISE GOD?

1. *Praise must be from the heart*, and the lips should express what the heart feels.
2. *We must praise God by a consistent life*, and by "letting our light shine before men," &c.
3. *Gratitude should constrain God's praise.*—We are indebted to him for unnumbered blessings.
4. *If we praise God in this world*, we are likely to praise him in a better world than this.

VII.

THE KING'S HIGHWAY OF HOLINESS.

Isaiah xxxv. 8, 9, 10.—" And an highway shall be there, and a way, and it shall be called the way of holiness; the unclean shall not pass over it; but it shall be for those: the wayfaring men, though fools, shall not err therein. No lion shall be there, nor any ravenous beast shall go up thereon, it shall not be found there; but the redeemed shall walk there. And the ransomed of the Lord shall return and come to Zion with songs, and everlasting joy upon their heads; they shall obtain joy and gladness, and sorrow and sighing shall flee away.

God's ways are not as our ways. His ways are safe, and we are required to walk in them, that we "may find rest unto our souls."

We may consider—1. The way; 2. The characters who walk in that way; and 3. The promises made to these travellers.

I. THE WAY IS—

1. *An highway.*—All may have free access to it—rich and poor, &c. It was designed by him who is infinite in all respects.
2. *It is an holy way.*—God, who marked it out, *is holy*, and he requires *us to be holy* in *heart* and *life*.
3. *A plain way.*—Inasmuch as "a fool need not err therein." Thank God, the most untutored may find out this way.
4. *It is a safe way.*—"No lion shall be there, nor any ravenous beast shall walk therein." The Great Enemy may make an effort to impede our progress in the divine life, but he can never succeed. The feeblest soul "shall overcome through the blood of the Lamb."

II. THE CHARACTERS WHO WALK IN THIS WAY.

1. *They are "ransomed"*—"not with silver or gold, but with the precious blood of Christ."
2. *They are holy.*—Saved from sin and wickedness. "The unclean shall not go up thereon." They walk in the ways of the Lord.
3. *They are "wayfaring men,"* travellers, with "no continuing city," not considering this their permanent home, but are here for the purpose of doing good.

III. Consider the Promises made to these Travellers.
1. *Promise of protection.*—While they "walk there,"—they are saved from "ravenous beasts."
2. *Salvation, finally, from sorrow and distress.*—"All tears shall be wiped away from their eyes." And they shall "obtain joy and gladness" in heaven, their eternal home.

VIII.
GOD'S COMMAND TO COMFORT HIS PEOPLE.

Isaiah xl. 31.—"Comfort ye, comfort ye my people, saith your God."

God's people have often been called to pass through sore trials, but they have always been sustained.

In the discussion of this subject we may consider:—1. God's people; 2. Their afflictions; and 3. The comfort they may obtain.

1. *God's people, first of all, are reconciled to him*—born of his spirit—and bear his image.
2. *They are his people, because they are sustained, protected, and guided by the God that made them.*
3. *His also, because they reverence him with a godly fear, and glorify him with their bodies and spirits, which are his.*

II. To Consider their Afflictions.
1. *The world, the flesh, and devil are a combination they have to overcome.*
2. *Providential Affliction.*—Abraham had his faith tried, and Joseph, Job, Jeremiah, Paul and Silas, John, and a host of martyrs who have died in the faith. How parents, like old Jacob, have had their domestic trials.

3. *We sometimes err in judgment, and errors in judgment sometimes lead to errors in practice,* which often lead to sorrow and humiliation.

III. CONSIDER THE ENCOURAGEMENT AND COMFORT WE MAY OBTAIN.

1. *God puts himself before us as a Father,* and gives us the endearing appellation of children. "And as a father pitieth his children, so the Lord pitieth them that fear him."
2. *God's people may be the instruments of comforting one another,* and they should be and are a source of comfort.
3. *His ministers,* especially, have *a comforting message.* They present various comforting considerations.

IX.

THE ENDURING CHARACTER OF GOD'S WORD.

Isaiah xl. 8.—"The grass withereth, the flower fadeth, but the word of our God endureth forever."

We have beautiful images in God's word: the withering of the grass and the fading of the flower are significant figures of human life.

There are two things to be considered: 1. The word of God; and 2. Its adaptation to human life.

I. GOD'S WORD. Is—

1. *A Revelation of his will to us,* and we may consider it as *permanent.*
2. *His word,* because—
   (1) It emanates *from* him, and
   (2) Leads *to* him. The Bible points to God as the only source whence all our blessings flow.

3. *It is proved to be his word by the way he acknowledges or endorses it,* as preached by his servants.

II. IT IS ADAPTED TO OUR STATE AND CONDITION.

1. *We are frail,* and liable to "wither" like "the grass," or "the flower" of that grass. God's word is a consolation under these circumstances. We have its blessed promise, that he "will never leave us, nor forsake us."

2. *We are probationers,* and have but a short time to remain in this world; but "his word abideth forever." The promises of that word "are yea, and amen, to them that believe."

3. *In the Day of Judgment we will be tried by that word.* "And though heaven and earth shall pass away, that word shall not pass away."

Infidels have banded themselves together in order to bring God's word into disrepute, but they are gone—have "perished" like the "grass," or "withered" like the "flower," but the word of our God continues to stand.

X.

THE ENDS OF THE EARTH INVITED TO LOOK TO GOD FOR SALVATION.

Isaiah xl. 22 —"Look unto me, and be ye saved, all the ends of the earth : for I am God, and there is none else."

Salvation is something we need, and if we obtain it not, there is no alternative but that we must perish. But this great need may be supplied on reasonable terms. Consider three things :—1. The salvation alluded to in the text ; 2.

The invitation to come and accept it; 3. The encouragement held forth in the text.

I. THE SALVATION REFERRED TO. It embraces—

1. *A deliverance from the guilt of sin.*
2. *From the Love of sin.*—How many who have loved to "roll it as a sweet morsel under their tongues, have had their delight in it taken away; and have been brought nigh to God. Salvation,
3. *Signifies deliverance from the remains of sin.*—We have an all-powerful Saviour who is "able to save to the uttermost," and "whose blood cleanseth from all sin." This will prepare the way for—
4. *Salvation from the consequences of sin,* which comprises our happiness in heaven. We come

II. TO GOD'S INVITATION. It is—

1. *As extensive as creation.*—It is offered in every land, and to every nation.
2. *It embraces all classes,* as well as all lands. Not only the rich, but also the poor and abject.
3. *The invitation embraces the greatest of blessings we can possibly enjoy*—greatest possible in *this life,* but it does not end there: its benefits follow us into the everlasting life which is to come.

III. THE ENCOURAGEMENT THE TEXT AFFORDS. Consider several particulars:

1. *We are invited by* GOD HIMSELF.
2. *The greatest of sinners possible have found mercy.*
3. *God is no respecter of persons.*—One has just as strong a warrant, and welcome as another.

XI.
IS THE GOSPEL MESSAGE BELIEVED?

Isaiah l. 1.—" Who hath believed our report?"

We have credited and heeded many less important reports; but how few have believed the most important and wonderful one of all.

Two things are to occupy our attention: 1. The report; and 2. The interrogation about the belief of it.

I. THE REPORT REFERRED TO.

  1. *The report is of great importance*, as it relates to man's *present* and *eternal* salvation. It describes man as a ruined sinner, exposed to the wrath of a sin-avenging God.

  2. *In this report a Saviour is proclaimed.*—The only deliverer for guilty man. He "bore our sins and carried our sorrows," &c.

  3. *Of the report we have the testimony of many witnesses* that Christ has power on earth to forgive sins.

II. THE INTERROGATION. "Who hath believed our report?" We remark:

  1. *A vast number of Jews believed the report in Apostolic times:* three thousand on the day of Pentecost, and even Saul of Tarsus.

  2. *Gentiles also were led to believe the report given of him in that day*, and turned "from dumb idols to serve the living and true God."

  3. *A great number in modern times have believed this report.*—They have the Old and New Testaments; they have heard them explained to them; their hearts have been softened and their eyes opened; and they have become eminent witnesses for Christ and his cause.

XII.
THE BLAST OF THE GREAT TRUMPET.

Isaiah xxvii. 13.—" And it shall come to pass in that day, that the great trumpet shall be blown, and they shall come which were ready to perish in the land of Assyria, and the outcasts in the land of Egypt, and shall worship the LORD in the holy mount at Jerusalem.

It may be inferred from this portion of Scripture, that greater displays of the power of religion will take place, and that many, who are enveloped in darkness, will embrace the truth. We notice two thoughts:—1. The great trumpet; and 2. Consider those who are to be blessed by the preaching of the Gospel.

I. THE GREAT TRUMPET.

1. *The trumpet is of God's appointing.*—Under the Mosaic dispensation the trumpets were to be of one piece, and were to be made of silver. This is designed to show that the Gospel is one in every country and in all time.

2. *This trumpet is the "great" one.*—This may indicate the great blessings proclaimed by the Gospel.

3. *The trumpet was to be blown.*—We infer from this that ministers would be raised up, who would proclaim a free and full salvation to a fallen world. God is able to call and qualify men for the important work. Though some, like Moses, may excuse themselves, yet others will say, " Here am I ; send me."

II. CONSIDER THOSE WHO WILL BE BLESSED BY THE PREACHING OF THE GOSPEL.

1. *They are those who are ready to perish.*—Those exposed

to hell on account of sin, being "in jeopardy every hour." Yes, not the safe, but those exposed to danger.

2. *They are those who "come"* burdened and heavy laden, weeping for their sins and transgressions, and casting their burden upon the LORD, they obtain salvation.

3. *They are from Assyria and the land of Egypt.*—They may be under strong delusion and hostile to the Christian religion, yet, being convinced of the error of their ways, they come to Christ and obtain salvation.

We infer from this subject:—

1. That the Gospel is designed to awaken the careless sinner who is exposed to the wrath of God.

2. That this Gospel will yet be preached in Mohammedan countries.

3. That the great trumpet is sounding, and many are coming who are ready to perish.

XIII.

IMPORTANCE OF SEEKING GOD WHILE HE MAY BE FOUND.

Isaiah lv. 6, 7.—"Seek ye the LORD while he may be found; call ye upon him while he is near."

We have many warnings, and we are admonished to attend to the things that make for our peace; yet, alas! how many neglect to lay these requirements to heart.

Let us attend—1st. To the duty enjoined; and 2nd. To the reasons assigned.

I. THE DUTY ENJOINED.

  1. *This does not devolve on all.*

    (1) Infants neither need, nor are they capable of seeking. Unconditional grace provides for them.

(2) Those in heaven are not again required to seek him, for they did seek him while on earth. Their prayers are turned to praises.

(3) It is too late for the damned in hell to seek him: their day of grace is passed and gone. But

2. *There are those who need to seek, may seek, and must seek*, and that with all their heart, if they would be saved.

II. THE REASONS ASSIGNED FOR THE REQUIREMENT.

1. *We may neglect until it is too late to seek*, and "mercy is clean gone forever," and we find our place in perdition.

2. *We ought to seek in our youthful days*—The mind and heart are then the most susceptible. God says, " They that seek me early shall find me."

3. *If we seek God timely we are sure to find him to the joy and comfort of our souls.*—This comprehends a free pardon, and we find him a stronghold, and our "refuge and exceeding great reward.'

XIV.
GOD'S CHARGE TO ZION'S WATCHMEN.

Isaiah lxii. 6.—"I have set watchmen upon thy walls, O Jerusalem, which shall never hold their peace, day nor night: ye that make mention of the LORD, keep not silence."

How many are complaining at the present; but why should living men complain? We are a favoured people. We are blessed with watchmen whom God himself has set upon the walls of our Zion; and they are not to hold their peace day nor night.

There are here two things to be considered :—1st. The watchmen and their duty; and 2nd. The lay members of the church.

I. THE WATCHMEN AND THEIR DUTY.

1. *The watchmen have their appointment from* " *Him* who weighs the mountains in scales and the hills in a balance, and takes up the isles as a very little thing."

2. *Watchmen should look out for opportunities to do good,* and to proclaim their message. Theirs is a work of great importance.

3. *Watchmen are to be instant in season and out of season :* they are to work for God both by day and *night* as well. They are to be faithful men in preaching and praying for the salvation of souls. But

II. CO-OPERATIVE DUTIES DEVOLVE ON THE LAY MEMBERS OF THE CHURCH.

1. *A church consists of those who have the word of God preached among them, and the ordinances of God administered to them.*

2. *It is said, when Zion travaileth, she shall bring forth children.*—Yes, it is the duty of every member of the church to pray, and labour, and wrestle for the salvation of those perishing around them.

3. *The church* " *makes mention of the Lord,*" for its members can "call Jesus, Lord, by the Holy Ghost given unto them." They can truly exclaim with Thomas, " *My* Lord, and *my* God !"

4. *The church may be considered as* " *God's elect*, that call upon him day and night." They are those whom he has promised to hear.

XV.
QUIETNESS AND ASSURANCE ATTENDANT ON RIGHTEOUSNESS.

Isaiah xxvii. 17.—" And the work of righteousness shall be peace; and the effect of righteousness, quietness and assurance forever."

Much has been said about the righteousness of Christ: we cannot exalt Christ too high ; yet, like antinomians, we may neglect to secure the salvation promised for us, while indulging a fallacious trust in the so-called righteousness of Christ.

We may consider the "*work* of righteousness" and the "*effect* of righteousness."

I. THE WORK OF RIGHTEOUSNESS.

  1. *God is righteous, and he has provided a means for having us accounted righteous* through the blood and righteousness of Christ.
  2. *Although corrupt by nature, a way is provided for our hearts to be purified by grace.*
  3. *The result of these will be, we shall*, as we are required, "live soberly, righteously, and godly in this present evil world."

II. THE EFFECT OF RIGHTEOUSNESS.

  1. *The effect of righteousness is peace* of conscience—peace with God, as we are reconciled to God.
  2. "*Quietness.*"—A tranquil state of mind, which may become "a joy unspeakable and full of glory."
  3. "*Assurance forever.*"—An abiding evidence of pardon —an earnest of heaven on the brink of death—and the attainment of a state of happiness which nothing can disturb or overthrow. We have "an house not made with hands, eternal in the heavens."

XVI.
OUR STAY WHILE WALKING IN DARKNESS.

Isaiah v. 10.—" Who is among you that feareth the LORD, that obeyeth the voice of his servant, that walketh in darkness and hath no light ? Let him trust in the name of the LORD, and stay upon his God."

This passage has engaged the attention of good and learned, and there has been a diversity of opinions as to what can be its real meaning. Some have thought it to be the state of a believer in obscurity and perplexity about temporal matters; others have construed it as applicable to the case of penitent sinners.

We will consider it as applicable to the latter. To *penitent inquirers.*

I. THEY " FEAR THE LORD," if no more. And this fear of the LORD is the *beginning* of wisdom.". Further,

II. THEY OBEY THE VOICE OF HIS SERVANTS.—Ministers are his peculiar servants ; and penitent sinners may obey their call to a certain extent.

Or it may apply to those who are in *providential darkness*, like Job, when he said, " O that I knew where I might find him ! "

III. THE COURSE POINTED OUT; or the remedy prescribed. "Let him trust in the name of the LORD, and stay upon his God." To trust in the name of the LORD is most important : it is synonimous with believing in Christ, the Saviour of a lost world. There is every warrant for trusting in Him who has an almighty arm. Let the penitent " *stay* upon his God," as he delights not in the death of the sinner, but would rather they turn and live.

We learn from this subject, that we may be "cast down, without being forsaken." We may be afflicted in body; and the soul and body being so connected, one affects the other; yet we are to trust in the LORD and "stay upon our God," and we shall find effectual succour.

XVII.
THE DUTY OF CRYING ALOUD.

Isaiah v. 1.—" Cry aloud, spare not, lift up thy voice like a trumpet, and show my people their transgression, and the house of Jacob their sins."

God's ministers ought to be earnest in warning sinners even as the Saviour was in an agony when he purchased salvation for those sinners.

We may consider:—1. The duty inculcated; 2. The reasons assigned for its performance.

I. THE DUTY HERE PRESENTED.
1. *Whatever we do, it ought to be done with energy.*—And above all, those who have been called by God to preach his Gospel, ought to be in earnest. Jesus was in earnest when he agonized in prayer until the sweat was as blood; in earnest when he bowed his head, cried it is finished, and gave up the ghost.
2. *We ought to deal candidly*, and enforce the truths of the Gospel with zeal, not shunning to declare the whole counsel of God.
3. *The Jews were in a backsliding state.*—Considering themselves righteous, they despised others. They drew nigh with their lips and honoured God with their bodies while their hearts were far from him.

4. *There are too many who imitate the Jews at present time*, who have a form of godliness but deny the power thereof, who must be aroused at every hazard.

II. CONSIDER THE REASONS FOR THESE WARNINGS.

1. *Man is a probationer.*—His probation may soon end; and as death leaves him, judgment will find him. And we ought to discharge our duty with fidelity, and deal plainly with him.

2. *Reasonable men will respect us the more*, if we preach plain, practical truths in a way that may prove effectual. And though some may become offended, in their sober after reflections they will give the minister credit for his home and faithful preaching.

3. *The earnest minister is the most successful in bringing souls to Christ.*—Though unpopular, it produces the most fruit. Such imitates the Master, who denounced the "hypocrites" as being in danger of the "damnation of hell."

Learn :

1. *God works by means,* and saves men by men.

2. *We ought to preach with a view to pleasing God,* and not man.

XVIII.

THE RELATION BETWEEN GOD AND HIS PEOPLE.

Jeremiah vii. 23.—" Obey my voice, and I will be your God, and ye shall be my people: and walk in all the ways that I have commanded you, that it may be well unto you."

Wickedness is described by the prophet, and the process of family idolatry; the children gathering the wood, the father kindling the fire, the mother kneading the dough, to make cakes to the queen of heaven, &c.

It is pleasing to see families engaged in the worship of God; but too often, as here described, they are idolatrous. Happily Jehovah has said, "Obey my voice, and I will be your God," &c.

The text includes a *commandment* and a *promise.*

I. THE REQUIREMENT IN THE TEXT.
1. *The commandment is divine in its origin.* Children are commanded to obey their *parents.* This is their imperative duty in all things lawful; but our parents may err, and then we are justified in disobeying them. God, however, is too wise to err, and too good to be unkind.
2. *Our obedience ought to be cheerfully rendered,* and not merely because the law rigorously requires it. It is "the willing and obedient" that shall eat the good of the land.
3. *Our obedience ought to be perpetual.*—How many promise fair, but fail. They begin in the spirit and end in the flesh. They become "weary in well-doing." Others hold out to the end, "ending in harness as good soldiers of Jesus Christ." Such go on "from strength to strength."
4. *True obedience is founded in knowledge.*—Jesus said, "My sheep hear my voice, and they follow me. A stranger will they not follow, for they know not the voice of strangers." "I know my sheep and am known of mine."
5. *This commandment is received by faith,* with the persuasion that it is from God; and they walk in his ways all the days of their lives.

II. THE PROMISE HERE MADE. "I will be their God." This includes:

1. *Defence.*—His power will be exerted for their succour from evil and harm of all kinds.
2. *To sustain and strengthen them* under all the weakness and infirmities which occasion the need of divine support. He empowers them with all strength in the inner man to do his will. It enables them to "run and not weary, to walk, and not faint."
3. *He will make them " his people."*—They are a peculiar people, and enjoy peculiar blessings and privileges of which the world knows nothing.
4. *It shall go well with them in life and death*, and be well with them in all eternity.

Let us all most earnestly seek, and strive, and pray that this may be our relation and our lot—at once and forever.

XIX.
THE CONTINUANCE OF SPIRITUAL DISEASE INEXCUSABLE.

Jeremiah viii. 22.—" Is there no balm in Gilead; Is there no physician there? Why then is not the health of the daughter of my people recovered?"

Man is a fallen creature, yet a remedy is provided for him. There is a physician and a medicine for his moral diseases, why then is his health not recovered?

We may consider—1. The disease; 2. The remedy; and 3. The inquiry.

I. CONSIDER THE DISEASE.

1. *It is a hereditary disease.*—It has descended from

father to son, from the first contaminated pair to this time—*and to this congregation.*

2. *It is a universal disease.*—It affects the whole human race, the whole man, the *soul* with all its *powers,* and the *body* with all its *members.* "The feet are swift to shed blood"—"with their tongues they have used deceit;" and "from the crown of the head to the soles of the feet there is no soundness in us; but we are full of wounds, bruises, and putrifying sores, which have not been bound up, neither mollified with ointment." The understanding is dark, the will perverse, and the affections alienated from God and goodness.

3. *This disease is contageous.*—Wicked parents contaminate their children; and they, in turn, lead other men astray. "Evil communications corrupt good manners;" and "one sinner destroyeth much good."

II. WE MAY CONSIDER THE REMEDY.

1. *There is the atonement made by Christ.*—The remedy is spoken of under the figure of "balm." The original "Balm of Gilead" was a drug obtained from a little shrub that grew in Mount Gilead. An incision was made in the bark from whence the gum exuded that was used as a medicine. This may apply to the healing nature of Christ's blood drawn from his wounded body on Mount Calvery, which opened a fountain for sin and all uncleanness.

2. *The qualities of this balm are all medicinal.*—Searching, drawing, and healing. Said Christ, "If I be lifted up, I will draw all men unto me." "The blood of Jesus Christ, his son, cleanseth from all sin."

3. *Christ is the Good and Great Physician.*—He is omnipresent and omnipotent, his skill and advice are

infallible. He knows how to apply the balm and to give it efficacy. Myriads have been healed and saved by him. He never lost a case that was honestly put into his hands.

III. WE MAY CONSIDER THE INQUIRY. "Why then is not the health of the daughter of my people recovered?"

1. *We cannot charge our perdition on God*—the FATHER—SON—or HOLY SPIRIT. All are concerned in some important part of the provisions for our salvation. And Deity has sworn by Himself that He has no pleasure in the death of them that die, but that he would rather that all should come to a knowledge of the truth and be saved.

2. *Nor can we charge our destruction on the faithful*—neither the *ministers* who have warned us, nor the good people who have set us a godly example and prayed for us.

3. *If lost, we will have to say Amen to the denunciation of our doom.*

XX.

THE HOPE AND SAVIOUR OF ISRAEL.

Jeremiah xiv. 8.—"O the hope of Israel and the Saviour thereof in time of trouble."

"Man is born to trouble, as the sparks fly upward." All, more or less, complain of trouble; but there is a remedy. We have a sovereign balm for every wound, a cordial for our fears."

1. Who may be understood by Israel? 2. And what by the hope of Israel?

I. WHO ARE WE TO UNDERSTAND BY ISRAEL ?

1. *The name was given to Jacob* at the time he wrestled with the angel and prevailed.
2. *There were certain marks by which ancient Israel was distinguished.*—There was circumcision; it imposed certain duties and sacrifices. These were confined to the descendents of Jacob, who constituted the Jewish Church. But the true Israelites under the present dispensation are those circumcised in heart, and who can call God their father, and Jesus Christ, Lord, by the Holy Ghost given unto them
3. *As Jacob was a praying man, and wrestled with God in earnest supplication,* so also the true "elect of God cry unto him day and night."
4. *God's ancient Israel were an afflicted people;* and the true Israel are distinguished in all ages, more or less, by affliction. "Many are the afflictions of the righteous."

II. WE MAY CONSIDER THE HOPE OF ISRAEL.

1. *As to hope itself.*—It is the desire for and expectation of some future good, with the possibility of obtaining it. We cannot hope for yesterday, but we may hope for to-morrow.
2. *But hope must have a basis,* and Christ is the foundation of our hopes. "On this rock I will build my church, and the gates of hell shall not prevail against it."
3. *When no human arm could deliver, Christ delivered his own.*—Hence martyrs have rejoiced at the stake.

XXI.

HUMAN COMPLAINTS AND THEIR CURE.

Lamentations iii. 39.—" Why should a living man complain ?"

Man is a compound—has many things to contend with in this life; but much is done to provide happiness for us even here. And we may secure a good hope for the life to come : " Why," therefore, " should a living man complain?"

Our complaints and the dissuasions against complaining.

I. THE PARTICULARS OF HUMAN COMPLAINTS.

1. *We have great cause to complain of ourselves*—that we have so little faith—and our love is cold—and that our usefulness amounts to so little.

2. *We sometimes complain of the inconsistent conduct of others.*

3. *But we should not complain* (as we are too often inclined to do), *of the dealings of God with us.* He can never mistake; nor can he do anything that is unjust or unkind.

II. THE DISSUASIONS AGAINST COMPLAINING.

1. *It is impious to complain of God*, who has done all that could be done consistent with human liberty and responsibility to secure our salvation.

2. *We are living men.*—We are not in perdition; and " While the lamp holds out to burn, the vilest sinner may return." We enjoy the society of our friends, and heaven may be made our eternal home, if we will.

XXII.
THE PROSPERITY OF CHRIST'S REIGN.

Jeremiah xxiii. 5.—" A king shall reign and prosper."

Christ Jesus was spoken of ages before he made his appearance in our world; and was presented under various titles. In our text he is called "a king," and it is said he shall prosper."

Two things are to be noticed : (1) Christ presented as a king ; and (2) The character of his reign.

I. HIS OFFICE AS A KING.

1. *We may mention some of the instances in which he was so presented in prophecy.*

2. *He himself claimed the title.*

3. *And by John the Revelator he is called the* " *King of kings and Lord of lords.*" He reigns in the church and in the material universe. " By ME kings reign, and princes decree justice."

II. THE CHARACTER OF HIS REIGN.

1. *He is essentially just ;* and therefore his reign is equitable. He is the " Judge of all the earth," who must " do right."

2. *Where there is rectitude there must be prosperity.* We have read of the rise and fall of empires; the kingdom of Christ is rising, but its fall will never come. After the lapse of eighteen centuries it shows vigour and progress still.

3. *Prophecy declares it is to fill the earth*, by extending " from sea to sea," and being established " upon the tops of the mountains and exalted above the hills."

13*.

XXIII.
BENEFITS OF SUBMITTING EARLY TO THE YOKE OF CHRIST.

Lamentations iii. 27.—" It is good for a man to bear the yoke in his youth."

God has given man in every stage of life precious pomises, but the realization of the benefits promised, depends on the fulfilment of the conditions—expressed or implied. If we would realize the benefits of true religion, we must bear the yoke from our youth upward. Two things will have to be ascertained : 1. What bearing the yoke signifies; and 2. What the "good" which follows comprehends.

I. To BEAR THE YOKE OF CHRIST IS, ETC.
   1. *A yoke implies government*, and to this we are to lovingly submit. "Take my yoke upon you, and learn of me."
   2. *We bear the yoke when we take up our cross and confess Christ before the world.*—It requires a public profession.

II. CONSIDER WHAT IS PROMISED.
   1. To bear the yoke in youth *will save us from many evils*; such as *drunkenness, licenciousness, Sabbath-breaking, and profane swearing.*
   2. *We will do more good* by presenting the first fruits to the Lord, thereby improving our gifts as we could not otherwise do.
   3. *There is a social good.*—We shall both *derive* and *promote* by bearing the yoke in our youth.
   4. *There is a personal good.*—We secure the approbation of good men and of the great good God. God will be our father—Christ our Saviour—and the Holy Ghost our comforter and sanctifier.

XXIV.
THE DUTY OF FEEDING CHRIST'S SHEEP.

John xxi. 16, 17.—" Feed my sheep," twice repeated.

Christ asked Peter directly if he loved him; and received a direct, explicit answer; finding he loved his Master, he authorized him to feed his sheep. None but the loving are qualified; and all who profess this love should endeavour to feed the sheep in some form.

We are to consider: 1. The sheep; 2. The shepherd; and 3. The food.

I. THE SHEEP.

1. *Sheep are innocent.*—They kneel when they lie down.
2. *They are fond of society and keep together.*
3. *They are profitable*—helpful to each other, and valuable to their owner. A blessing to the world.

II. THE SHEPHERD.

1. *None but converted men,* who "care for the sheep," are fit for this office.
2. *The best gifts, as well as the largest amount of grace, is desirable*; and the talents bestowed should be cultivated and improved.
3. *Fidelity to their trust is required;* they must "know nothing among men, but Christ and him crucified."

III. THE FOOD TO BE GIVEN THEM.

They are to have—
1. *Doctrinal teaching.*
2. *Practical enforcement, and the encouragement of the promises.*

XXV.
CAUTION AGAINST QUENCHING THE SPIRIT.

1 *Thessalonians* v. 19.—" Quench not the spirit ! "

The Scriptures of the Old and New Testaments are full of cautions and admonitions, but none more significant and important than the one in the text, " Quench not the spirit."

To feel the force of this caution, let us, 1. Consider the spirit; 2. Show how it may be quenched; and 3. The consequences.

I. CONSIDER THE SPIRIT.
  1. *The spirit is a person*, but is put before us as the element fire. It has the qualities of fire; it gives *light* and *heat*.
  2. *It is purifying;* and the spirit is the source and agent of moral purity to us.
  3. *Fire renovating;* and to be born of the spirit is to have our hearts renewed in righteousness and true holiness.

II. HOW THE SPIRIT MAY BE QUENCHED.
  1. *Fire may be extinguished by separating its parts.*—This may apply to dissensions in the Church.
  2. *Smothering* (with earth, or ashes), *will put out fire.* Worldly mindedness : being burdened with the " thick clay " of the earth, has extinguished the fire of the Holy Spirit in many a heart.
  3. *It will even go out if you neglect to supply the proper fuel.*—Many a person and many a family have extinguished the fire upon the altar of their hearts by restraining prayer and neglecting the means of grace.

4. *But the most direct way to put out fire is to throw on water*—its opposite. The Spirit is "truth," and "holiness," and *goodness*; and whatever we indulge in contrary to these—all falsehood, all sin, all injustice and unkindness we indulge in is directly and effectually adapted to quench the Spirit in our hearts.

III. THE CONSEQUENCES AND EFFECTS OF QUENCHING THE SPIRIT.
1. *By quenching we bring ourselves into condemnation.*
2. *By the same we jeopardise our salvation.*
3. *Yea, we put ourselves beyond God's mercy*, and say amen to our own eternal damnation.
4. *But if led by the Spirit*, we obtain all necessary help against temptation, to bear trials, to watch and pray, and to overcome at last.
5. *It is our privilege to cherish the Holy Spirit*, and thus receive His consolations through life.

In conclusion, let us learn that in this matter we may either to insure our everlasting happiness, or fix our destiny beyond happiness and hope

⁎ These specimens of Father Corson's sermons might have been increased to twice the number, and more; but as the book is large enough without them; and as all the other objects for introducing the specimens already given, mentioned in another place, will be answered by the few as well as the many, the reader will excuse me for retaining them among the other MSS in my antiquarian archives.—THE EDITOR.

WORKS BY THE SAME AUTHOR,
EITHER PUBLISHED, OR ON SALE
AT THE METHODIST BOOK ROOM, TORONTO.

REASONS FOR METHODIST BELIEF AND PRACTICE
RELATIVE TO WATER BAPTISM.
Expressed in Plain Words and Arranged in a Summary Manner.

BY JOHN CARROLL.

"*RENDER A REASON.*"—PROV. xxvi. 26.

46 pp. 18mo. Price 15 Cents.

TESTIMONIALS TO "METHODIST BAPTISM."

"This little tractate contains the Methodist views of the BAPTISMAL QUESTION—well and forcibly put. The individuality of the writer is here and there apparent, but the argument is well calculated to counsel those who are in any wise perplexed on the subject to which it refers. W. MORLEY PUNSHON,
"President Wesleyan Conference."

"This little work, METHODIST BAPTISM, published by the Rev. John Carroll, has my approval as a correct exposition of 'Our Position,' in regard to that ordinance. As to his arguments in support thereof, I deem them sound and conclusive; but of this every reader must form his own judgment. I freely commend the work to the candid consideration of every enquirer after Scriptural truth.
"JAMES RICHARDSON,
"TORONTO, Nov. 3, 1870. Bishop M. E. Church in Canada."

"TORONTO, Nov. 3rd, 1870.
"I have read this publication of Rev. John Carroll, on METHODIST BAPTISM, and I think it admirably adapted to assist Methodists and others in forming a correct opinion of the question of which it treats. I can confidently recommend it. WILLIAM ROWE,
"Gen. Sec. of P. M. Church."

"TORONTO, Nov. 4th, 1870.
"This little volume is an honest, direct, clear avowal and defence of Methodist belief in the nature, mode, and subject of Christian Baptism; and after carefully reading it over, has my hearty concurrence. Its wide circulation among the Methodist people of this Dominion, will silence many a doubt, and answer many a question by which thoughtful enquirers after truth are often confused and perplexed. I wish it a wide circulation. WILLIAM McCLURE,
" Theological Tutor, M. N. Connexion."

"There is a great deal of thought, fact, and argument crowded into a small space."—*Christian Guardian.*

HISTORY OF
METHODISM IN CANADA;
OR,
"CASE AND HIS COTEMPORARIES."

BY THE REV. JOHN CARROLL, D.D.

A complete set of the five volumes of CASE AND HIS COTEMPORARIES can now be obtained at the Book Room at the low price of $4.90 for the whole work, or $1 for a single volume. The fifth volume extends from the reconstruction of the Union, in 1847, to the incorporation of the Lower Canada District and the Hudson Bay Territory Missions with the Canada Conference, closing with the death of the Rev. William Case in 1855. The five volumes embrace a very minute and the only complete HISTORY OF METHODISM in the "two Canadas" during the first sixty-five years of its existence, and portray all the itinerant labourers and very many of the lay co-operators, to the number of nearly 1,300 in all. The books are written in Dr. Carroll's easy, racy, graphic style. The fifth volume is furnished with an extensive Alphabetical Index to the whole five volumes, which makes it now very easy for reference to the multitudinous matters the volumes contain.

Usual discount to Ministers and the Trade. Agents wanted to sell these and other books, to whom a liberal discount will be made.

Opinions of the Press, Relating to the first Two Volumes.

"Mr. Carroll has performed a valuable service. Around the Rev. William Case, as the principal figure, he has grouped a large body of the founders and leaders of Canadian Methodism."—*Methodist Quarterly.*

"Mr. Carroll wields a ready pen, and his style is popular and pleasing. CASE AND HIS COTEMPORARIES are the common property of Methodism."—*Canada Christian Advocate.*

"Mr. Carroll's style is chaste and racy, and exceedingly natural, and he will not lack a host of readers."—*Cobourg World.*

"It is neatly got up as to its typography and binding. We anticipate for the work an extensive circulation."—*Hastings Chronicle.*

"We take pleasure in ranking the author among our choice friends. The book merits an extensive sale."—*Guide to Holiness.*

"It gives a very graphic, interesting, and entertaining account of the origin and early history of the Methodist Church in Canada. The typography and the binding are creditable, and the style is Mr. Carroll's—easy, racy, lively and graphic."—*Waterloo Chronicle.*

"Our esteemed Bro. Carroll appears to have an especial fitness for the work he has chosen. His delineations of character are of photo graphic vividness and fidelity. It is fitting to lay a wreath on the graves of those who have fallen on the field, and to twine a garland for the silvery locks of those who are left behind."—*Recorder.*

AUTHOR'S "FINAL WORD TO THE READER."

"My long cherished desire and purpose are achieved at last. The unparalleled production of a history of sixty-five years' course of operations, and a portraiture of the actors in its accomplishment combined, is before the reader. It is as if the 'Nonconformist's Memorial,' and 'Baxter's Life and Times,' or 'The History of the Puritans,' should have been woven into one. I pretend not to say whether this is an excellence, or defect, but there it is. My original and fondest wish was to preserve a memorial of each of the itinerants who had laboured in Canada from 1790 to 1855; next, I adopted the idea of presenting the public life, pre-eminently, of the most influential among them, and one who exercised his ministry fifty years; but in the accomplishment of these two objects, I accomplished a third, and more important one than either, the history of the Church as as well as its ministry. If such things are of any importance, then I say that I have furnished the great Methodist Church (so far as it relates to 'the two Canadas' especially) an account of its rise and progress and a memorial of all its ministers, something which no Church in existence possesses but herself, at least that I know of. A complete Alphabetical Index enables the reader to trace out any single one of these ministers in whom he may feel interested."

THE STRIPLING PREACHER;

OR,

A SKETCH OF THE LIFE AND CHARACTER

WITH

THE THEOLOGICAL REMAINS

OF THE

REV. ALEXANDER STURGEON BYRNE,

(*Written and Compiled at the Request of the Conference.*)

Toronto, 1852, pp. 255, 12mo.

PRICE, - - - SIXTY CENTS.

"The author has succeeded admirably in furnishing the Wesleyan community with an interesting addition to its biographical literature." *Christian Guardian.*

A NEEDED EXPOSITION;

OR,

THE CLAIMS AND ALLEGATIONS OF THE CANADA EPISCOPALS CALMLY CONSIDERED.

BY ONE OF THE ALLEGED "SECEDERS."

(JOHN CARROLL.)

"And the bramble said unto the trees, If in truth ye anoint me to be king over you, then come and put your trust under my shadow ; and if not, let fire come out of the bramble and consume the cedars of Lebanon."— *Parable of Jotham.*

"And there passed by a wild beast that was in Lebanon, and trode down the thistle."—*Parable of Jehoash.*

"A NEEDED EXPOSITION."

" This is the title of a pamphlet by the Rev. John Carroll, D.D., in which he examines the claims of the M. E. Church of Canada to be the original Methodist Church of Canada, and the allegation of the Episcopal Methodists that the Wesleyan Methodist Church of Canada seceded from the Episcopal Methodist body. Dr. Carroll has done good service by giving in a brief space the main historic facts bearing on the case, especially for the benefit of youthful readers, who might not be cognizant of the history of the case. Dr. Carroll's personal knowledge of the transactions relating to the union of Canadian Methodism with the Wesleyan Church in England, and the formation of the M. E. Church of Canada by Mr. Reynolds, Mr. Gatchell, Mr. Bailey and other seceders from the Wesleyan Methodist Church of Canada, and his intimate acquaintance with the whole history of Canadian Methodism, peculiarly qualify him for this work. He states the facts with great fairness, giving statements from Webster's History of Methodism, most favourable to the Episcopal claim. We cannot see how any impartial reader can carefully read Bro. Carroll's pamphlet, and not be convinced that the Episcopal claim has no historic foundation. The case is not argued at any length; but the chief facts bearing upon the question are given correctly. It must be remembered, that the question is not now whether the Episcopal Methodists were justified in forming a new denomination or not—nor whether certain objections against the terms of union urged by the seceders were well taken or not—but whether the Wesleyan Methodist Church, after the union, was really and legally the same Church which had previously existed as "the Methodist Episcopal Church of Canada;" and whether the present M. E. Church of Canada was not organized and formed some time after the union of the Canada Conference with British Wesleyan Methodism. We can only give a very brief summary of the main historic facts, by which Dr. Carroll proves that the Wesleyan Church was legally and substantially the same Methodist Church that had previously existed under another name; and that the present M. E. Church had no existence as an organization till some time after the union. It is clearly shown—that the changes adopted in 1833 were made to promote union, and to prevent friction and rivalry between English and Canadian Methodism; that this union was fully discussed for over a year before it was consummated; that the steps to bring about the union were taken in a legal and disciplinary manner; that there was no opposition in the Church to the proposed union except some slight objections to some minor changes; that the measure was agreed to unanimously, by a legally constituted General Conference, on motion of Rev. J. Richardson, late bishop in the M. E. Church; that for some time after the union the present M. E. Church had no existence, as its founders,—Reynolds, Gatchell and others—continued in connection with the Wesleyan Methodist Church for the greater part of that year; that the time and place when the present M. E. Church was organized is well known; that the four men that formed themselves into a General Conference were not "travelling preachers," and had no right to seats in a General Conference; that a Committee of the General Conference of the United States,

at Cincinnati, in 1836, after examining the facts, declined to recommend the recognition of the Canadian M. E. Church as the representative of the original M. E. Church of Canada; that in 1837 all the surviving ministers of the American Methodist Church, who had been present at the organization of that Church, also Bishop Hedding, Dr. Fisk and other eminent ministers in the United States, declared their explicit conviction that the change of name and substitution of an annual president for a bishop, and other changes, did not destroy the identity of the Canadian Methodist Church; that the highest Canadian court of law gave a similar decision in the Church property trials; and that the original seceders were at first only dissatisfied about some limitation of the privileges of local preachers, the formation of an independent Church being an afterthought. No art can destroy the force of these facts." * * *
—*Christian Guardian.*

" Dr. John Carroll issues from the Methodist Book Room, Toronto, a pamphlet entitled, "A Needed Exposition," in which he most calmly considers the claims and allegations of the M. E. Church in Canada. This little document sets the facts of a division existing in the Methodist ranks in Canada, in a clear, unmistakable light. The false position of the Canadian Episcopal Methodists, and the false position in which they place the Wesleyan Methodists, are presented and corrected by the unanswerable argument of historical facts, documents and testimonies. The compact little book of seventy-two pages, obtainable for twenty-five cents, is a valuable historical chapter for instruction and preservation."—*W. D. Malcom, in Vermont Christian Messenger.*

DR. CARROLL'S " NEEDED EXPOSITION."

The Nashville *Christian Advocate* has an appreciative notice of the Rev. John Carroll's pamphlet on the history of the separation and organization of the Canadian Episcopal Methodist Church. The Nashville *Advocate* admits the force of the historical facts, but demurs somewhat to the counsel which Dr. Carroll gives to the Canadian Methodist

Church, and to his complaint about the American General Conference receiving delegates from the Canadian M. E. Church. After referring to the fact established that the Canadian M. E. Church originated in the disaffection of four or five local preachers, who would not submit to the action of the Canadian Conference of 1833, by which the British economy was substituted for the American, our Nashville brother says:—"The author claims that the present Canada Conference of the Wesleyan Methodist Church is the only true representative of primitive Canada Methodism—as we have always considered it in this country. We smile at the pains taken by Dr. Carroll to prove by Ezekiel Cooper and other fathers of American Methodism that we do not consider Episcopacy (strongly attached to it as we are) essential to the Church or to Methodism. A delegated General Conference cannot "do away with" it, or *unfrock* any member of the Episcopal College without charges alleged and proved; but the Church in convention can modify its government in any way it seems proper. Whether or not it was proper for the Canada brethren, in 1833, to renounce our economy, and affiliate with the mother Connexion in Great Britain, is no concern of ours. We wish that the British Methodists had adopted Mr. Wesley's Episcopal plan, as we have done; but they must judge what is best for themselves. We allow none outside of our Connexion to dictate to us, and we are not disposed to dictate to others."

N.B.—"PAST AND PRESENT" and "THE BESIEGER'S PRAYER" are just now out of print.—ED.

THE
SCHOOL OF THE PROPHETS;

OR,

FATHER McROREY'S CLASS AND SQUIRE FIRSTMAN'S KITCHEN FIRE.

A FICTION FOUNDED ON FACTS.

BY JOHN CARROLL.

A BOOK FOR THE METHODISTS.

"In this book our indefatigable and always racy and instructive brother, the Rev. John Carroll, appears in a new role. The story is a clear picture of life in early Canadian Methodist circles, with which the writer is so familiar. His quick perception, graphic delineation, and keen sense of the humorous, are admirable qualifications for the task he has undertaken. Additional interest will be given to the book by the recognition of the characters who figure under assumed names. In many cases these will be apparent, in most they will become so by a reference to Cornish's 'Hand-Book' and 'Case and his Cotemporaries.' Under a thin veil of fiction much valuable information is given, and there are wholesome lessons for both head and heart in these pages. We bespeak for the book a wide circulation. It gives a graphic account of and accurate presentation of the lights and shadows of itinerant life in the old heroic days of pioneer Methodism in this land—days, the vivid conception of which is fast fading from the minds of men—of which, indeed, the younger generation have scarcely any conception at all. Of the incidents recorded here, the author can say in the words of the Latin poet, ' All which I saw, and part of which I was.' There is just spice enough of the tender sentiment in the story to give it additional interest."— *Canada Methodist Magazine.*

"This 'fiction founded on facts' purports to be a historical narrative covering the early history of Methodism in Canada. Some names well known to American Methodism are introduced, while many other characters have fictitious names, and may only be recognized through their personalities. 'THE SCHOOL OF THE PROPHETS' held its first sessions around Squire Firstman's Kitchen fire, where used to gather from their distant circuits, to meet the elder, the itinerants, young and old, to discuss theological questions, and questions of Church polity, and to renew their courage and strength through the generous hospitality of this well known Methodist hotel. Rev. John Carroll tells the story, ' much of which he was himself.' As a literary production, it is open to criticism. As a picturesque account of the journeyings, difficulties, and besetments of the heroes who carried the Gospel through a wild and sparsely settled land, its reading will revive pleasant memories in the minds of the aged who still linger on the shores of time, and may prove an incentive to the younger generation of preachers, who, not having like hardships to encounter, may still find other and more malignant foes to fight and conquer."—*Christian Advocate and Journal.*

"There is not a dry line in the book."—*Hamilton paper.*

www.ingramcontent.com/pod-product-compliance
Lightning Source LLC
Chambersburg PA
CBHW022048230426
43672CB00008B/1108